# Talking Bodies

Emma Rees
Editor

# Talking Bodies

Interdisciplinary Perspectives on Embodiment,
Gender and Identity

*Editor*
Emma Rees
Institute of Gender Studies
University of Chester
Chester, UK

ISBN 978-3-319-63777-8     ISBN 978-3-319-63778-5   (eBook)
DOI 10.1007/978-3-319-63778-5

Library of Congress Control Number: 2017948251

Cover design by Fatima Jamadar

Printed on acid-free paper

This Palgrave Macmillan imprint is published by Springer Nature
The registered company is Springer International Publishing AG
The registered company address is: Gewerbestrasse 11, 6330 Cham, Switzerland

# CONTENTS

# EDITOR AND CONTRIBUTORS

## About the Editor

**Emma Rees** is Professor of Literature and Gender Studies at the University of Chester, where she is Director of the Institute of Gender Studies. In 2013 her second book, *The Vagina: A Literary and Cultural History* was published, and a revised, paperback edition came out in 2015. She has published widely in the field of gender and representation, was the inaugural Political Writer in Residence at Gladstone's Library in Wales, and is currently working on a monograph that looks at feminism's fractures. She runs the biennial international, interdisciplinary Talking Bodies conference.

## Contributors

**Graham Atkin** attended the School of English and American Studies at the University of East Anglia, Norwich. He completed his Ph.D. at the University of Liverpool, under the supervision of Nick Davis, on Spenser's *Faerie Queene*. Graham has taught for over 20 years in the English Department at the University of Chester on a range of courses in Renaissance, Shakespeare, and American literature. He has published on Spenser and Shakespeare and is currently working on the topic of loneliness in American literature. Graham is particularly interested in the way that the allegorical imagination evident in earlier American writers, such as Hawthorne and Melville, draws on English literary Renaissance inspirations.

**Quinn Eades** is a researcher, writer, and award-winning poet whose work lies at the nexus of trans, queer, and feminist theories of the body, autobiography, and philosophy. Eades is published internationally, and is the author of *all the beginnings: a queer autobiography of the body* (2015), and *Rallying* (2017).

**Maria Krebber** holds a Master's degree in Italian Studies, German as a Foreign Language and the History of Art. She studied at the Friedrich-Schiller-Universität Jena (Germany) and the Universidade de Coimbra (Portugal). Currently, she is a researcher at CELGA-ILTEC (Research Center for General and Applied Linguistics—Institute for Theoretical and Computational Linguistics) and is working on her Ph.D. in Applied Linguistics/Discourse Analysis at the University of Lisbon (Portugal). Her thesis focuses on the discursive construction of female identities in the light of the great social changes that occurred in Portugal in the last quarter of the twentieth century.

**Marzia Mauriello** holds a Ph.D. in Ethnoanthropology from the University of Rome, La Sapienza. She is adjunct professor of Medical Anthropology at the University of Magna Græcia of Catanzaro (Italy) and of Body Languages at the University of Naples Suor Orsola Benincasa (Italy). Her research focuses on the processes of construction, deconstruction, and representation of gender identities in the contemporary world, with particular reference to Mediterranean urban cultures. Over the course of more than eight years of ethnographic fieldwork in Naples, she has published articles and chapters on the transgender experience and on homosexuality. Her first monograph, on gender in early twentieth century Neapolitan theatre, *Drammi di genere. Femminile e maschile nel teatro di Raffaele Viviani*, was published in 2016.

**Nina Nyman** is currently working as the editor-in-chief of *Astra*, a 98-year-old feminist magazine published in Swedish in Finland. She graduated in 2012 with a Master's degree in Gender Studies from Åbo Akademi University, Finland by way of Utrecht University, the Netherlands and Københavns Universitet, Copenhagen. Nyman is currently training as a midwife; she has recently given birth herself. She has five tattoos of her own, and lives in the small coastal town of Ekenäs, Finland.

**Renita Sörensdotter** holds a Ph.D. in Social Anthropology and is a lecturer and researcher at the Centre for Gender Research at Uppsala University, Sweden. Her research interests are theoretically located in the field of intersectionality, with a special focus on queer, crip, class and age. She researches in the fields of sexual health, including sexual practices and (re)negotiation, sexual orientation as constructed, bodies as active, and sexual dysfunction in relation to sexual norms. Recent research projects focus on vulvar pain and youth health clinics. She has also been developing methods for how to work with norm critical pedagogy with a focus on intersectionality and teaching in a non-oppressive way.

**Abigail Tazzyman** is a research associate in the Health Management group at Alliance Manchester Business School. In 2009 she graduated with a BA in History from the University of Oxford and in 2011 she completed a Master's at the Centre for Women's Studies, University of York, for which she was awarded the Palgrave/Macmillan Women's Studies Prize. She completed a Ph.D. in Women's Studies at the University of York entitled 'Fitting In: Young British Women's Reported Experience of Body Modification', for which she was awarded funding by Funds for Women Graduates (FfWG) in her final year. Abigail organised the 2013 international conference 'Body Projects', bringing together both academics and artists working on and researching the contemporary female body, its relation to body modification, and its situation in the contemporary world. Abigail is also the co-organiser of 'Teaching Women's History', an Arts and Humanities Research Council (AHRC) skills development programme which investigates the inclusion of women in the curriculum and provides teaching resources through its website.

**Jemma Tosh** is a chartered psychologist and Director of Psygentra Consulting Inc. She is the author of *Perverse Psychology: The Pathologization of Sexual Violence and Transgenderism* (Routledge, 2015) and *Psychology and Gender Dysphoria: Feminist and Transgender Perspectives* (Routledge, 2016). *Perverse Psychology* was shortlisted for a British Psychological Society Book Award in 2016 and Jemma was awarded the Psychology of Women Section Postgraduate Prize in 2011 for her Ph.D. research. She is editor of the *Journal of Psychology, Gender, & Trauma*, and her research interests include gender, sexuality, sexual violence, intersectionality, and critical psychology.

**Melisa Trujillo** is post-doctoral fellow at the University of Toronto. She received her Ph.D. in Sociology at the University of Cambridge, where her doctoral research was supported by a full Economic and Social Research Council (ESRC) studentship. Her Ph.D. examined the body hair removal practices of young feminist-identifying women in the UK and interrogated the links between feminist identifications and women's embodied experiences and choices. As well as conducting multiple research projects during her studies in the fields of gender and embodiment, she was also the co-author of a research project commissioned by Mary Honeyball, Member of the European Parliament, on the links between newspaper adverts for sexual services and trafficking for sexual exploitation. Melisa is fascinated by the intersections between gender, race, identity and embodiment.

**Naomi Wolf** received a DPhil from the University of Oxford in 2014. She holds a BA from Yale and was a Rhodes Scholar. She has written eight bestselling non-fiction books, and has presented her academic research on the criminalisation of male homosexuality in Victorian Britain, at the University of Chester and at Oxford University; to the Ashmolean Museum; and as a keynote for the first LGBTQ Seminar at Rhodes House in Oxford. She was a fellow at the Barnard Center for Research on Women in New York; received a Rothermere American Institute, Oxford University, Research Fellowship; and was Extraordinary Fellow at New College, Oxford. A book based on her DPhil, *Outrages* (2018), is published by Houghton Mifflin and Virago.

# LIST OF FIGURES

# LIST OF TABLES

# CHAPTER 1

# Varieties of Embodiment
# and 'Corporeal Style'

*Emma Rees*

Late in 1819 the poet John Keats contracted tuberculosis. He moved from London to Rome the following year in an eleventh-hour attempt to prolong his life in a warmer climate, but as the last surviving letter he wrote suggests, he was keenly aware that such optimism was unfounded. 'I have an habitual feeling of my real life having passed', he wrote in November 1820, continuing: 'I am leading a posthumous existence' (Bate 1963, p. 680). By February of 1821, he was gravely ill: he died on the 23rd, aged just 25. As the poet's physical health deteriorated, his artistic and intellectual powers remained relatively unaffected. His sonnet fragment, 'This living hand', in its subtle balancing of antitheses, is poignantly—*urgently*—suggestive of the immortality that only creativity can provide:

> This living hand, now warm and capable
> Of earnest grasping, would, if it were cold
> And in the icy silence of the tomb,
> So haunt thy days and chill thy dreaming nights

E. Rees (✉)
Institute of Gender Studies, University of Chester, Chester, UK
e-mail: e.rees@chester.ac.uk

© The Author(s) 2017
E. Rees (ed.), *Talking Bodies*, DOI 10.1007/978-3-319-63778-5_1

> That thou would wish thine own heart dry of blood
> So in my veins red life might stream again,
> And thou be conscience-calm'd – see here it is –
> I hold it towards you. (Keats 2007, p. 237)

What's so forcefully affective about this spectral little sliver of a poem is its afterlife and its vivid suggestion that Keats's own hand is reaching out from the page, reducing the two hundred years between then and now to one corporeal gesture. In its insistent immediacy, the poem disrupts both spatial and temporal principles. That invitation – 'see here it is' – ruptures the penultimate line, foreshadowing the final line's caesura that's stopped in its act of becoming. Like the hand that drew the hands that drew the hands in M.C. Escher's famous lithograph, Keats's poetic form draws attention to its own immanence, and embodiment operates without bodies. The powerful irony at the heart of this kind of creative immortality is, of course, that neither poet nor artist knew about it—their bodies were all too mortal, but both images—the 'living hand' and the hands that draw hands that draw hands—endure.

My own tap-tapping of my laptop's keys as I write this chapter, with hands that always feel uncomfortably and unreasonably cold, regardless of the time of year, echoes the scratch-scratching of Keats's own act of writing. Our corporeal hands are what make our communication across epochs possible. And yet, as I read Keats's poem and as you read this paragraph, those hands are—metaphorically in one case, and very literally in the other—no more. The body of the text exceeds the body of the writer; writing becomes both tomb for, and immortalisation of, the body. Judith Butler wrote of 'the marks on the page' that 'erase the bodily origins from which they apparently emerge, to emerge as tattered and ontologically suspended remains' (1997, p. 11). She asks: 'Is this not the predicament of all writing in relation to its bodily origins?', and concludes that 'There is no writing without the body, but no body fully appears along with the writing that it produces' (Butler 1997, p. 11).

What Keats's fragment demonstrates, then, is that while mortality is a constant, there is for the dull, sublunary, embodied artist, the potential for a sort of immortality: art is transcendent and simultaneously finite and in flux (Keats—again—put this beautifully: 'Beauty is truth, truth beauty' (2007, p. 192)). This immortality means that what a 'body' is becomes unshackled from what may hitherto have appeared to be inviolably natural 'truths' about it; it becomes infinitely mutable and renewable. The essays in *Talking Bodies* all contribute in diverse and significant ways to this renegotiation of thinking about the body, moving the narrative—and the body—forward. The contributors, like their subjects, come from a range of backgrounds and intellectual traditions. In their work they trace how bodies come to carry meaning; how they are differently disciplined and regulated; and how they operate as, and exceed, embodied language. Whether we *have* bodies or *are* bodies is, of course, a question which has been asked by human beings for millennia, and the idea of what 'embodiment' is, and does, is key when it comes to formulating answers for it.

The idea for this volume arose during the inaugural Talking Bodies conference at the University of Chester in 2013. Delegates from around the world met to discuss what the body, or the idea of the body, meant to them in their research. And over the course of the discussions the body was framed by numerous different discourses, from the anatomical to the sociological, and from the sexual to the epistemological. It is on and in the body that the major questions about human beings being human are asked and answered: questions of death, sex, community, cruelty, or religion. Dominant cultural forces inscribe meanings—multiple, fluid meanings—onto and into the body. One might venture that this present volume is a collection of broadly poststructuralist essays—but to claim this would be to delimit it by aligning it with one school of thought (albeit a school which thrives on multiplicity and possibility), when, in fact, many schools and disciplines find expression here.

Susan Bordo is a powerful advocate for the need for writing on the body to be meaningfully—materially—anchored. '[T]he study of cultural representations alone, divorced from consideration of their relation to the practical lives of bodies', she writes, 'can obscure and mislead' (Bordo 2003, p. 183). The movement not only of bodies beyond and outside of theory, but also of academic practice beyond and outside of rigidly disciplinary silos, is crucial, and is something that the interdisciplinary essays in this present collection do well. The essays are to some extent a response to the claim made more than twenty years ago by Caroline Bynum, who wrote that 'no one in the humanities seems really to feel comfortable any longer with the idea of an essential "bodiliness"' (1995, p. 2).

Ideas of reification—of 'thingness', or of Bynum's 'bodiliness'—are dominant when we talk about bodies: being a body and having a body are the same and different and the same. There is a danger that if we move too far into the realm of a Foucauldian 'discursive' composition of the body, we risk losing all sense of biology and facticity. Put simply, the body needs to be put back into writing about the body. Our largest organ—the skin—is simultaneously in contact with the world and with ourselves. Its inside and outside are inseparable. Like de Saussure's sign and signified, skin-self and skin-world are co-dependent and (in)separable: 'Language can be compared with a sheet of paper: thought is the front and the sound the back; one cannot cut the front without cutting the back at the same time; likewise in language, one can neither divide sound from thought nor thought from sound [...] Linguistics then works in the borderland where the elements of sound and thought combine; *their combination produces a form, not a substance*' (2011, p. 113; italics in original). The skin, then, is the language of the body—that which keeps us 'in', and that which allows us to interact. It is the 'borderland' of being—the liminal space that is simultaneously both us and the world; separate from, and integrated with, others. The redolent indeterminacy of the skin was also a source of fascination to another important commentator in the field of embodiment, Donna Haraway, who characteristically tried to transcend it: 'Why should our bodies end at the skin', she asked, 'or include at best other beings encapsulated by skin?' (1991, p. 178).

Not only has the meaning of the body been in flux across the millennia, but it can also change radically in one lifespan. In her affecting memoir, *A Body, Undone*, the academic Christina Crosby records the struggles she encountered following an accident that left her paralysed. Crosby sees the skin as 'an organ of sense that runs imperceptibly from inside my body to the outside' (2016, p. 198), and argues that: 'Body and mind are simultaneously one and the same and clearly distinct. Thinking my body, I am thinking in my body, as my body, through my body, of my body, about my body, and I'm oriented around my body. I'm beside myself' (2016, p. 198). This messily complex imbrication of self and body suggests a sentiment not dissimilar to that of Sylvia Plath's protagonist Esther Greenwood who, in *The Bell Jar*, marvels at her body's resilience and what she characterises as its truculent nature. 'Then I saw that my body had all sorts of little tricks', the narrator states, 'such as making my hands go limp at the crucial second, which would save it, time and again, whereas if I had the whole say, I would be dead in a flash. I would simply have to ambush it with whatever sense I had left, or it would trap me in its stupid cage for fifty years without any sense at all'

(Plath 2005, p. 153). This radical disaggregation of 'I' and body, and the relentless facticity of the self, were closed down by Plath shortly after her novel's publication, courtesy of the domestic gas oven in an unremarkable kitchen in London.

Crosby writes: '*I* feel alienated, sometimes profoundly alienated, from "myself"' (2016, p. 18; italics in original). She responds to the paradox by imagining a 'bodymind', constituting 'the whole person' (Crosby 2016, p. 5), not unlike Elizabeth Grosz's Möbius band. Grosz writes that: 'The Möbius strip model has the advantage of showing that there can be a relation between two "things"—mind and body—which presumes neither their identity nor their radical disjunction' (1994, p. 209), since:

> The Möbius strip has the advantage of showing the inflection of mind into body and body into mind, the ways in which, through a kind of twisting or inversion, one side becomes another. This model also provides a way of problematizing and rethinking the relations between the inside and the outside of the subject, its psychical interior and its corporeal exterior, by showing not their fundamental identity or reducibility but the torsion of the one into the other, the passage, vector, or uncontrollable drift of the inside into the outside and the outside into the inside. (Grosz 1994, p. xii)

Grosz's metaphor is so effective precisely because language fails in the face of embodiment. Writing on the body always necessitates an approximation due to the insufficiency and contingency of the raw linguistic materials. Take Shakespeare's Leontes, in *The Winter's Tale*, for example. Talking to his son, the king grasps at, but cannot find, the right words for articulating his pre- or ultra-linguistic emotions. Language cannot truthfully express the somatic primalism of the sucker punch of paranoid jealousy. The body 'depends on language to be known [but] the body also exceeds every possible linguistic effort of capture' (Butler 1997, p. 4). Leontes's feelings are so all-consuming that the visceral rapidly surpasses the linguistic, and both structure and meaning collapse in the anguish of suspicion:

> women say so,
> That will say anything. But were they false
> As o'erdyed blacks, as wind, as waters, false
> As dice are to be wished by one that fixes

No bourn 'twixt his and mine, yet were it true
To say this boy were like me. Come, sir page,
Look on me with your welkin eye. Sweet villain,
Most dearest, my collop! Can thy dam? May't be
Affection? - Thy intention stabs the centre,
Thou dost make possible things not so held,
Communicat'st with dreams - how can this be?
(Shakespeare 2010, 1.2.130–40)

The dashes, or hesitations, barge in on the pentameter, gesturing at a profound disruption of coherent thought. Affect is articulated only in the false starts, in the unspoken moments of the speech—its hyphens, and liminal spaces. It is at once behind, and beyond, and embedded in, language.

This moment of linguistic catastrophe in the face of overwhelming emotion, where mind and body act coextensively, highlights language's deficiencies. It is a moment of all-consuming embodiment or, as Merleau-Ponty expressed it, of an overthrow of Cartesian dualism: 'I am not in front of my body, I am in my body, or rather I am my body [...] I am myself the one who holds these arms and these legs together, the one who simultaneously sees them and touches them' (2012, p. 151). Leontes is not *expressing* jealousy; he *is* jealousy. For Merleau-Ponty, bodies are not merely *in* the world, but are *of* it. In other words, we only know the world because of its contiguity with our bodies: 'The interior and the exterior are inseparable. The world is entirely on the inside, and I am entirely outside of myself' (Merleau-Ponty 2012, p. 430).

The story of bodies is, viewed through a Foucauldian lens at least, a story of societies, and of how those in power exercise and maintain their authority. 'Historians long ago began to write the history of the body', writes Foucault:

they have shown to what extent historical processes were involved in what might seem to be the purely biological base of existence; and what place should be given in the history of society to biological 'events' such as the circulation of bacilli, or the extension of the lifespan. But the body is also directly involved in a political field; power relations have an immediate hold upon it; they invest it, mark it, train it, torture it, force it to carry out tasks, to perform ceremonies, to emit signs. (Foucault 1991, p. 25)

The Foucauldian body is a site of social inscription, ensnared in culture. The gendered body is, equally, discursively fashioned. Gender is less *thing* than *act*: 'an ongoing activity embedded in daily action' (West and Zimmerman 1987, p. 130). Its self-conscious construction of what it is, in the face of what it is not, firmly places difference at its core, and 'Doing gender means creating differences between girls and boys and women and men, differences that are not natural, essential, or biological' (West and Zimmerman 1987, p. 137). In Pierre Bourdieu's formulation of *habitus* and cultural capital, gender difference was socially constructed on the site of a body which was the locus of 'embodied class' (Bourdieu 1984, p. 437). The power of the 'body hexis' is both played out, and instantiated, by the individual's 'life-style' (Bourdieu 1984, p. 173), and is evident, for example, in the ways in which men and women occupy space differently according to gendered socialisation, which makes the body a 'cultural product' (Grosz 1994, p. 24).

Developing Foucault's ideas in *Discipline and Punish*, the late feminist critic Sandra Lee Bartky wrote that 'a generalized male witness comes to structure woman's consciousness of herself as a bodily being' (1998, p. 38), to the point where 'women cannot begin the re-vision of our own bodies until we learn to read the cultural messages we inscribe upon them daily and until we come to see that even when the mastery of the disciplines of femininity produces a triumphant result, we are still only women' (1998, p. 44). Or as Judith Butler famously put it, 'gendered bodies are so many "styles of the flesh" [...] Consider gender, for instance, as a *corporeal style*, an "act," as it were, which is both intentional and performative, where "*performative*" suggests a dramatic and contingent construction of meaning' (Butler 2007, p. 190; italics in original). This idea of thinking not about what a body is, but about what it can do, is crucial, since women especially, faced by the 'man-standard', must 'create only by making possible a becoming over which they do not have ownership, into which they themselves must enter; this is a becoming-woman affecting all of humankind, men and women both' (Deleuze and Guattari 1987, pp. 321, 117).

The tyranny of the notion of a bodily norm means that, in the act of being human, our very humanity—our age, weight, ability—sets us up to fail. Simone de Beauvoir's agonised question, asked of herself as she grew older—'Can I have become a different being while I still remain myself?'—is particularly redolent in this regard (1996, p. 283). The maintenance of an idea of 'the norm' is utterly dependent on a reversible polarity that posits the existence of a 'not normal' other which, in order to shore up the social artifice and contingency of the norm, is rendered alien, stigmatised, or abject. Julia Kristeva has written powerfully on how, for example, the ageing body's sexuality may be read as abject (Kristeva 1982), and it remains the case that, for both men and women 'successful aging' [*sic.*] is equated with continued sexual function (Katz and Marshall 2003, p. 7). The representation of non-normative bodies throws up a challenge to the hegemonic, neoliberal status quo; they are bodies that queer the pitch in more ways than one (Ahmed 2006; Halberstam 2011).

The body in pain, too, challenges the idea of consistent or normative bodies, since pain returns us to a radically divided subject position, emphasising the usually 'latent distinction between a self and a body, between "me" and "my body." The "self" or "me," which is experienced on the one hand as more private, more essentially at the center, and on the other hand as participating across the bridge of the body in the world, is "embodied" in the voice, in language' (Scarry 1985, pp. 48–49). As Elspeth Probyn has argued, 'recognition of the body in its physiological matter has tended to disappear under the weight of its cultural importance' (2004, p. 240)—and there can be a danger that: 'in placing the body and representations of it on equal analytic footing, postmodern analysis does away with the need to investigate people's actual embodied experiences' (Sanders with Vail 2008, p. 184). Susan Bordo has also written persuasively on this idea of the body's facticity in the face of abstracted analyses. 'When bodies are made into mere *products* of social discourse', she warns, 'they remain bodies in name only' (Bordo 2003, p. 35; italics in original).

One of the most creative attempts to accommodate and challenge the paradox of being/having a body—of envisioning a posthuman utopia—remains Donna Haraway's 'Cyborg Manifesto'. First published in the mid-1980s, the 'Manifesto' imagines a mode of being a body that moves a body beyond itself. It's readily apparent that we're still a long way away from the idea of humanity being cyborgs, those genderless, queer figures envisaged by Haraway: '[W]e are all chimeras', that is, 'theorized and fabricated hybrids of machine and organism; in short, we are cyborgs. The cyborg is our ontology; it gives us our politics' (1991, p. 150). Haraway's fantasy was an effective riposte to humanity's grand framing narratives that were predicated on what she terms 'antagonistic dualisms' (1991, p. 180). The collapsing of dualisms might move us to see 'Our bodies, ourselves', and that 'bodies are maps of power and identity. Cyborgs are no exception. A cyborg body is not innocent; it was not born in a garden; it does not seek unitary identity' (Haraway 1991, p. 180).

So human/animal, artificial/natural, corporeal/incorporeal, and organic/inorganic become not antithetical dualisms but markers of continuity and coalition, as difference is replaced by hybridity and affinity, and 'Cyborg imagery can suggest a way out of the maze of dualisms in which we have explained our bodies and our tools to ourselves' (Haraway 1991, p. 181). But to articulate this new world order nevertheless requires recourse to phallogocentrism and, as Haraway writes, 'Grammar is politics by other means. What narrative possibilities might lie in monstrous linguistic figures for relations with "nature" for ecofeminist work?' (Haraway 1991, p. 3). So ultimately the cyborg fails just as the human body fails—hamstrung by its dependence on the unreliable medium of language.

It's against this backdrop of varieties of embodiment and 'corporeal styles', then, that *Talking Bodies* is positioned. I've brought together ten writers from different intellectual traditions to contribute to these key debates from an array of approaches and concerns. The chapters range across the disciplines, from historicist literary analyses, through anthropological and ethnographic investigations, across Europe and into North America and the Antipodes, and via creativity and scientific method. But at its heart, this book contains essays united in their quest to frame and reframe embodiment—that is, to scrutinise how we *do* and talk about bodies—from the nineteenth century through to the present day, and into the future.

In the opening chapter, Naomi Wolf poses the question: 'Edith Wharton: an Heiress to Gay Male Sexual Radicalism?'. Wolf persuasively demonstrates how the lives and works of both Oscar Wilde and Walt Whitman had a powerful influence on Wharton's own writing. Perhaps Wharton's most famous novel, for example, *The House of Mirth* (1905), echoes Wilde's trial, and elements of his play *Lady Windermere's Fan* (1893). By situating Wharton in a nexus of influential *fin de siècle* writers and thinkers, Wolf shows how she began to rethink female sexuality, moving away from the constrictions of 'New Woman' morality towards a celebration of European aestheticism and liberated sexuality, reimagining these movements to suit her own position, and the positions of her protagonists, as heterosexual women. The reimagining was, however, repeatedly frustrated by the obstinacy of corporeality. As Wolf writes: 'One can almost hear Wharton [...] asking the shades of Wilde and Walt Whitman to theorise further on behalf of women who, in pursuing that ideal, risk pregnancy, unsafe and illegal abortions and forms of venereal diseases to which lesbians were not subject—taking the "case" of heterosexual women's reality into account'.

Whitman's compatriot and close contemporary (the lifespans of the two men are almost exactly concurrent), Herman Melville, is, of course, best known for his epic novel *Moby-Dick* (1851). Five years earlier, however, Melville's intriguing debut, *Typee*, had been published. In his chapter, 'Losing Face Among the Natives: "something about tattooing and tabooing" in Melville's *Typee*', Graham Atkin develops a new reading of this semi-autobiographical South Sea adventure, considering the ways in which precarious nineteenth-century ideas around 'civilisation' were challenged by the islanders' use of tattoos. As Margo DeMello argued in *Bodies of Inscription*, tattoos have long been caught up in debates around racial and cultural superiority, with colonisers 'constructing a narrative about tattooed people as savages, a narrative that is later turned on its side when white tattooed people start to display themselves in sideshows' (2000, p. 47). The heroes of *Typee*, Tommo and Toby, find their conceptions of self-identity irrevocably disrupted by the threat of non-consensual, highly-visible body modifications at the hands of a cannibalistic Typeean tattooist. In his analysis of how cultural crisis can be emblematised by and on the human body, Atkin draws on material from a range of disciplines.

The fragility of the body-self in terms of gender is a key theme in Marzia Mauriello's chapter, 'What the Body Tells us: Transgender Strategies, Beauty, and Self-consciousness'. Mauriello demonstrates how the Neapolitan *femminielli*, traditional figures of men 'impersonating' women, can be seen as important precursors not only for today's trans women, but also for individuals embodying the idea of a third gender. The *femminielli*, Mauriello argues, are a subculture under threat, but their existence nevertheless continues to trouble gendered embodiment, and serves as a concrete example of how changing the body in order to position oneself as 'Other' is a rejection of the rigid binarism of phallogocentrism. Judith Butler has argued that 'the doctrine of construction implies that the body is not only made *by* language, but made *of* language, or that the body is somehow reducible to the linguistic coordinates by which it is identified and identifiable, as if there is no non-linguistic stuff at issue' (1997, p. 3; italics in original); the *femminielli* stand as exemplars of how individuals understand, inhabit, and ultimately construct, their own bodies as 'non-linguistic stuff' reified, nonetheless, partially through language.

The self/body relationship is at the heart of Nina Nyman's contribution to this volume, 'Tattoos: an Embodiment of Desire'. Nyman uses interviews to determine what processes women go through prior to, and during, getting tattooed, asking important questions about how these same women perceive their bodies once tattooed. What emerges is evidence that the process of tattooing can radically influence women's relationships with their own bodies: agency and control are key, here. Nyman explores how, for these women, desire became less a matter of individual sexual preference, and more a development of the bodily positivity associated with the very act of being tattooed. Nyman's participants, in Foucauldian terms, acquire the mastery and knowledge of themselves—or of their *selves*—an acquisition that 'may be called the political technology of the body' (Foucault 1991, p. 26).

The gendered complexities of the political technology of the body are Abigail Tazzyman's focus in her chapter, 'Learning Womanhood: Body Modification, Girls and Identity'. Girls learn the script of 'femininity', Tazzyman argues, in their first attempts at bodily modification. Early engagement with body modification impacted greatly on Tazzyman's interviewees' identities as young women. She uses her data, drawn from interviews with thirty young British women, to argue that body modifications are way stations in a socially-determined performance of 'womanhood'. Finally, Tazzyman expands on Geza Lindemann's (1997) tripartite, phenomenologically-informed demarcation of the body, in order to elucidate her own, pioneering, identification of a fourth element: the 'ideal' body.

The 'ideal body' is, almost by definition, unattainable. Susan Bordo, in her important work *Unbearable Weight*, powerfully described the tyranny not only of unachievable idealism, but also of 'normality' (2003). Women who do not conform—the anorexic, the hysterical, or the agoraphobic woman—have, and *are*, bodies that 'are speaking to us of the pathology and violence that lurks just around the corner, waiting at the horizon of "normal" femininity' (Bordo 2003, p. 175). Maria Krebber develops this idea of 'normality' and asks what would happen were we to reframe it. In 'The Construction of a Personal Norm of Physical and Psychological "Well-Being" in Female Discourse', Krebber argues for an epistemology that rejects Western body image norms by constructing instead a norm of well-being. Her analysis is based on interviews with Portuguese mothers and daughters who were asked to reflect on their relationships with their own bodies. Krebber skilfully demonstrates how her interviewees navigated beauty image norms, engaging in disciplinary practices that—ironically—shored up precisely the norms they ostensibly critiqued.

In 2001 Dalia Judovitz reflected on the apparently infinite capacity for socio-cultural adaptation that the human body undertakes. 'The fate of the body as an idea', she wrote, 'like that of subjectivity to whose emergence it is linked, is haunted by the foreclosure of its past meanings and history' (Judovitz 2001, p. 1). The idea of this adaptability in relation to the online, 'virtual' world is at the heart of Jemma Tosh's chapter. In 'No Body, No Crime? (Representations of) Sexual Violence Online', Tosh ventures online to investigate how the word 'rape' has been co-opted and redefined in virtual environments, focusing on the prevalence of sexual violence as a feature of platforms like *Grand Theft Auto*. Her chapter interrogates the debate around whether what goes on in these spaces is sexual violence, or a *representation* of it, situating her findings in relation to wider debates around gender, sexual identity, and inequality.

From communal platforms online to the intimate space of the bedroom, then, the body is prey to numerous powerful circulating discursive practices. From these discourses arise ideas about 'normality', as we have seen, and, when chronic pain is part of the equation, 'normality' can function insidiously in the individual's life. For her chapter on how vulvar pain challenges norms of sexual behaviour, Renita Sörensdotter interviewed 21 women. In 'Heteronormativity as a Painful Script: How Women with Vulvar Pain (re)Negotiate Sexual Practice', Sörensdotter argues that how we have—or expect to have—sex can be core to our embodied identity. If vaginal intercourse is the heterosexual norm, then how does the woman whose chronic pain prevents her from participating in it, interpret her 'abnormality'? And how does she rewrite the heteronormative script in the light of her body's sexual encounters with the bodies of others?

What the contributors I feature in this collection have done is little short of remarkable: they have elicited verbal responses that convey the 'feelingness' of embodiment—they have navigated a way through the linguistic snares that we saw entrap Leontes, Shakespeare's paranoid king. How to develop the self-in-words is the focus of the penultimate chapter in the collection, Quinn Eades's honest and powerful

'Queer Wounds: Writing Autobiography Past the Limits of Language'. Considering the relationship of trauma to narrative, Eades in effect writes a manifesto for pushing language to, and beyond, the limits of representation; for 'writing wounds' in the spirit of Derridean *hymenography*, focusing not only on those wounds, but on their narratives, too. *Talking Bodies* concludes by looking forwards. In 'The Trouble with Body Image: the Need for a Better Corporeal Vocabulary', Melisa Trujillo reconsiders the idea of 'body image'. She discusses the relative merits of the concept, arguing forcefully for a new way of talking about bodies. What, she asks, are the limitations of talking about bodies in terms of (dis)satisfaction? And how embodied is 'body image'?

Do I have a body, or am I my body? What is beyond doubt is that 'it is always the body that is at issue—the body and its forces, their utility and their docility, their distribution and their submission' (Foucault 1991, p. 25). From dissatisfaction to sexual satisfaction; from physical pain to the agony of 'nonconformity'; and from consensual modification to socially enforced activities and behaviours, the body is at the centre of the ten powerful analyses gathered here. My contributors ask—and answer—many questions: what happens when my body will not be compliant? What if my body's language is not my idiolect? What does it mean when my body talks? The neoliberal cult of the individual has made the body a private combat zone; we're caught in a perpetual struggle to contain it or to bring it into line; to discipline or to punish it. In the essays that follow there are uniting themes, of course, but there are also dissensions and tensions across the landscape of the book, resulting in an immensely productive polyphony. *Talking Bodies* is a radically interdisciplinary volume, not least because bodies cannot be divorced from the potent cultural forces which circulate around—and through—them. Being a body or having a body? Each enterprise is universal, yet each is at the same time profoundly individuated. The essays that follow all provide answers to—or at the very least, ways of living with—such powerful contradictions.

## REFERENCES

Ahmed, Sara, 2004. *The Cultural Politics of Emotion*. New York: Routledge.
Ahmed, Sara, 2006. *Queer Phenomenology: Orientations, Objects, Others*. Durham: Duke University Press.

Bartky, Sandra Lee, 1998. 'Foucault, Femininity, and the Modernization of Patriarchal Power', in Rose Weitz (ed.), *The Politics of Women's Bodies: Sexuality, Appearance, and Behavior*. Oxford: Oxford University Press, pp. 25–45.

Bate, Walter Jackson, 1963. *John Keats*. Massachusetts: The Belknap Press of Harvard University Press.

De Beauvoir, Simone, 1996. *The Coming of Age*, trans. Patrick O' Brian. New York: Norton.

Bordo, Susan, 2003. *Unbearable Weight: Feminism, Western Culture, and the Body*. Berkeley: University of California Press.

Bourdieu, Pierre, 1984. *Distinction: A Social Critique of the Judgement of Taste*, trans. Richard Nice. Cambridge: University of Harvard Press.

Butler, Judith, 1997. 'How can I deny that these hands and this body are mine?'. *Qui Parle*, 11:1, 1–20.

Butler, Judith, 2007. *Gender Trouble*. Abingdon: Routledge.

Bynum, Caroline, 1995. 'Why All the Fuss about the Body? A Medievalist's Perspective'. *Critical Inquiry*, 22:1, 1–33.

Crosby, Christina, 2016. *A Body, Undone: Living on after Great Pain*. New York: New York University Press.

De Saussure, Ferdinand, 2011. *Course in General Linguistics*, trans. Wade Baskin and eds. Perry Meisel and Haun Saussy. New York: Columbia University Press.

Deleuze, Guy, and Félix Guattari, 1987. *A Thousand Plateaus: Capitalism and Schizophrenia*, trans. Brian Massumi. London: Continuum.

DeMello, Margo, 2000. *Bodies of Inscription: A Cultural History of the Modern Tattoo Community*. Durham: Duke University Press.

Foucault, Michel, 1991. *Discipline and Punish: The Birth of the Prison*, trans. Alan Sheridan. New York: Vintage.

Grosz, Elizabeth, 1994. *Volatile Bodies: Toward a Corporeal Feminism*. Bloomington: Indiana University Press.

Halberstam, J., 2011. *The Queer Art of Failure*. Durham: Duke University Press.

Haraway, Donna, 1991. 'A Cyborg Manifesto: Science, Technology, and Socialist-Feminism in the Late Twentieth Century', in *Simians, Cyborgs and Women: The Reinvention of Nature*. New York: Routledge, pp.149–81.

Judovitz, Dalia, 2001. *The Culture of the Body: Genealogies of Modernity*. Ann Arbor: University of Michigan Press.

Katz, Stephen, and Barbara Marshall, 2003. 'New Sex for Old: Lifestyle, Consumerism, and the Ethics of Aging Well'. *Journal of Aging Studies*, 17: 3–16.

Keats, John, 2007. *Selected Poems*, ed. John Barnard. Harmondsworth: Penguin.

Kristeva, Julia, 1982. *Powers of Horror: An Essay on Abjection*, trans. Leon S. Roudiez. New York: Columbia University Press.

Merleau-Ponty, Maurice, 2012. *Phenomenology of Perception*, trans. Donald A. Landes. London: Routledge.

Plath, Sylvia, 2005. *The Bell Jar*. London: Faber and Faber.

Probyn, Elspeth, 2004. 'Shame in the habitus'. *The Sociological Review*, 52:2, 224–48.

Sanders, Clinton R., with D. Angus Vail, 2008. *Customizing the Body: The Art and Culture of Tattooing*. Philadelphia: Temple University Press.

Scarry, Elaine, 1985. *The Body in Pain: The Making and Unmaking of the World*. Oxford: Oxford University Press.

Shakespeare, William, 2010. *The Winter's Tale*, ed. John Pitcher. London: Methuen (Arden Shakespeare).

West, Candace, and Don H. Zimmerman, 1987. 'Doing Gender'. *Gender and Society*, 1:2, 125–51.

# CHAPTER 2

# Edith Wharton: An Heiress to Gay Male Sexual Radicalism?

*Naomi Wolf*

The American novelist Edith Wharton (1862–1937) began writing her short stories in 1891. Oscar Wilde's trial for gross indecency was in 1895. I believe Wilde's trial, and his plays, alongside the work of Walt Whitman, had a formative impact upon Wharton's most substantial work, which followed the period of his greatest successes.

Throughout her post-1905 work, and to the end of her career, Wharton at times imitates Wilde's phrasing, not always successfully. She attempts Wildean paradoxes: in *The Fruit of the Tree* (1907), the household confidante Mrs Ansell notes that '[M]ost divorced women marry again to be respectable', to which Mr Langhope, the heiress's father, replies, nearly quoting Wilde, 'Yes—that's their punishment' (Wharton 2004, p. 243). In a later conversation between the same two characters, Mrs Ansell asks, 'Do you really mean that Bessy should get a divorce?', to which Langhope replies: 'divorce does not frighten me very much. It is as painless as modern dentistry' (Wharton 2004, p. 280). In 'The Reckoning' (1902), in a Wildean aside, the narrator Julia Westall recalls that '[S]he had once said, in ironical defense [*sic*.] of her marriage,

N. Wolf (✉)
University of Oxford, Oxford, UK

© The Author(s) 2017
E. Rees (ed.), *Talking Bodies*, DOI 10.1007/978-3-319-63778-5_2

that it had at least preserved her from the necessity of sitting next to [her husband] at dinners' (Wharton 2007, p. 178).

The Wilde trial, with its focus on members of the demimonde seeking to blackmail one another, had echoes in Wharton's *House of Mirth* (1905). The same theme—of stolen letters with sexually implicating content being used to blackmail a character—had also been central to the plot of Wilde's *Lady Windermere's Fan* (1893). Because of the conflict of social expectation—that Lily Bart must marry for money—as opposed to her sexual desire (she wishes to be with Lawrence Selden)—Lily tries to engage in blackmail. With letters stolen from their owner—as Wilde's (and Alfred Douglas's) letters had been stolen for the purpose of blackmail—Lily Bart seeks to blackmail the society matron Bertha Dorset into acknowledging her socially.

In 1903 Wharton met the writer Vernon Lee in Italy, and began to read John Addington Symonds. By 1905, she had begun her intimate friendship with Henry James and the circle of male homosexual writers around him, and by 1908, she was reading Whitman and Nietzsche, and she began her affair with Morton Fullerton. Through these influences, Wharton was drawn away from the moralism of one strand of the 'New Woman' framing of sexuality (and away from American discourses about sexuality in fiction, which were generally framed in moralistic terms in this period, regardless of the gender of the writer), and towards British and European aestheticism and sexual liberationism. It is after this period that we begin to see the multiple echoes and palimpsests of Wilde in her work.

As Wharton is drawn more and more firmly onto the Wildean/ Whitmanesque path, the differences between her position and that of 'New Woman' sexual morality become ever clearer. In 'The Reckoning', *Summer*, *The Age of Innocence* and *The Gods Arrive*, her heroines do not act out the 'wrongs of' narrative. On the contrary, Wharton's heroines in these texts do indeed suffer for their decisions to live out a measure of sexual self-directedness; their sexuality does punish them, as it always punished the heroines of the 'wrongs of' school. But there the resemblance ends. Though they are sometimes victimised sexually, Edith Wharton's heroines are never sexual victims. She never presents the subject as regretting her sexual decisions, nor do her heroines assert that punishment has made sexual experience not worth having. Nor does the authorial voice ever take this moralising position. On the contrary; the authorial voice finds the 'abundant recompense' in that experience, no matter how ultimately painful.

There are direct echoes of Wilde's *Lady Windermere's Fan* in Wharton's short story, 'Autre Temps, Autre Moers' (c.1920), where Mrs Lidcote, the central character, is a 'ruined' mother who returns from the exile forced upon her by her sexual transgression, in order to save her daughter Leila from scandal. 'The Other Two' is a Wharton short story about two ex-husbands, and one current husband, of the central female character. It illustrates a post-Wildean world in which the female sexual subject has escaped the patriarchal sexual economy and patriarchal sexual control. Indeed, the heroine of the story runs the sexual economy and the three men are subordinated to her sexual arrangements. Here is the sexual anarchy implied by Wilde and feared by critics of the New Woman and opponents of Wilde at his trial: here is a scenario of a world in which the dominant sexual law has broken down. Mrs Waythorn appropriates herself and her own sexuality.

Wilde wrote *The Picture of Dorian Gray* between 1890 and 1891. Wharton engaged in several direct rewritings of this novel, including 'The Portrait' (c.1919) and 'The Rembrandt' (1922). 'The Portrait' centres on a painter who cannot bring himself to render the face of a scurrilous robber baron, Mr Vaid, even though a substantial commission depends upon it. The reason the painter cannot complete the portrait is that the robber baron is too evil. Wharton appropriates *Dorian Gray*'s moral world in relation to the visual arts, in taking wholesale a magical-realist dimension in which the final appearance of a work of visual art is affected by moral actions. It ends with a scene of his daughter throwing back the drapery in confrontation with the moral truth about her father, a direct echo of the last scene in *Picture of Dorian Gray*. In 'The Rembrandt', an art advisor keeps a secret about the worthlessness of a copy in order to do a kindness to an impoverished, genteel lady—but in the process corrupts his own reputation and his own soul. In both narratives Wharton appropriates and engages with Wilde's construction of a painting as a mirror of, or catalyst to, moral decay.

Indeed, Wharton also rewrote *Lady Windermere's Fan* twice—once, as we saw above, in 'Autre Temps, Autre Moers', and then again in *The Age of Innocence*. In this novel, which Wharton wrote in 1920, but which was set in the 1870s, there are direct equivalencies of Wharton characters to Wilde characters. The sexually jaded, worldly, 'fallen' but admirable Ellen Olenska corresponds to the sexually jaded, worldly, 'fallen' but admirable

Mrs Erlynne of *Lady Windermere's Fan*. The sexually and intellectually innocent daughter figure May Welland corresponds to the sexually
and intellectually oppressed innocent daughter figure Agatha. In *Lady
Windermere's Fan*, Mrs Erlynne sacrifices herself, in order to protect her
daughter, and she does so by sacrificing her sexual reputation. In *The Age
of Innocence*, Ellen Olenska also sacrifices herself, to protect her cousin
May Welland, and she also does so by sacrificing her sexual reputation.

Far more interestingly than these generic echoes that simply reveal
an intensity of influence, however, is what happens when Wharton uses
Wilde to ask questions about the nature of female sexual liberation.
Wharton used Wilde in order to engage in a necessary, indeed central,
argument about what happens to the aestheticist/sexual liberationist
project once it is undertaken by heterosexual women. One can almost
hear Wharton frustratedly asking the shades of Wilde and Walt Whitman
to theorise further on behalf of women who, in pursuing that ideal, risk
pregnancy, unsafe and illegal abortions and forms of venereal diseases to
which lesbians were not subject—taking the 'case' of heterosexual wom-
en's reality into account. In 'The Reckoning', Wharton poses a challenge
back to Wilde.

Many social historians, such as Lillian Faderman in *Surpassing the Love
of Men*, have established that in the nineteenth century, both in Britain
and in the United States, relationships between women that we would
today identify as 'lesbian', were socially nearly normative; I would add
that there was also no law prohibiting female-female sexual relationships
before the twentieth century in either country. One could argue that
prior to reliable contraception and safe abortion, heterosexual and lesbian women were more dramatically differently situated in terms of bio-
graphical and biological experience than they are today. Wharton's work
struggles overtly with the historical risks of the heterosexual female body,
including risks of unwanted pregnancy and unsafe abortion.

In *The Picture of Dorian Gray*, Lord Henry Wotton's speeches about
the overarching value of individualism and impulse, when he argues that
'Pleasure is Nature's test, her sign of approval. [...] I represent to you all
the sins you have never had the courage to commit', appal the painter
Basil Hallward: 'But surely, if one lives merely for oneself, Harry, one
pays a terrible price for doing so?' (Wilde 1989, pp. 106–107). This
argument about sexual individualism and its costs is picked up directly as
if in a counterpoint by Wharton in 'The Reckoning' which could be read

as a direct argument by Wharton in response to the provocation posed by Wilde and Whitman about female sexual autonomy. Wharton is drawn to the Whitmanesque/Wildean vision of sexual transcendentalism, but frightened too by its implications, as women would have been in the pre-Marie Stopes era.

The question that 'The Reckoning' poses in reaction to Wilde's provocations is not merely a question: she knows that the answer, in 'The Reckoning' as in *Summer*, and *The Age of Innocence*, and *The Gods Arrive* (1932), is ruin. 'The Reckoning' is the tale of a 'New Woman' character who takes the Wildean project seriously and at face value: she embraces a Wildean/Whitmanesque vision of a sexually liberated and autonomous future—and ends up left by her lover for a younger woman, socially ostracised and alone.

One must cast a glance backward at Joris-Karl Huysmans' 1884 novel *À Rebours* to read the gender politics of 'The Reckoning'. Huysmans' nihilistic novel explores the logical consequence of following the Decadent search for sensation for its own sake, in the absence of other values, to its logical, excessive conclusion. In *À Rebours*, an excess of sensual stimulation leads to the hero's descent into isolation, chaos and a kind of sensory burnout. The text explores extreme possibilities of a man's withdrawal from nature; it addresses openly the previously tabooed subjects of male hostility to women and domesticity. One can argue that the writing of *À Rebours* became possible because technology and modernity allowed the development of certain kinds of misogyny, or certain kinds of isolation from bonds with women, that social conditions did not allow for previously.

This is the nightmare scenario that underlies *fin de siècle* anxiety about male homosexuality and about 'New Woman' sexuality, but it is also an anxiety that informs Wharton's dark insight in 'The Reckoning'. But Wharton is asking a fundamental female heterosexual question: if you say 'yes' to self-expression, what, if any, are the protective limits? If everything becomes permitted, why keep any promises? If any sensory gratification is valid, why bond with any one person? It's an argument about the implications of sexual transcendentalism that we are still having today, in almost exactly the terms that Wilde first posited it and Wharton first interrogated it: if we open the door to 'liberation' for men and for women from the double standard, from the burdens of domesticity, and so on, do we not usher in ultimately a dystopia of narcissism and loneliness?

It is in some of the short stories that Wharton's engagement with Wilde is most direct, and, understandably, most angry at times. In 'The Reckoning', the Wildean hypothesis of liberated social arrangements is played out over the complete arc of a heterosexual relationship—leaving the woman who has embraced his credo in a traditionally victimised and abandoned position at the end. It is as if Wharton is dramatising the Wildean hypothesis or provocation as an algebra equation on a literary blackboard—but substituting 'woman' for one of the terms, and showing that the end sum is the same old position of seduction, betrayal, disempowerment and enslavement to a merciless biology. She is not rejecting the Wildean call—but merely, with the love of truth that characterises her polemic, showing how in following it, the same path leads women to different end points than it leads men—and that the end point for women is mined by many of the traditional sexual traps and punishments that have always awaited women who have 'transgressed': abandonment, loss of love, loss of social place, loneliness.

'The Reckoning'—even the title carries the double meaning of an algebra or mathematical sum in which a real bottom line cost is totalled up after a hypothetically new kind of equation—is the story of a female sexual liberationist, Julia Westall. Julia Westall, now married to a leader of the sexual avant-garde, the magnetic and dashing Clement Westall, had left her stodgy, conventional first husband, John Arment, because he was locked, and locked her, in the ways of the past. Her current husband, a Wildean sexual liberation propagandist, offers a message to the adoring society ladies around him that conflates the provocative message of Wilde himself in 'The Critic as Artist', and in his newspaper interviews, with the somewhat more commodified version of that message that Morton Fullerton's letters reveal he communicated to the women and men around him, himself.

Conventional gender norms ensnare Julia, as she sees the sexual knowledge that seduced her, also seducing her younger rival. This existential threat makes Julia, in a moment of great authorial irony, suddenly side with conventional norms about protecting young women from the sexual knowledge that could come to challenge her own security. It is Una Von Sideren for whom Clement will leave Julia; a young woman who had approached Julia as a role model for the sexually-awakened woman. Wharton identifies sexual textuality with sexual arousal and experience—the young woman was aroused by the speech of Una's husband—yet sees it as potentially destructive as well as potentially liberating.

After Julia hears from her husband that he is, in a very unrevolutionary way, leaving her for a younger, prettier and less intellectually gifted woman, this erstwhile female sexual *avant-gardiste* finds that she has fallen—inevitably, as many of Wharton's female readers will have recognised—into a traditional wifely posture in a highly traditional scenario:

> Life could not be broken off short like this, for a whim, a fancy; the law itself would side with her, would defend her. The law? What claim had she upon it? She was the prisoner of her own choice. She had been her own legislator, and she was the predestined victim of the code she had devised. But this was grotesque, intolerable – a mad mistake, for which she could not be held accountable! [...] She had been allowed to go free when she had claimed her freedom [...] Ah, but the difficulty lay deeper! [...] She was the victim of the theories she renounced. It was as though some giant machine of her own making had caught her up in its wheels and was grinding her to atoms. (Wharton 2007, p. 186)

Her own 'new pact' of freedom and sexual choice—of Wildean liberation, her own right to leave her conventional husband and the deadly pact of their marriage—had turned on her like a 'great wheel', that metaphor of being trapped in time and biology that is so familiar, in a Jungian sense, to women when they think about sexual and emotional freedom. Her 'freedom' to which she had pledged a Wildean allegiance, had turned into her husband's right—now unstoppable, without social constraint of any kind, without the opprobrium against infidelity and divorce that both inhibits individual freedoms and sustains marriages—to a 'whim' and 'fancy' for this not-radical, not 'new world' choice of a younger, prettier and less demanding acolyte for a wife.

Extraordinarily, the story ends with Julia seeking out her first husband, whom she had left with a callous blitheness when she had first been swept up in Clement's advocacy of Wildean freedoms and her right to a highest allegiance being to her own self's sense of pleasure and expression. She seeks his forgiveness ('Clement' has, going by his name, 'always already' forgiven himself). She is aware of the 'horrors' of the conventional domestic drawing room that once constrained her. Julia's dialogue with her former husband has the feel of a theoretical treatise or a polemic, questioning what happens in real life to real women when they embrace Wildean 'freedoms' and allow their

men to do the same. The logic of the outcome, Wharton may be arguing, is the risk of emotional chaos and destruction that weighs more
heavily on heterosexual women than on heterosexual men. This may
be because a higher law—an 'inner law', which goes above the material
law, and also above the Wildean law of attraction and play has not yet
seized the day.

As feminist theorists of sexuality would perceive again and again as
they would come 'anew' to this theoretical crisis about the implications
of sexual liberation for heterosexual women versus heterosexual men,
in the 1970s, 1980s and 1990s (and they would have to keep 'arriving'
at this problem, since prior female sexual-liberationist theoretical work
around this problem, such as this work by Wharton here, tends to be
'erased' by the culture), a masculine vision of sexual and emotional freedom may not be sufficient for real liberation for heterosexual women.
There may be further sexual-liberationist work to be done than Wilde's
and his acolytes' such as Fullerton's (and Westall's)—and it may be, perhaps, this call to a higher emotional 'inner law' that is not subject to the
'whims' of impulse and attraction, but a progressive, not regressive, new
ethics that acknowledges the body in the context of will and emotional
commitment.

At the end of the story, Julia leaves their former home; her former
husband makes a gesture as if to reach out to her but 'the footman, who
was evidently alive to his obligations, advanced from the background to
let her out'. Julia is not yet in the new world she has barely glimpsed;
she is in a world of incommensurate choices for women: conventional,
stifling security, or liberationist existential danger: 'The footman threw
open the door, and she found herself outside in the darkness' (Wharton
2007, p. 192).

In reading Wharton as a manifesto-maker for a female version of the
male homosexual liberationists' credo, we should keep in mind the ways,
obvious in retrospect, that women could not engage as unequivocally
with this imaginative call as many of their male peers could. The risks
male writers ran in heeding Whitman's and Wilde's call were legal. But
the risks run by heterosexual women were often of another kind: bastard
children, illegal abortions, more severe prognoses for contracting venereal diseases, the risk of passing on the consequences of such diseases to
their children, permanent social exile, the loss of children in a divorce,
the loss of sustenance itself. But this tension—a woman writer allured,

but terrified, by the attraction of the Whitmanesque/Wildean vision of sexuality—plays out in Wharton in different ways than it did in, for example, Christina Rossetti.

In her letters to Fullerton, this tension appears as a discourse in which Wharton's most private voice connects the possible fulfilment of female sexual desire with the fulfilment of a female artistic self—a most Wildean view—but simultaneously reveals her fears that this same fulfilment of female sexual desire will lead to a form of annihilation of self in other ways. Her fictions and short stories often shine a light on this incommensurate reality: depicting, as in 'Autre Temps, Autre Moers' and *Hudson River Bracketed* (1929), heroines who choose sexual and thus creative fulfilment, but who pay the price with social annihilation. Given the time, with its opening and closing legal and social doors in relation to gender norms, its shifting and contested legal and social limits on sexuality, for both genders, both this hope and this anxiety were utterly realistic, and engaging with both were necessary work for an imagination as potent and a social-critical sensibility as subversive as Wharton's.

But as insensitive as Fullerton was as a lover in the relationship, and later as a cad outside of it, he served magisterially, in a literary dimension, as a male muse to this writer. Wharton's work, after her relationship with Fullerton, defines in text after text a seductive, desirable male love object whose role in the narrative is to serve as a locus of projection, idealisation, obsession, and source of inspiration to the female lover and artist, sometimes at the expense of this subject's (now object's) own complexity and humanity, in just exactly the (much-criticised) ways in which male artists have used the female muse figure and the male gaze. These letters prefigure scenes of Wharton's sexually transgressive heroine Halo Tarrant delighting in observing the beauty of her lover Vance Weston in *Hudson River Bracketed* and *The Gods Arrive*; just as they prefigure the scene of the sexually transgressive heroine of *Summer* (1917), Charity Royall, unseen by her own beautiful lover Lucius Vance, hiding in the ivy outside of his window, like a voyeur or even a stalker, and observing him in the lamplight, in a room described with the language of Eros and intimacy. Wharton uses male figures as sources of aesthetic and erotic inspiration in relation to her female lovers/artists, in a way that is parallel to Wilde's painter, Basil Hallward, using the beautiful Dorian Gray as a muse for his own creative gift in *The Picture of Dorian Gray*, in the way that Wilde draws on Hellenic sculpture in 'The Critic as Artist'; in the way that Walter Pater in *Greek Studies* releases an almost ecstatic rush of literary description to depict in the reader's imagination the beauty of the naked male form in Aegean sculpture as a provocation to his critical imagination.

Wharton's use of the same gazer/gazed upon trope—casting the beautiful male body as creative muse that Wilde also used as a spur to transcendental creativity, suggests that perhaps 'objectification' of this kind cannot be dismissed simply as a product of sexism, but may rather be a far more complex and allegorical yearning of the artistic imagination that transcends gender and perhaps even culture. The female erotic muse figure in heterosexual male writing is assigned the role of eliciting male creativity; the beautiful male muse does the same for the male homosexual transcendentalists. We should not be surprised though we may find the issue complicated that a male muse serves the same purpose for heterosexual women artists.

Women's writing about Eros, dating from Wharton, will have a strain of emotional (as opposed to legal) fear and needy dependency that the male homosexual transcendentalists do not share in their work—and we can surely speculate that the physical 'bondage' of childbirth that a woman of Wharton's period risks is one reason for this difference in literary styles. For when Wharton imagines losing that connection, she invokes the opposing language of 'liberation'—the language of slavery, indeed, 'bondage'. Wharton fears that her freedom is his bondage. When the artist is taken in the arms of her lover, she feels—and writes—that she has no more will. Thus, she explains, since she needs to communicate a message clearly, she must do so in writing rather than within the reach of touch—touch annihilates clarity of speech. This dilemma, of how a woman can speak to a man about her ideas, even as she is in an erotic relationship with him, resurfaces in Wharton's fiction. In the male homosexual transcendentalists of desire, ideas and Eros are coextensive; Wilde and Whitman both describe sexual connection as emerging out of, or extending, intellectual connection. Indeed, the male sexual transcendentalists' charm and their enduring influence derive from the ringing affirmation of self and individual vision through sexual awakening.

But for this heterosexual woman writer, in the fictive world, as in the social world, one's status as a speaker to a man is at cross purposes with one's role as a female lover of a man. Again and again in *Summer*,

Charity Royall will try to speak to Lucius Harney, to communicate something important to him, and he will be unable to hear her—her self will be diminished because of the static caused by his physical lust for her. Verbal and sexual connection with the male lover work, in *Summer* and in Wharton's private letters, tragically to undermine each other (Wharton 1988, p. 145).

The tension between the realisation of pleasure and the potential loss of self, clarity, autonomy, and signature, is the conundrum posed to the female imagination by the nature of female sexual experience. From Wharton's prose in the later novels, notably the confident voice in *Summer* and the assertive characterisation of Halo Tarrant's attachment to her lover in *The Gods Arrive*, we see that female sexual awakening can create voice and autonomy; yet from Wharton's personal papers we see that in relation to a living man—one who is frustratingly not subject to the authorial will—erotic awakening, with the dependency it can entail, can also threaten to annihilate the artist's self, vision and will. This seems to me to be a female writer's problem; male literary accounts, both homosexual and heterosexual, of sexual awakening, do not tend to draw upon language of submission, loss of will, yielding, loss of boundaries or loss of self. Hence the appeal of Nietzsche as a complement to Whitman in Wharton's pantheon, as being the darker but the more reliable guide into states of freedom. Is this distinction in literary phrasing about sexual transcendence—the male-homosexual tradition of sexual transcendence as divine revelation of self, the female heterosexual tradition of sexual transcendence as a loss of or overwhelming of a sense of self—biologically inflected? Male writers of any sexuality do not tend to describe sexual transport as a loss of self. If there is indeed something unique to the female physical experience in a passionate sexual context that can lead to a sense of loss, even if momentary, of identity, boundaries, will and self, then it poses even more of a problem to the female artist than it does to the female philosopher or theologian.

What if one paradox at the heart of female sexuality and creativity, as some heterosexual women writers' work suggests, is that the very qualities that determine the tools of the artist—will, self, boundaries, consciousness, identity—can be swept away by sexual passion, even if momentarily, in an erasure of sense of self that can also be intensified by the prospect of unwanted pregnancy and possibly lethal abortion?

Fullerton had told Wharton she would write better for having learnt about her own sexual response. Indeed, she did write better about the relations between men and women after the experience of awakened sexual love, and in later work she as much as states this: her philosophical position post-1910 is that women are better for the experience of sexual love. She presents this highly countercultural argument frequently as she counterpositions the sexual and literary 'blank slate' anti-heroines such as May Welland with the 'impure' but imaginatively rich fallen women heroines of her oeuvre, from Madame Olenska to the near-prostitutes and kept women of the *Old New York* novellas (1924). In taking up this highly dangerous and novel position for a woman writer in this period, she will take up the banner that Wilde had necessarily let fall after his imprisonment and then his death: she will, fifteen years later, echo him, occupy his same rhetorical and argumentative ground about the correlation between female sexual experience, wisdom and character, and will pay homage to the heroic near-prostitutes and kept women of Wilde's three signature plays, *A Woman of No Importance*, *An Ideal Husband*, and *The Importance of Being Earnest*.

Seven years after her affair with Fullerton ended, Wharton would have Charity Royall also assert proudly her own identity, even though it has elements of 'fallenness' in it, and assert her allegiance to her sexual awakening. Wharton portrays Charity as having the egotism of an artist, and the shamelessness of a woman who rejects the sexual double standard: Charity, like Wilde's heroines in the 'fallen woman' plays, proudly claims her identity and her past, even though the society around her defines it as 'shameful'. Wilde's three most successful plays also represent female protagonists who are proud of their identities and histories in the face of social norms that would define both as negative, because they are fallen.

'What did it matter where she came from, or whose child she was, when love was dancing in her veins, and down the road she saw young Harney coming toward her?' Charity asks herself (Wharton 2001, p. 160). Charity's sense of her significance as an erotic agent and subject is more important than more superficial markers of heritage, social status and occupation. Charity claims her subjective perception and her autobiographical history proudly, even though her mother is an archetypal 'fallen woman', actually a prostitute. When Lucius Harney and Charity Royall go up into 'the Mountain'—that place outside of respectable social norms—and encounter the promiscuous, degraded, impoverished Mountain people who are her real tribe, she refuses to disavow the truth of her antecedents: 'I ain't—I ain't ashamed. They're my people, and I ain't ashamed of them', she sobs (Wharton 2001, p. 166). She is able to stand up for her identity even when her guardian calls her a whore: 'It helps me not to care a straw what lies you tell about me', she retorts (Wharton 2001, p. 179).

Subsequent to the affair with Fullerton, there was a shift in how Wharton represented her heroines. Wharton began to position them as gazing at the objects of their desire, and as initiating erotic contact. Wharton had been reading Nietzsche in the summer of 1909; eight years later, on the eve of a war that posited the destruction of the traditional, repressive world in which she had been raised, in *Summer*, Wharton creates a Nietzschean figure of female sexual assertiveness in Charity Royall. Indeed Wharton's 1908–1909 letters to Fullerton have explicit echoes of Nietzsche as well as of Wilde, or rather, of the credo of the seductions in *The Picture of Dorian Gray*: 'How strange to feel one's self all at once *"Jehnseits von Gut und Bose"* [Beyond Good and Evil ...] It would hurt no one—and it would give me my first last draught of life [...] Why not? I have always laughed at the "mala prohibita"—"bugbears to frighten children". The anti-social act is the only one that is harmful "per se" [...] And, as you told me the other day—*and as I needed no telling!*—what I have given you is far far more' (Lewis 1993, p. 221). Though the letter is a fragment, we can guess that the conclusion is another Wildean assertion that love trumps conventional morality, that the value of experience trumps the dullness of 'goodness'. In the character of Charity Royall, Wharton constructs a heroine who repeatedly insists upon her right to sexual pleasure; upon her right to defend herself against sexual assault and incest; and one who self-consciously articulates what amounts to a series of manifestoes on the rightness of her own identity as a sexual being. Indeed, in this figure Wharton creates an almost supernaturally empowered defender of female sexual integrity.

Nominally though, this is a story about female victimisation. Charity Royall was, rather mysteriously, adopted by Lawyer Royall, a dour, negative authority figure, and his now-deceased wife, taken from her surviving, impoverished mother on The Mountain (who, as the narrative progresses, we learn is a loose woman or perhaps even professional prostitute), and brought up in the small hamlet of North Dormer where nothing ever happens and from which no one ever seems to escape. Charity is positioned as being penniless, completely dependent upon Lawyer Royall, and with no relatives, mentors or professional options, which makes her blazing self-defence and insistence on her right to an autonomous sexuality all the more implausible in reality, but all the more plausible if we read her as being a kind of dream work Wharton was conjuring toward another kind of world than the one that existed when she wrote this novel. In this way, Charity Royall is an act of magical invocation of a better world in which to house female sexuality. The utopian and dystopian quality of the narrative is underscored by Wharton's clearly symbolic, even allegorical names for her characters and places: 'Charity', *caritas*; 'Royall', king, patriarch; 'Lucius', light; 'Dormer', sleeper.

The story opens with Lawyer Royall drinking too much and trying to force his way into Charity's room, for sexual purposes. With strength for the time of this writing, Charity repudiates her would-be assailant, shames him, and insists on protection from his further encroachments, demanding that he hire a woman to keep house, essentially as security. Throughout *Summer*, Wharton describes Lawyer Royall in terms of sexual revulsion from a female perspective: he is described in unattractively violent and tumescent terms: his 'rumpled grey hair stood up above his forehead like the crest of an angry bird' and 'the leather-brown of his veined cheeks was blotched with red' (Wharton 2001, p. 171). The scene of a fearless and guiltless female response, within the fantasy world of fiction, to an attempt at incest or sexual assault, is far different from the cowed, guilty reactions of contemporary young women in similar 'real-life' situations, such as that recounted in Freud's case history of 'Dora', or in Virginia Woolf's account in her letters of the incest she experienced at the hands of her brother; and it is difficult to name another such scenario in the 1910s of female sexual resistance in another novel of the period.

In my reading, while there is certainly a great cost for Charity's sexual self-assertion, this is not a novel about victimisation but about resistance. Charity is not only portrayed as a sexual avenger with 'her own revolts and defenses' [*sic.*] (Wharton 2001, p. 154); Wharton also depicts the girl as an artist. We receive a highly nuanced presentation, through Charity Royall's eyes, of the connection between female desire and artistic perception. In the Whitmanesque tradition, Charity Royall is a mystic sensualist who is a woman of the earth; she is scarcely educated, and, though implausibly, Wharton describes her as working as a librarian and we can recall the erotic description in Wharton's memoir of the library of her childhood as a place of blissful and unmediated innocent feminine sexual pleasure. She is also represented, in dream logic as being barely literate, which in the long feminine literary tradition equating literary knowledge with sexual knowledge, suggests that she is sexually unawakened too.

Yet in scene after scene, in a narrative that parallels awakening creative and sensual consciousness in male protagonists ranging from the voice of Whitman's 'Calamus' poems, to Jude in Hardy's *Jude the Obscure*, Wharton represents Charity Royall's physical desire as being intimately connected to her artistic vision. If one unpacks Wharton's at times oblique prose, one can see Charity embody the same challenge that Wilde had issued, if less directly, in *Lady Windermere's Fan* and *A Woman of No Importance* two decades before: the confrontational proposal that there are worse—that is, far more immoral—things a woman can be than a whore. We can hear the Wildean argument that being an unjust, brutal or obtuse person, as 'respectable' as one might be, is actually more shameful and dirtier than being simply sexually transgressive. One can also hear the echo of the Wildean assertion that it is lack of imagination or narrow-mindedness that actually sully the soul, rather than sexual expressiveness. Wharton makes the case, as Wilde had done in his plays of 1892–1893, that the 'proper' choices—those of forced chastity, forced marital servitude to a boor, or merely generalised hypocrisy—are actually morally dirtier than a life of conscious prostitution lived with inner integrity. As radical as that message was in 1892 and 1893 from a homosexual male playwright's pen, it was just as radical, and virtually unprecedented, from a woman's pen in 1914.

In the scenes of lovemaking in the farmhouse ruin, Charity is portrayed as being reborn and redeemed through a sexual awakening, connecting in the Wildean/Whitmanesque tradition, identity, nature, spirituality and sexuality, as Wharton's private letters to Fullerton reveal she herself felt that she had been: 'The only reality', writes Wharton, 'was the unfolding of her new self, the reaching out to the light of all her contracted tendrils' (Wharton 2001, p. 214). After she becomes an awakened sexual being, Charity integrates her knowledge, sexual and intellectual, and begins to attend to what stirs or diminishes her own sexual response: 'Sometimes she envied the other girls their [...] long hours of inarticulate philandering [...] but when she pictured herself curling her hair or putting a new ribbon in her hat for Ben Fry or one of the Sollas boys the fever dropped and she lapsed into indifference' (Wharton 2001, p. 152).

Harney, of course—true to his role in the 'wrongs of' plotline—does eventually leave Charity. The worst, as in so many of Wharton's fictions about 'fallen women', really does take place. But again Charity faces the truth of her situation; that of a poor girl seduced and abandoned by a middle-class man without euphemism and without regret for her sexual experience: 'She had given him all she had—but what was it compared to the other gifts life held for him? She understood now the case of girls like herself to whom this kind of thing happened. They gave all they had, but their all was not enough; it could not buy more than a few moments' (Wharton 2001, p. 223). Even when she understands that she is pregnant, she does not abandon the experience she has gained. By remaining true to the avowal of her pleasure, in a critical and novel way in the tradition of representations of female sexuality in women's fiction, Charity has remained true to herself.

Charity at length went to consult an abortionist, and fled at the prospect of sacrificing her baby. 'Her soul recoiled from the vision of the white-faced woman among the plush sofas and gilt frames. In the established order of things as she knew them she saw no place for her individual adventure' (Wharton 2001, p. 243). Wharton is making a hermeneutical and theoretical point here about female sexuality and women's writing: a woman can have the Whitmanesque epiphany about the unity of mind and body, of the carnal and the divine, but, as Wilde himself found to his sorrow in 1895, there was still 'no place' in the social world to house that epiphany.

Charity faces—and considers—becoming an actual prostitute in order to support her child; she had considered and rejected a visit to an abortionist. She tries to escape to her mother and the mountain, but her mother is dying a grotesque death, portrayed as if she has been worn out from sexual slavery, and there is indeed no escape. At the time Wharton was writing, there were no alternative endings if a woman dared step out of her constrained sexual role. After this crisis, there is indeed no exit for Charity; her would-be abuser/father/lover, Lawyer Royall, comes to get her back and she gives in; 'for the most part she had only a confused sensation of slipping down a smooth and irresistible current; and she abandoned herself to the feeling as a refuge from the torment of thought' (Wharton 2001, p. 263). Reader, she marries him. The deed is done, in an atmosphere of 'unreality' (Wharton 2001, p. 272).

The ending is implausible: Wharton has Charity concede, improbably, that Lawyer Royall is a good man after all. Having made the case that there is no escape for a woman like Charity, it is as if Wharton cannot bring herself to linger long on the no-escape resolution that awaits her formerly brave, formerly independent heroine. Wharton seems to give up, finally, on narrative just as her heroine did on hope. Yet up until the last three or four pages of her text, when the punishments for female sexual assertion inevitably introduce themselves, Wharton succeeded in creating a vivid polemicist for female sexual rights. By the time some of these most sexually radical Whartonian works were being created, both Whitman and Wilde had been dead for over a decade. Both reputations were in eclipse and neither writer consciously or overtly cultivated female sexual-revolutionary heiresses or mentees. But Wharton nonetheless picked up the banner these radicals—radicals we would now identify as gay men—had left to posterity, and used their provocations, challenges and rhetorical strategies to imagine a way forward even for female sexual liberation within the context of an awakening artistic consciousness.

## REFERENCES

Lewis, R.W.B., and Nancy Lewis, 1993. *Edith Wharton: A Biography*. New York, NY: Fromm International.

Wharton, Edith, 1988. *The Letters of Edith Wharton*, eds. R.W.B Lewis and Nancy Lewis. New York, NY: Simon & Schuster.

Wharton, Edith, 2001. *Summer*. New York, NY: Modern Library Classics.

Wharton, Edith, 2004. *The Fruit of the Tree*. Amherst, NY: Prometheus Books.

Wharton, Edith, 2007. *The New York Stories of Edith Wharton*, ed. Roxana Robinson. New York, NY: New York Review of Books Press.

Wilde, Oscar, 1989. *The Picture of Dorian Gray*, in *The Major Works*, ed. Isobel Murray. Oxford, UK: Oxford World's Classics.

# CHAPTER 3

# Losing Face Among the Natives: 'Something About Tattooing and Tabooing' in Melville's *Typee*

*Graham Atkin*

Herman Melville's first novel *Typee*, published in 1846, remained his most popular work until the 1930s. Now Melville is, of course, most famous for his later epic *Moby Dick*, but this was not always so. *Typee* is an intriguing South Sea adventure based on the author's own experiences and narrated by 'Tommo', who, with his companion Toby, jumps ship and wanders into the valley of Typee, home to a tribe of suspected cannibals. In this essay I will focus on the novel's twenty-ninth (or is it thirtieth? I will explain this gnomic uncertainty later) chapter in which Tommo describes his encounter with a Typeean tattooist and then discusses 'the mysterious "Taboo"', a 'remarkable system' 'so strange and complex in its arrangements' (Melville 1994, p. 173). Tommo's encounter with the man, who seems determined to tattoo his very *face* (the word is deliberately emphasised by Melville), leaves him 'convinced that in some luckless hour I should be disfigured in such a manner as never more to have the *face* to return to my countrymen even should an

G. Atkin (✉)
University of Chester, Chester, UK
e-mail: g.atkin@chester.ac.uk

© The Author(s) 2017
E. Rees (ed.), *Talking Bodies*, DOI 10.1007/978-3-319-63778-5_3

opportunity offer' (Melville 1994, p. 172). The threat of non-consensual body modification, understandably perhaps, deeply troubles our narrator and he decides he must attempt to escape from his hosts. Melville's story is far more than a traveller's yarn. In following the experiences of a narrator far from his own 'civilisation', and increasingly fearful for his bodily safety, the reader of *Typee* is confronted with unsettling issues of personal and cultural identity in crisis.

This early advertisement (Fig. 3.1) from the publishers of *Typee* (Harper and Brothers, New York) serves as an admittedly selective and biased indication of the novel's early reception. We read that:

> Typee is a happy hit, whichever way you look at it – whether as travels, romance, poetry or humor. The *bonhommie* of the book is remarkable. It appears as genial and natural as the spontaneous fruits of the island. – *Morning News*

> Some of these pictures but require us to call the savages celestials, to have supposed Mr. Melville to have dropped from the clouds, and to fancy some Ovidian grace added to the narrative in order to become scenes of classic mythology. – *London Spectator*

> Enviable Herman! A happier dog it is impossible to imagine than Herman in the Typee valley. – *London Times*

Even in this brief sample from contemporary commentators, some of the preoccupations of modern critics are alluded to, such as the desire to classify the text in literary generic terms. The *Morning News*'s use of 'whichever way you look at it' raises the vital matter of perspective and viewpoint in a text we must remember Melville calls 'a peep at Polynesian life'. The indefinite article and the diminutive, humble 'peep' suggest that Tommo-Melville presents his own view and perspective and invites us to look with our own eyes and see for ourselves. Melville even gives us the names of his co-authors, Porter and Stewart, and the titles of their writings, so that we might know his textual sources directly.

As many readers of this volume on *Talking Bodies* may be unfamiliar with Melville's early tale, I thought I would give you a brief account of the narrative. I will then move on to pay some closer attention to the aforementioned chapter (29 or 30, depending on which edition of this remarkably 'fluid' text you read). In commenting on this chapter I will draw on a range of material from the fields of anthropology, psychology, literary criticism, sociology and linguistics.

## BY HERMAN MELVILLE.

## TYPEE.

*One Volume, 12mo, Muslin, 87½ cents ; Paper, 75 cents.*

"Why I never chanced upon Mr. Melville's work before, is one of the inscrutable mysteries of my fate. While luxuriating in its perusal, I looked back upon myself in my ante-Typee-cal existence, with positive commiseration. There are those, I am aware, who doubt the authenticity of this charming narrative. 'Oh, ye of little faith!' I have a solemn conviction of its truth—a pertinacious belief in the entire work—an humble, unquestioning reliance on the word of the narrator."—*Correspondence of* "Grace Greenwood" *to the Home Journal.*

Chateaubriand's Atala is of no softer or more romantic tone—Anacharsis scarce presents us with images more classically exquisite.—*New York Mirror.*

Typee is a happy hit, whichever way you look at it—whether as travels, romance, poetry, or humor. The *bonhommie* of the book is remarkable. It appears as genial and natural as the spontaneous fruits of the island.—*Morning News.*

The air of freshness and romance which characterizes Typee, gives it the appearance of an improved edition of our old favorites, Peter Wilkins and Gulliver.—*Richmond Republican.*

A charming book—full of talent, composed with singular elegance, and as musical as Washington Irving's Columbus —*Western Continent.*

Enviable Herman! A happier dog it is impossible to imagine than Herman in the Typee valley.—*London Times.*

Some of these pictures but require us to call the savages celestials, to have supposed Mr. Melville to have dropped from the clouds, and to fancy some Ovidian grace added to the narrative in order to become scenes of classic mythology.—*London Spectator.*

Such is life in the valley of the Typees; and surely Rasselas, if he had had the good luck to stumble on it, would not have gone further in his search after happiness.—*Douglas Jerrold's Magazine.*

The whole narrative is most simple, most affecting, and most romantic. Ah! thou gentle and too enchanting Fayaway, what has become of thee?—*Lon. Gent's. Mag.*

Since the joyous moment when we first read Robinson Crusoe, and believed it all, and wondered all the more because we believed, we have not met with so bewitching a work as this narrative of Herman Melville's.—*London John Bull.*

A book full of fresh and richly-colored matter.—*London Athenæum.*

This is really a very curious book. The happy valley of our dear Rasselas was not a more romantic or enchanting scene.—*London Examiner.*

This is a most entertaining and refreshing book. The writer, though filling the post of a common sailor, is certainly no common man.—*London Critic.*

The style is racy and pointed, and there is a romantic interest thrown around the adventure, which to most readers will be highly charming.—*American Review.*

It bears the unexhausted characteristics of talent.—*National Intelligencer.*

The story is eventful—wonderful; some of the deeds performed by the author and his companion almost surpass belief.—*Cincinnati Herald.*

### Harper & Brothers, Publishers, New York.

**Fig. 3.1**  An early advertisement from the publishers of Melville's *Typee*

As Tommo, Toby, Captain Vang and the rest of the crew approach the Marquesas Islands, Melville's powers of description, of signification, fail. This, perhaps, defines the ineffability of paradise: 'No description can do justice to its beauty' (Melville 1994, p. 9). The women who live in this paradise are not only women, but 'Mermaids'. Their greeting party is full of an innocent open playfulness that will, sadly, be corrupted by the sailors. They are 'a shoal of "whinhenies" (young girls)' swimming towards the vessel. Tommo 'almost fancied they could be nothing else than so many mermaids'. They 'succeeded in getting up the ship's side, where they clung dripping with the brine and glowing from the bath, their jet-black tresses streaming over their shoulders, and half enveloping their otherwise naked forms. There they hung, sparkling with savage vivacity, laughing gaily at one another, and chattering away with infinite glee' (Melville 1994, p. 11).

Tommo and his friend Toby escape from the foul despot Vang, who himself has no respect for the natives or the contract between a ship's captain and his crew. Here is Tommo on Captain Vang's tyrannical treatment of his men: 'His prompt reply to all complaints and remonstrances was the butt-end of a hand-spike, so convincingly administered as effectually to silence the aggrieved party' (Melville 1994, p. 13). The society of the ship is a crew 'composed of a parcel of dastardly and mean-spirited wretches, divided among themselves, and only united in enduring without resistance the unmitigated tyranny of the captain' (Melville 1994, p. 13). This is the society from which the like-minded friends, Tommo and Toby, flee. The two friends set off on their Homeric journey to an ideal home beyond the hills, and *Typee* tells the story of Tommo's adventures, his residence with the Typee tribe, and his eventual escape. Even at this early stage, however, there are anxieties about men who eat human flesh, and Tommo, and we, the readers, share that horrifying fear of the breaking of perhaps the ultimate taboo, the consumption of the human body.

*Typee* begins with the narrator Tommo waiting his chance to escape the tyrannous Captain Vang. The sailors are due some shore leave, but before they are let off the ship for a day they are 'harangued' by their 'worthy captain' who tries to convince them to stay on board:

Ten to one, men, if you go ashore, you will get into some infernal row, and that will be the end of you; for if these tattooed scoundrels get you a little ways back into their valleys they'll nab you – that you can be certain of. Plenty of white men have gone ashore here and never been seen any more. There was the old *Dido*, she put in here about two years ago, and sent one watch off on liberty; they never were heard of again for a week – the natives swore they didn't know where they were – and only three of them ever got back to the ship again, and one with his face damaged for life, for the cursed heathens tattooed a broad patch clean across his figurehead. (Melville 1994, pp. 21–22)

The narrative takes a thrilling turn when our heroes Tommo and Toby flee the ship: 'On we toiled, the perspiration starting from our bodies in floods, our limbs torn and lacerated with the splintered fragments of the broken canes' (Melville 1994, p. 25) and 'I will not recount every hair-breadth escape, and every fearful difficulty that occurred before we succeeded in reaching the bosom of the valley' (Melville 1994, p. 49).

The question which haunts Tommo and Toby when they meet the natives is 'Typee or Happar?' They hope the answer will be 'Happar', as these are reputed to be a friendly tribe. The Typeeans, on the other hand, are notorious cannibals. Reflecting on the narrative ambivalence of Melville-Tommo's 'peep at Polynesian life', critic John Samson comments, 'the question could as easily be "Calvin or Rousseau?" "Missionary or Sailor?"' (Samson 1984, p. 279). Whether the natives are friendly noble savages or vicious bloodthirsty cannibals may depend more on how you see them than how they are. As with Hawthorne's *Scarlet Letter* and the ambiguous purport of the embroidered 'A', there are problems of signification and interpretation at the heart of Melville's *Typee*.

The simplicity of Tommo's comments is noteworthy: 'They were a boy and a girl, slender and graceful, and completely naked, with the exception of a slight girdle of bark' (Melville 1994, p. 51). Tommo tells how he 'uttered a few words of their language with which I was acquainted, scarcely expecting that they would understand me, but to show that we had not dropped from the clouds upon them' (Melville 1994, p. 52). With this he wins their trust. Later they will meet others of the tribe, including Chief Mehevi and Kory-Kory. The first detailed account of the tattooing of these islanders comes when Tommo sees a tattooed Typee warrior.

Melville-Tommo, in his account, pays close attention to the tattooing, in particular the tattooing of the chief's face (for it transpires that this is Mehevi himself):

that which was most remarkable in the appearance of this splendid islander, was the elaborate tattooing displayed on every noble limb. All imaginable lines and curves and figures were delineated over his whole body, and in their grotesque variety and infinite profusion, I could only compare them to the crowded groupings of quaint patterns we sometimes see in costly pieces of lace-work. The most simple and remarkable of all these ornaments was that which decorated the countenance of the chief. Two broad stripes of tattooing, diverging from the centre of his shaven crown, obliquely crossed both eyes – staining the lids – to a little below either ear, where they united with another stripe, which swept in a straight line along the lips, and formed the base of the triangle. (Melville 1994, p.60)

Tommo does not desire to be a Typeean warrior. Instead he wants to be an untattooed lover, with his wounded leg healing gradually, while he enjoys physical pleasures with the sexually free and generally naked women of the island, in particular his beloved Fayaway. Tommo decries the small marks of tattooing on Fayaway's divine form, and the practice of tattooing generally, in an earlier chapter that intensifies our sense of his horror at the prospect of being tattooed in Chap. 30:

Were I asked if the beauteous form of Fayaway was altogether free from the hideous blemish of tattooing, I should be constrained to answer that it was not. But the practitioners of this barbarous art, so remorseless in their inflictions upon the brawny limbs of the warriors of the tribe, seem to be conscious that it needs not the resources of their profession to augment the charms of the maidens of the vale. (Melville 1994, p. 68)

Behind the Paradise lurks a sinister and dark threat, for the ultimate taboo of cannibalism haunts the account. Tommo-Melville acknowledges this with a certain dry humour:

The reader will, ere long, have reason to suspect that the Typees are not free from the guilt of cannibalism; and he will then, perhaps, charge me with admiring a people against whom so odious a crime is chargeable. But this only enormity in their character is not half so horrible as it is usually described. (Melville 1994, pp. 160–161)

He goes on to say: 'I assert that those who indulge in it [cannibalism] are in other respects humane and virtuous' (Melville 1994, p. 161). It perhaps seems an odd claim, but Melville is an odd writer, a strange mixture of Rousseauian optimism and harsh Calvinism.

This brings me to the crucial chapter I wish to consider more closely now. Chapter 29 or 30.[1] In my own reading experience this chapter struck me as a key moment in the narrative, one which awoke me, as Tommo is awoken, to a new and present danger. Decisions have to be made. If Tommo is to survive as Tommo then he must escape. And it is the threat of tattooing, arguably as much as, or possibly more than, the threat of cannibalism, which spurs Tommo on to escape. Either alternative, assimilation by tattooing, or death and devouring in cannibalistic ritual, will result in the end of Tommo-Melville. Like Ishmael, we know he will live, for he is telling us the story. But we do not know whether he might decide, or be forced, to become tattooed across the face and join the band of brother warriors and their island civilisation.

You can see from this table (Fig. 3.2) that reflections on Tattooing and Taboo have been added as the novel develops through stages 1–7 (and I would just like to praise here the extraordinary scholarship of Bryant in *Melville Unfolding*). The chapter I am particularly concerned with here is, in the final editions of the novel, Chap. 30, but it began as Chap. 17 and then became Chaps. 19, 21 and 26 (with further reflections on taboo added), and then became Chap. 27 before ending as Chap. 30.[2] It is a climactic moment in the narrative in which Tommo's reflections on the native Typeean customs shift to a compulsion to escape the 'paradise' which, through his increasing anxiety, has been lost to him. It is the fear that he will lose his human 'face divine', through the zealous evangelistic art of Karky's tattooing, that convinces Tommo that he can no longer stay with Fayaway, Mehevi, Kory-Kory and the others. It is in this moment, as T. Walter Herbert Jr. astutely observes, that:

> Instead of finding a life of psychic freedom among the Typees where 'the grand principles of virtue and honor' hold sway amenably with his own deepest impulses, Tommo now has to contend with efforts to draw him into an alien and confining social structure. (Herbert 1980, p. 170)

What fills our narrator with horror in this key Chap. 30 is the thought that he may end up looking something like one of the tattooed figures he has seen—Karky's living canvases. We wonder whether Melville actually himself came face to face with a Karky of his own and experienced a similar threat. Certainly it was a threat to all who fell in with these Polynesian island tribes, as we see in the case of Lem Hardy, and we think also of Captain Vang's warning to his men. The 'face divine' is mentioned by Tommo 'as the poets call it'. This is disingenuous on Tommo-Melville's part, for Melville is well aware that it is not just any poet, but Milton himself, the ultimate poet of paradise known and paradise lost. And in this encounter with Karky paradise is lost for Tommo, and he knows he wants to leave. The process of Tommo's assimilation by the tribe (with cannibalism as the ultimate form of assimilation) has come into sharp consciousness for our hero in Chap. 30, and as we read we tingle with the excitement of the fear of this hideous threat.

It is on the experience of reading the novel that I particularly want to reflect. In reading *Typee* we are placed in the position of Tommo: we encounter both place and people for the first time, as he does. We meet Chief Mehevi and are served by Kory-Kory and we fall in love with the beautiful Fayaway. We encounter Marnoo (a liminal figure, like us (Tommo), who is strangely 'taboo' and can therefore come and go as he pleases) and we are perplexed by him and affronted by his rude disdain for us. We fear the cannibalistic Typeeans. We fear the predatory artist Karky, with his tools of tattooing, relentlessly pursuing us to tattoo broad bands across our divine faces. We lunge at MowMow's throat with the boathook in a terrible final outburst of violence in our desire to escape. And throughout we are puzzled and confused by the mysterious taboo, and by its connection to the observance of tattooing. But then we are in good company, with Tommo and Sigmund Freud. Here is Tommo on the subject (we will hear from Freud later):

> Although convinced that tattooing was a religious observance, still the nature of the connection between it and the superstitious idolatry of the people was a point upon which I could never obtain any information. Like the still more important system of the 'Taboo', it always appeared inexplicable to me. (Melville 1994, p. 173)

Melville has added to his climactic Chap. 30 the description of the impossibilities of understanding even a small part of the strange language of these alien cultures by commenting on the 'intricacy of these dialects' when he says he saw a 'tabular exhibition of a Hawiian [*sic.*] verb, conjugated through all its moods and tenses'. Tommo-Melville claims that it 'covered the side of a considerable apartment, and I doubt whether Sir William Jones himself would not have despaired of mastering it'.[3] To this key chapter Melville also later added (at Stage Five of the creative process, following Bryant's analysis (see Fig. 3.2)) the dark humour of

The Growth of *Typee*

| Stage | | | | | | | | | | | | | | | | | | | | | | | | | | | | | | | | |
|---|---|---|---|---|---|---|---|---|---|---|---|---|---|---|---|---|---|---|---|---|---|---|---|---|---|---|---|---|---|---|---|---|
| Stage 1 | | 1 | | 2 | 3 | 4 5 | 6 7 | 8 9 | 10 11 12 | | 13 A/B | 14 | 15 A/B | | | | | | | | | | | | | | | 16 | 17 | 18 | | | |
| 2 | | 1 | | 2 | 3 | 4 5 | 6 7 | 8 9 | 10 11 12 | | 13 13A | 14 13B | 15 | 16 15A pop gun | | | | | | | | | | | | 17 15B tattoo | | 18 | 19 | 20 | | | |
| 3 | | 1 | | 2 | 3 | 4 5 | 6 7 | 8 9 | 10 11 12 | 13 fruit | 14 | 15 | 16 | 17 | | | | | | | | | 18 fish | | 19 | | 20 | 21 | 22 | | | | |
| 4 | 1 | 2 Stewart | 3 | 4 Stewart | 5 | 6 7 | 8 9 | 10 11 | 12 13 14 | 15 | 16 | 17 | 18 | 19 | | | | | | | | | 20 | | 21 | | 22 | 23 | 24 | | | | |
| 5 | 1 | 2 | 3 | 4 | 5 | 6 7 | 8 9 | 10 11 | 12 13 14 | 15 | 16 | 17 | 18 | 19 | | 20 | 21 | 22 | 23 | 24 | | 25 | | 26 taboo | | 27 | 28 | 29 | | | | |
| 6 | 1 | 2 | 3 | 4 | 5 | 6 7 | 8 9 | 10 11 | 12 13 14 | 15 | 16 | 17 Porter | 18 | 19 | | 20 | 21 | 22 | 23 | 24 | | 25 | 26 Porter | 27 | 28 Porter | 29 | 30 | 31 | | | | |
| 7 | 1 | 2 | 3 | 4 Porter | 5 | 6 7 | 8 9 | 10 11 | 12 13 14 | 15 | 16 | 17 | 18 | 19 | 20 | 21 | 22 | 23 | 24 | 25 | 26 | 27 Porter | 28 | 29 | 30 | 31 | 32 | 33 | 34 | | | |
| | Escape to mountains and Typee | | | | | | MS | | | Tommo and Toby, Fayaway and Marnoo | | | Dance and ruins | Feast of the calabashes | | | Typee customs | | | | | Escape from Typee | | | | | | | | | |

**Fig. 3.2**  The growth of *Typee* from *Melville Unfolding* (Bryant 2008, p. 36)

Captain Vang's violent rejection of the Taboo's power: 'Oh, hang your taboo [...] talk taboo to the marines' (Melville 1994, p. 176).

When we begin reading this key chapter of Melville's first novel in the Wordsworth Classics edition we find the following heading: 'A professor of the fine arts—His persecutions—Something about tattooing and tabooing—Two anecdotes in illustration of the latter—A few thoughts on the Typee dialect' (headings differ between editions of the novel).

The chapter begins:

In one of my strolls with Kory-Kory, in passing along the border of a thick growth of bushes, my attention was arrested by a singular noise. On entering the thicket, I witnessed for the first time the operation of tattooing as performed by these islanders. (Melville 1994, p. 170)

'The operation of tattooing' is 'performed' for us in the following description: 'I beheld a man extended flat upon his back on the ground, and, despite the forced composure of his countenance, it was evident that he was suffering agony' (Melville 1994, p. 170).

So much for the man being tattooed. But next we are introduced to his tormentor, Karky, the tattoo artist 'with a heart as callous as that of an army surgeon' who delights in his 'performance, enlivening his labours with a wild chant, tapping away the while as merrily as a wood-pecker' (Melville 1994, p. 171).

> His tormentor bent over him, working away for all the world like a stone-cutter with a mallet and chisel. In one hand he held a short slender stick, pointed with a shark's tooth, on the upright end of which he tapped with a small hammer-like piece of wood, thus puncturing the skin, and charging it with the colouring matter in which the instrument was dipped. (Melville 1994, p. 170)

> As soon as he perceived me, supposing that I sought him in his professional capacity, he seized hold of me in a paroxysm of delight, and was all eagerness to begin the work. When, however, I gave him to understand that he had altogether mistaken my views, nothing could exceed his grief and disappointment. But recovering from this, he seemed determined not to credit my assertion, and grasping his implements, he flourished them about in fearful vicinity to my face. (Melville 1994, p. 171)

'Fearful vicinity to my face': the phrase startles us as we are confronted with Tommo's new predicament. Karky flourishes his instruments about in fearful vicinity to Tommo-Melville's face and the effect on Tommo is profound: 'The incident opened my eyes to a new danger; and I now felt convinced that in some luckless hour I should be disfigured in such a manner as never more to have the *face* to return to my countrymen, even should an opportunity offer' (Melville 1994, p. 172). His encounter with Karky the tattoo artist forces Tommo to confront his 'difference' from his hosts. Having relaxed with Fayaway and happily tested the strengths of the Taboo by pleading with Chief Mehevi for special dispensations, Tommo now finds himself fearful of being defaced and subsumed by the Typeean culture. Mehevi and 'several of the inferior chiefs' declare that Tommo 'should be tattooed' (Melville 1994, p. 172). Tommo has a moment of epiphany: 'The whole system of tattooing was, I found, connected with their religion: and it was evident, therefore, that they were resolved to make a convert of me', and this leads our hero to ruminate further:

Although convinced that tattooing was a religious observance, still the nature of the connection between it and the superstitious idolatry of the people was a point upon which I could never obtain any information. Like the still more important system of the 'Taboo', it always appeared inexplicable to me. (Melville 1994, p. 173)

This kind of deep cultural analysis of the Typees is further developed by Tommo-Melville:

The capricious operations of the taboo are not its least remarkable feature: to enumerate them all would be impossible. Black hogs – infants to a certain age – women in an interesting situation – young men while the operation of tattooing their faces is going on – and certain parts of the valley during the continuance of a shower – are alike fenced about by the operation of the taboo. (Melville 1994, p. 175)

So, not only are tattooing and tabooing 'inexplicable', but the operations of the taboo are worryingly 'capricious'. However, Tommo is given a choice of patterns by which his visage should be adorned: 'a choice of patterns' between a 'face spanned by three horizontal bars' or to 'have as many oblique stripes slanting across it' or 'like a true courtier' Tommo 'might wear a sort of freemason badge upon my countenance in the shape of a mystic triangle'. The pressure he is under to be tattooed in this way means that 'at last my existence became a burden to me' (Melville 1994, p. 173; please see Fig. 3.3 for examples of Marquesan facial tattoo designs).

To get a sense of the impact facial tattooing can have I encourage readers to search the internet for images using the term 'Leeds United Tattooed Man'. With a cross of St. George on one cheek, a Union Jack on the other, a 'three lions' badge and a Leeds United FC crest on each side of his forehead, this man, whose name I have been unable to ascertain, makes quite an impression when you come face to face with him, even if that confrontation is with a screen you are gazing at on the internet. It is difficult to see this man as anything but identified by his tattoos, he *is* Leeds United Tattooed Face Man to me. Taking this man at face value you would fly in the face of reason not to assume that this man identifies himself as a Leeds United Football Club supporter, an Englishman and an England football supporter. The shock is caused not by the fact that this man is tattooed, but by the fact that his *face* is

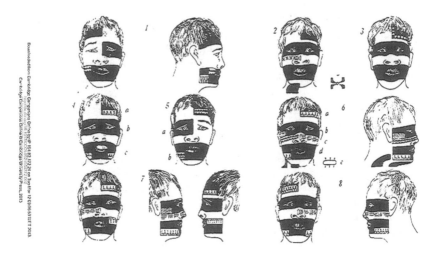

**Fig. 3.3**   Tattoo designs in the Marquesas (Levine 1998, p. 21)

tattooed, and tattooed so fully that his 'identity' seems somehow defined by the overlaid, ornamented surface of the front of his head.

A new face on the matter of the old art of tattooing is provided by Carl Zimmer's *Science Ink: Tattoos of the Science Obsessed*. Zimmer's book is one example of Western society's changing attitudes towards tattoos. Yale lecturer Zimmer noticed tattoos on his scientist friends at a pool party and started a blog about it all. He has unearthed a huge variety of intricate biological and biochemical tattoos adorning scientists around the world.[4] I see more tattoos around me than ever before (not many of them intricate biochemical designs, it must be said) on men and women. Nina Nyman, elsewhere in this volume, takes a provocative and fascinating look at the relationship of tattooed women with their bodies. Now tattoos are not as taboo as they once were in the West, even tattoos on women, but is there still something, for us all, men and women, that is taboo about tattooing the *face*? Perhaps it is something to do with the fact that the facial tattoo is very hard to conceal. Most other tattoos are possible to keep under wraps (when necessary or desired), and are often only revealed when clothes are removed to some extent. But the facial tattoo is not easy to hide.

Confronted with such a full and startling tattoo style as that of Leeds United Tattooed Face Man or a Marquesan Warrior (see Fig. 3.3) I think I might find it difficult not to quail. These face tattoos seem to be the marks of the warrior, indeed tattooed tears on the faces of Los Angeles gang members denote their victims and are perhaps a modern instance of these bare-faced marks of the warrior. How would I feel were I to be afraid that those I lived with might forcibly tattoo my face in this startling way? They want me to belong with them. They want me to change my appearance in the most radical way so that I fit in better. Perhaps I could then marry into the royal family, and have heirs galore in this tropical paradise. This is the situation in which Tommo-Omoo-Melville finds himself. I use Tommo-Omoo-Melville here, borrowing from James E. Miller (1962) in *A Reader's Guide to Herman Melville*, as a way to describe the character/narrator, wanderer/rover ('Omoo' is the Marquesan word for a rover or wanderer), and author figure who relates his sailor's yarn to us with the kind of scientific attention to detail that convinces us that what we are being told is essentially true. Or if not true, then credible. And for the time that we are reading and immersed in such a tale we are willing to believe in its verisimilitude and place ourselves in the tale with Tommo-Omoo-Melville, for there is a little of the inquisitive character, the narrator, the rover, the wanderer, the storyteller, the author, in us all. And is there part of me that fears bands of tattooing across my face, and part of me that fears (any part of me) being eaten? Faced with such a fearful assimilation by the tribe would I, Lem Hardy-like, acquiesce, or would I, Tommo-Melville-like, flee with an urgency that might show a violent face if any Mow-Mow should attempt to pursue and detain me?

*Omoo* (1847) is Melville's sequel to *Typee*, and Miller argues that we should see the two books as essentially two parts of the same narrative, *Typee-Omoo*. In *Omoo*, Tommo, now escaped from Typee, encounters Lem Hardy, a man who has made a different choice from Tommo. Hardy has remained behind, become tattooed, and married into the royal family of the tribe he encountered. He has lost his face among the natives. Though born in England, he has deserted his ship at Hannamanoo and, after ten years ashore, become a military chief and war-god of the island. He is looked upon with horror by the sailors as his face is dramatically tattooed: 'A broad blue band stretched across his face from ear to ear, and on his forehead was the taper figure of a blue shark, nothing but fins from head to tail' (Melville 1982, p. 353). The sailors' horror is 'no ways abated when informed that he had voluntarily submitted to this embellishment of his countenance' (Melville 1982, p. 353). From Tommo and his fellow sailors there is a 'revulsion at this white man's reversion to savagery even though there is sympathy for the unmerited misfortune that plagued him in the civilized world', according to Miller (1962, pp. 34–35). Lem Hardy has chosen another path from Tommo, and in their meeting Tommo is brought face to tattooed face with what succumbing to the entreaties of Karky the tattoo artist might have possibly meant for him.

The mention of 'the human canvas' causes the reader to think of an idea behind the practice of tattooing, an idea that the body is *the* site of Art. Karky embodies this, and he has a sense of pride and quality in his work 'touching up the works of some of the old masters of the Typee school, as delineated upon the human canvas before him' (Melville 1994, p. 171).

Tommo's reflections on the 'capricious operation of the taboo' sit neatly alongside the thoughts of others on the topic. Melville-Tommo observes that: 'The savage, in short, lives in the continual observance of its dictates, which guide and control every action of his being' (Melville 1994, pp. 173–174). However, he later admits that he: 'Cannot determine, with anything approaching to certainty, what power it is that imposes the taboo [...] I am wholly at a loss where to look for the authority which regulates this potent institution' (Melville 1994, p. 176). Having pondered the 'taboo' Tommo-Melville has concluded, like Freud, that 'in fact the whole subject is highly obscure' (Freud 1953, p. 22). Freud's famous ruminations on the mystery of the 'taboo' are surprisingly resonant with Tommo-Melville's:

> The word 'taboo' denotes everything, whether a person or a place or a thing or a transitory condition, which is the vehicle or source of this mysterious attribute. It also denotes the prohibitions arising from the same attribute. And, finally, it has a connotation which includes alike 'sacred' and 'above the ordinary', as well as 'dangerous', 'unclean' and 'uncanny'. (Freud 1953, p. 22)

In a brilliant passage, dripping with humour and profundity, Tommo-Melville wryly mocks taboos, laws and religions of all kinds as he tests Mehevi's understanding of the bedrock of his own belief system:

> Although the 'taboo' was a ticklish thing to meddle with, I determined to test its capabilities of resisting an attack. I consulted the chief Mehevi, who endeavoured to persuade me from my object: but I was not to be

repulsed; and accordingly increased the warmth of my solicitations. At last
he entered into a long, and I have no doubt a very learned and eloquent
exposition of the history and nature of the 'taboo' as affecting this particular case; employing a variety of most extraordinary words, which, from
their amazing length and sonorousness, I have every reason to believe were
of a theological nature. (Melville 1994, p. 107)

This challenging of the 'taboo' here is over the matter of Tommo taking
Fayaway out in his canoe, but the tattooing encounter with Karky reveals
the face of the Typeean culture to Tommo with altogether more clarity.
Now he feels the culture to be a force and his wry theological musings
over the nature of the taboo are replaced by a frightened desire to flee.
The fear of tattooing, especially facial tattooing, forces Tommo into recognition of his essential difference from the Marquesan Islanders.

Tommo-Melville fears that the tattooing planned for him will rob
him of his "face divine", and the change this fear produces in him is profound: 'I was fairly driven to despair; nothing but the utter ruin of my
"face divine" as the poets call it, would, I perceived, satisfy the inexorable
Mehevi and his chiefs, or rather their infernal Karky, for he was at the
bottom of it all' (Melville 1994, p. 172). Paradise has become Hell for
Tommo, so that his 'existence became a burden to me; the pleasures I
had previously enjoyed no longer afforded me delight, and all my former desire to escape from the valley now revived with additional force'
(Melville 1994, p. 173). At the opening of Book Three of *Paradise Lost* it
is Milton, the preeminent English poet of Paradise, who mourns missing
the sight of the 'human face divine' now denied him in the 'ever-during
dark' of his blindness (Milton 2004, III.44–45). Tommo fears his
own 'human face divine' will be disfigured, and that, whether he likes
it or not, he will have quite literally lost his face. His only consolation
is 'a choice of patterns' (Melville 1994, p. 172). In fleeing this fate will
Tommo be moving towards Civilisation and will he be losing Paradise?
As Miller comments: 'the Garden remains at the last unfound, the perfect innocence undiscovered' (Miller 1962, p. 21). In Melville's novel
Tommo finds a kind of Eden, with no roads, no villages, no labour, no
money, however, in order to save his very sense of himself as a civilised
white man, he must turn his face away and flee. His choice is stark, either
paradise must be lost, or he must be.[5]

Tommo here is no longer able to maintain the cool reflective distance he achieved in earlier parts of his tale, such as when he eats bananas

and philosophically reflects on the 'immeasurable distance' between the French Admiral Du Petit Thouars and the King of the Nukuhevans:

> At what an immeasurable distance, thought I, are these two beings removed from each other. In the one is shown the result of long centuries of progressive civilization and refinement, which have gradually converted the mere creature into the semblance of all that is elevated and grand; while the other, after the lapse of the same period, has not advanced one step in the career of improvement. 'Yet, after all', quoth I to myself, 'insensible as he is to a thousand wants, and removed from harassing cares, may not the savage be the happier man of the two?' Such were the thoughts that arose in my mind as I gazed upon the novel spectacle before me. In truth it was an impressive one, and little likely to be effaced. I can recall even now with vivid distinctness every feature of the scene. The umbrageous shades where the interview took place – the glorious tropical vegetation around – the picturesque grouping of the mingled throng of soldiery and natives – and even the golden-hued bunch of bananas that I held in my hand at the time, and of which I occasionally partook while making the aforesaid philosophical reflections. (Melville 2007, p. 45)

This is Melville's 'joking self-effacement' as he contrasts the civilised and the savage man while presenting an ironic 'portrait' of the observer himself. A narrator eating bananas philosophically reflects, containing in himself the simple and the complex, a perfect encapsulation of the pastoral paradox. Herbert captures it well:

> In *Typee* the crisis of meaning is located within Melville himself: he finds his mind radically divided between horror and profound admiration for the islanders, as it is also divided between hatred for civilization and a frantic desire to return to it [....] What we find in Melville is a change of focus: he is fascinated as much by white responses to the Marquesans as by the Marquesans themselves. He shifts the emphasis so that it rests upon the encounter, the experience of contact, rather than upon the Marquesans as a thing observed. (Herbert 1980, p. 158)

And Sanborn puts it thus:

> Tommo's resistance to tattooing is driven not only by a fear that it will blot out the sign of his soul, but also by a fear that it will blot out a highly visible sign of his social privilege: his white skin. (Sanborn 1998, p. 104)

We have to agree that 'it is now signification itself, understood as pervasive and persistent, that sends Tommo backpedaling [*sic.*] away from the object of his romance' (Sanborn 1998, p. 105).

We wonder whether Tommo can find signs of 'civilization' among his own people. His own 'worthy Captain', on hearing that 'there were a considerable number of fowls in the valley' which 'being strictly tabooed, flew about almost in a wild state' is 'determined to break through all restraints, and be the death of them' (Melville 1994, p. 175). The 'nautical sportsman' shows his disdain for the natives' sense of the sacred by 'shooting down a noble cock, that was crowing what proved to be his own funeral dirge'. To the 'affrighted savages', who are shrieking 'Taboo', the Captain replies 'Oh, hang your taboo [...] talk taboo to the marines' as he bangs away with his 'most formidable looking gun', and 'down came another victim. At this the natives ran scampering through the groves, horror-struck at the enormity of the act' (Melville 1994, p. 176). This intervention of Vang's in the great taboo debate was inserted by Melville at stage five of the creative process (see Fig. 3.2 for Bryant's analysis). We read, perhaps with the same wry smile with which Melville wrote, that 'All that afternoon the rocky sides of the valley rang with successive reports, and the superb plumage of many a beautiful fowl was ruffled by the fatal bullet' (Melville 1994, p. 176). This is the man, Captain Vang, 'who thus outraged their most sacred institutions', and so the natives drive him from the stream where the contaminating Captain seeks to refresh himself as he is 'thirsting with his exertions' for 'his lips would have polluted it' (Melville 1994, p. 176).

It is clear here where Melville's sympathies lie. The civilised worthy Captain defiles Paradise. He becomes taboo, both dangerous and polluting, by ignoring the sacred prohibitions which protect the fowls. Here fair is foul and fowls are fare. Just as when they first arrived on the Islands it is the white man that brings filth. He may be fair of face, lacking the broad bands of tattooed marks across his figurehead, but the sailors' polluting example as they ruin the natives is the truly contaminating contact:

> Our ship was now given up to every species of riot and debauchery. The grossest licentiousness and the most shameful inebriety prevailed, with occasional and but short-lived interruptions, through the whole period of her stay. Alas for the poor savages when exposed to the influence of these polluting examples! Unsophisticated and confiding, they are easily led into

every vice, and humanity weeps over the ruin thus remorselessly inflicted upon them by their European civilizers. Thrice happy are they who, inhabiting some yet undiscovered island in the midst of the ocean, have never been brought into contaminating contact with the white man. (Melville 1994, p. 12)

They may not be tattooed, but Tommo-Melville, Captain Vang and the rest of these worthy white men should be well and truly tabooed.

Tommo-Melville fails to comprehend the system of tattooing and the mysterious nature of the taboo. It is a world of which he is not really qualified to speak. A South Seas myth shows the deep but confusing, even contradictory, origins of tattooing and its connection to deep-rooted beliefs and taboos in the Polynesian islands. According to legend it was two goddesses, originally Siamese twins, who introduced tattooing to Fiji. The twins repeat over and over their message as they swim: 'Tatau fafine, ae le tatau tane', which translates as 'Tattoo the women, but don't tattoo the men'. But as they swim, and are distracted by diving for shells, their message becomes jumbled so that it now ran: 'Tatau tane, ae le tatu fafine', or, 'Tattoo the men, but don't tattoo the women'. And that is why, down to this day, Samoan men are tattooed but not Samoan women (Rubin 1988, p. 155).

Photographic portraits of David Porter, Charles S. Stewart and Herman Melville all survive. Melville used Porter's *Journal of a Cruise* and Stewart's *Visit to the South Seas* to augment his own material for *Typee* and build the novel to its final form. Unfortunately no portrait of the Queen of Nukuheva's magnificent hieroglyphical buttock tattoos exists to present to the reader. Only Melville's account of the incident remains:

> The royal lady, eager to display the hieroglyphics on her own sweet form, bent forward for a moment, and turning sharply round, threw up the skirt of her mantle, and revealed a sight from which the aghast Frenchmen retreated precipitately, and tumbling into their boats, fled the scene of so shocking a catastrophe.[6]

This rearguard action from the Queen of Nukuheva, full in the face of the formal French, in all their pomp and facings (lapels and cuffs), casts an early tattooed female moon across the narrative. Melville's disorientated reader tumbles away in laughing shock, while simultaneously wanting to decipher the signs the royal lady so energetically displays.

## NOTES

1. The reason for my uncertainty is that, to be perfectly honest with you, dear reader, I first read *Typee* in the Wordsworth Classics edition, which claims to be 'Complete and Unabridged', but is not. I frequently tell my own students not to use Wordsworth Classics editions, but a good edition with a decent introduction and discursive notes. However, this was the edition that I happened to pick off my shelves some years ago. So my experience of the novel has involved a re-reading with additional parts, mostly wry and darkly humorous observations and links to source materials which Melville added at later stages of the book's composition.
2. And mysteriously appearing in the Wordsworth Classics edition as Chap. 29.
3. These comments are not in the Wordsworth Classics edition of *Typee*, but are reproduced at the end of the full version of Chap. 30 which appears in the Filiquarian Classics edition of the novel. H. Melville, *Typee: A Peep at the Polynesian Life* (Milton Keynes: Filiquarian Publishing, LLC, 2007), p. 301.
4. 'Applied Science: why intricate biological tattoos are the latest trendy accessory', from *The Independent*, 15 July 2014, p. 25.
5. Living with the Typeeans is, at least initially for Tommo, a Utopia that reminds the reader of Gonzalo's vision in Shakespeare's *The Tempest*, and Montaigne's in 'Of the Cannibals' before him. There are echoes of the otiose Golden Age in Tommo's indolent bliss, but this happy state does not last.
6. This lively and enjoyable incident is sadly omitted from the Wordsworth Classics edition of the novel, but appears in Melville, *Typee: A Peep at the Polynesian Life* (Milton Keynes: Filiquarian Publishing, LLC, 2007), pp. 15–16.

## REFERENCES

Bryant, J., 2008. *Melville Unfolding: Sexuality, Politics, and the Versions of Typee.* Ann Arbor, Mich.: University of Michigan Press.

Freud, S., 1953. *Totem and Taboo and Other Works* in *The Complete Psychological Works of Sigmund Freud, Volume XIII.* London: The Hogarth Press.

Herbert, T. W. Jr., 1980. *Marquesan Encounters: Melville and the Meaning of Civilization.* Cambridge, Mass.: Harvard University Press.

Levine, R. S. (ed.), 1998. *The Cambridge Companion to Herman Melville*. Cambridge: CUP, 1998.

Melville, H., 1982. *Typee, Omoo, Mardi*. New York: Library of America.

Melville, H., 1994. *Typee*. Ware: Wordsworth Classics.

Melville, H., 2007. *Typee: A Peep at the Polynesian Life*. Milton Keynes: Filiquarian Publishing LLC.

Miller, J. E., 1962. *A Reader's Guide to Herman Melville*. London: Thames and Hudson.

Milton, J., 2004. *Paradise Lost*. Oxford: Oxford World's Classics.

Rubin, A. (ed.), 1988. *Marks of Civilization: Artistic Transformations of the Human Body*. Los Angeles, CA: Museum of Cultural History, University of California.

Samson, J., 1984. 'The Dynamics of History and Fiction in Melville's *Typee*', *American Quarterly*, Vol. 36, No. 2 (Summer, 1984), pp. 276–290.

Sanborn, G., 1998. *The Sign of the Cannibal: Melville and the Making of a Postcolonial Reader*. London: Duke University Press.

# CHAPTER 4

# What the Body Tells Us: Transgender Strategies, Beauty, and Self-consciousness

*Marzia Mauriello*

## THE BEAUTIFUL BODY

The word 'transgender', which first appeared in the United States in the 1970s and the 1980s (Valentine 2007; Stryker 2008; Feinberg 1996), is considered an umbrella term that generally indicates people embodying a gender variance that is not in line with the heteronormative dichotomy of 'masculine' and 'feminine'. This binary has its roots in Western societies, where discursive practices around masculinity and femininity as two incommensurably opposed sexes developed in the eighteenth and nineteenth centuries (Foucault 2006 [1976]; Laqueur 1990). With the passage from sexual isomorphism to dimorphism, gender identity came to be definitively associated with the body and its genitals.

The idea of an individual's gender being inextricably tied to the body is the effect of how the modern world has learnt to look at the body as the core of a person, representing once and for all the identity of an individual. This culturally and historically determined perspective is deeply related to the way the view of the body changed in the eighteenth

M. Mauriello (✉)
University of Naples Suor Orsola Benincasa, Naples, Italy
e-mail: marziamauriello@gmail.com

E. Rees (ed.), *Talking Bodies*, DOI 10.1007/978-3-319-63778-5_4

century, modifying the idea of female genitalia as introverted versions of those of the male. Before that, according to Thomas Laqueur, 'to be a man or a woman was to hold a social rank, a place in society, to assume a cultural role, not to be organically one or the other of two incommensurable sexes' (Laqueur 1990, p. 8).

Subsequent developments in Western medical technology helped to maintain sex and bodies in an oppositional, binary structure (male versus female). In relation to this, trans people embody, as do intersex people, a 'transgressive' gender identity that subverts the dominant sex/gender dyad: anyone who 'alters' the 'normal' sex/gender representation can be considered subversive (Barnes 2001, n.p.). This is due to the analogy, compellingly investigated by Mary Douglas in *Purity and Danger* (1966), between anomaly and danger: anyone embodying what is perceived as an anomaly is implicitly dangerous, as these individuals cannot be conceivably included in a determined cultural and social frame. Whitney Barnes observed that 'Western medical technology serves to impose and reinforce the socially expected sex/gender dyad by attempting to prevent the existence of adult individuals whose sex/gender alignment is deemed "inappropriate"' and that 'this ideology is not a product of medical advances; rather the technological and medical advances are the products of this ideology' (2001, n.p.). According to Barnes, psychology and medicine are, in this respect, both the cause of, and the means to reinforce, the socially constructed sex/gender dyad.

Clear proof of this process is the effort made by the biomedical world to include trans experience in the realm of abnormality *tout court*. As Bernice Hausman affirms, 'psychiatric sexologists involved with intersexuality in the 1950s and 1960s', suggested an 'expanded definition of sex' that 'allowed would-be transsexuals to claim a disjunction between sexual signifiers in the register of the psyche' (1992, p. 301). The transgendered body came to be abnormal in its embodying an 'internal difference indicative of aberrant psychological sex' (Hausman 1992, p. 301). In the early 1950s, the idea of 'transsexualism', at least in the form that we know it today, appeared on the Western medical scene, as some people started demanding medical sex changes. The term 'transsexual' was coined by physicians; it was introduced in 1949 by D.O. Cauldwell in his article 'Psychopathia transexualis', but until the early 1950s it was not differentiated from transvestism (Ekins 2005). This change occurred a few years later when transsexualism was finally considered a medical syndrome, after the surgery of George/Christine Jorgensen in 1952 by

Harry Benjamin. Sex Reassignment Surgery (SRS) became the new way through which, as Judith Halberstam points out in their usage of the term 'technology of gender', medical technologies regulated sexual dimorphism (Halberstam 1991).

As Hausman observes:

> Both plastic surgery and endocrinology, as technologies and as professional specialties, actively worked to further somatogenic theories of behavior. It is precisely the production and instantiation of this discursive network, the overlapping theories that claim the body as the basis for mental and emotional actions and attitude, that set the stage for the emergence of transsexualism in 1950s. (1992, p. 288)

What needs to be underlined here is the consideration that the body comes to represent the core of identity for transsexuals; it is still the body that, if appropriately 'cured', constitutes the only means to be 'happy', since happiness depends on the self-realisation that might come from a perception of being 'beautiful enough'. During my fieldwork among the transgender community in Naples, what is perceived mainly by the subjects themselves is that *a beautiful body* significantly contributes to making transsexual people satisfied. Specifically, this is the kind of satisfaction that might lead to self-realisation and a more general happiness.

If we consider the 'beautiful' to be that which gives back a sense of harmony and familiarity (Etcoff 2010), then for certain subjects the 'incompleteness' of their body—for them clearly perceived as an anomaly when it does not reflect the real (ideal) image of the Self—is deeply associated with the idea of 'strangeness' that often stands for 'ugliness'. For many transsexuals their original body is not perceived as 'familiar' but, on the contrary, as the very source of their anomaly (Chiland 2011). If a person is reduced to a body as a reflex of Western modernity, then the relation between sex and gender is obviously part of the process, because it is what contributes to the process of construction of identity. This is why for a trans woman (male to female, or 'mtf') changing sex means eliminating what more than anything else is considered the quintessence of masculinity—the phallus—and constructing what is considered the quintessence of femininity—the vagina.

If the word 'transgender' generally indicates people embodying a gender variance, the usage of this term, when considering the subsequent developments of transsexualism, is sometimes confusing.

As a matter of fact, the terms *transgender* and *transsexual* came to indicate two separate experiences; two different ways of conceiving of and considering the individual's body—in relation both to the idea of beauty on the one hand, and to sexuality on the other. Sexuality can be thought of as deeply related to beauty, since the evaluation of a person's seductive power often lies in self-confidence, which derives from a reassuring way of thinking about one's body. This is where the difference between transgender and transsexual people lies: transsexuals are individuals who declare themselves uncomfortable with their 'wrong' body, first of all with its genitals, which represent the embodiment of what psychiatrists call *gender dysphoria*.[1] Transsexuals wish to modify those parts, once and for all, through SRS. Transgender people, on the other hand, are subjects who in some cases partially modify the body, but who do not change their primary sexual characteristics.

In the last seven years I have been conducting ethnography among the transgender community of Naples, in the south of Italy.[2] During fieldwork, three possible categories of transgender people who do not modify their genitals have been singled out[3]:

1. mtf transgender people who like themselves the way they are. They do not feel the need to change their genitals as they consider themselves 'beautiful' in the specific sense of 'feminine *anyway*' (despite their male genitals), and they do not associate their genitalia with monstrosity. Some of them might also love the 'ambiguity' of their condition of 'hybridism'. The transgender people falling into this category whom I have met and interviewed are usually highly educated or older (generally between 30 and 60 years old). What many of them told me is that they grew accustomed to their 'different' body (with particular reference to genitalia) and eventually accepted it the way it is. These people seem to have elaborated on, and internalised, the idea of going beyond the dichotomy female/male, since during interviews they often underlined their *right to be different*;

2. transgender sex workers, who say that keeping their male anatomy means earning more. They say clients like the idea of having sex with a 'half-and-half', also for strictly broadening the 'sexual scope', since these 'so-called heterosexual'[4] clients like to be 'passive', that is, to play a 'female role' in sexual intercourse;

3. transgender people who are afraid of not being able to achieve orgasm after SRS. Many of them have reported stories of their transsexual girlfriends who, after SRS, were not satisfied with what they had done. They explained that the dissatisfaction can be due to bad vaginoplastic surgery results, or, and in this case it appears more serious, to regret for having changed their body, even in relation to the impossibility of feeling sexual pleasure. In the worst case scenario, some transsexual women ended up with identity problems. Significantly, during fieldwork, none of the post-op transsexual women I met revealed any of these possible problems to me. When I expressed to my mtf transgender informants my doubts about post-op transsexuals feeling sexual pleasure, they replied that post-op transsexual women often lie about this matter.

There is another category to be added to the three listed above, which can be included in the transgender experience but with some significant differences, concerning both individual and social dimensions. This category belongs specifically to the tradition of Naples and can be considered part of the cultural history of that city.

## ANTE LITTERAM TRANSGENDERS: THE NEAPOLITAN FEMMINIELLI

In the past thirty years, significant changes have occurred in Naples, a city emblematic of the south of Italy, especially since the earthquake in 1980, which partially changed the face of Naples. In areas where the underprivileged class used to live (the so-called Quartieri Spagnoli [*Spanish Quarters*]), many people were forced to abandon their homes for safety, moving to the outskirts of the city.

For some of these people, the cultural, social and economic reality of the Spanish Quarters' *vicoli* (masc. pl.) —typical narrow streets in the very centre of Naples mostly inhabited by the underclass (a kind of inner periphery that formed a microcosm, a real anthropological enclave)— suddenly largely disappeared. More generally, some of the old habits tied to the traditional structures of these particular places also changed (Valerio-Zito 2010; Zito-Valerio 2013; Romano 2013). Those *vicoli* were also the realm of the *femminielli* (masc. pl.), whom we define as *ante litteram transgenders*, members of the urban underprivileged class of Naples; they lived their gender variance in this specific and deeply culturally determined environment, where there was, and partially still is, an acceptance of these 'different' individuals, males living as females.

In relation to what field research and interviews have revealed, the *femminielli* reproduce, through specific *mise-en-scènes*, those rituals that mark the milestones of life, so-called rites of passage, such as birth; the transition to adulthood represented by marriage; and death. *'O spusarizio* ('the wedding', in Neapolitan dialect) is the celebration of a marriage between two *femminielli* who, on that day, play the role of a woman and of a man; the ceremony is not celebrated for real, but it is a representation that involves all the community, in this case the people of the *vicolo* (masc. sing.) or the quarter where the *femminielli* live. Guests join them to celebrate the fake marriage outside a church and, after the 'religious' celebration, they all go to a restaurant to celebrate. Each of the guests is involved in the ceremony, and is invited to play a specific role connected to the wedding (Carrano-Simonelli 2013 [1983]).[5]

Nine months later, the *mise-en-scène* of the *figliata* ('the birth') takes place. It celebrates the birth of the 'married' couple's offspring. The newborn, usually a wooden puppet with a huge phallus, is delivered of a *femminiello* (masc. sing.), with all the community members celebrating the event.[6] Concerning ceremonies related to death, one of my informants told me about the *femminiellis'* custom of staging—in the course of what they call *campagnate*, a kind of special event where they all meet and usually eat together in some popular restaurants around Naples (Romano 2013)—what they call *il pianto al finto morto* ('the fake dead's mourning'), pretending to mourn a man who is usually chosen to be a kind of dupe.[7] Their relationship with death is also linked to celebrating traditional Neapolitan artists (principally those in music and theatre) by going to the cemetery on the occasion of All Souls' Day (2 November); in this way, they show respect for, and a line of continuity from, what they consider tradition. And the *femminielli* themselves also assert that they are the repository of Neapolitan artistic culture (Mauriello 2014). Three out of five that I have met and interviewed are artists themselves—actors or singers.[8]

As Laurence Senelick asserts:

> In some cultures the relegation of gender-liminal individuals to the realm of performance provides them with a social context. A constitutive relationship between structure and agency. By acting out this gender

marginality, such an individual achieves a kind of alternative prestige as a repository of artistic and cultural tradition. (Senelick 2000, p. 29)

Cultural performances, ritual forms and *mise-en-scènes*, together with the knowledge of a certain artistic tradition and its staging, help the figure of *femminielli* in defining their identity as related to specific practices. Their exuberance, their role of fortune teller and fortune bearer, together with the cheerfulness that characterises them,[9] make the *femminielli* common guests at traditional Catholic ceremonies such as baptisms, first communions, and weddings (Mauriello 2014).

The first witnesses to this figure of corporeality that can easily be identified with a real *third gender*, with all the limitations that this definition implies, date back to the late sixteenth century. Giovanni Battista Della Porta wrote about this figure in *De Humana Physiognomonia,* published in 1586 (Zito-Valerio 2013, p. 26). In the author's description, where these figures are defined as 'effeminate men', some features that still distinguish these subjects, who are still part of what is called the marginal proletariat, the so-called self-defined *popolino* (literally 'common people') of Naples, are very well depicted.[10]

Living as women means playing the roles traditionally associated with them. In this case, it means helping women to take care of children and doing all the domestic chores that a woman is 'meant' to do. However, it also means, for the *femminielli*, staging their femaleness, or better, femininity, in a histrionic and almost grotesque way. What the *femminielli* represent is a body style, which is idealised to the point of becoming hypertrophic. This hypertrophy apparently serves to confirm an identity which, because of its indefiniteness, in making this category of people associated with liminality, has a constant need to be continuously represented through overexposure (that is, through a constant staging in an exuberant way). The *femminielli* of the tradition are not 'complete' transvestites but they wear female accessories (scarves, nail polish, earrings, jewellery, and so on) on male clothing. Their movements, their gestures and the way they walk reproduce, often in exaggerated ways, a perceived female model, and their speech bears a typically effeminate intonation. Such exuberance is most probably the cause and effect of the inclusion of this figure in the social and economic reality of the Neapolitan underclass, accompanied by 'the investiture of a kind of sacredness that often, in societies of anthropological interest, characterises liminal figures in a gender perspective' (Mauriello 2014, p. 439).

A comparison of the figure of the *femminielli* of Naples with those of non-Western cultures is possible if we consider the fact that in the under-class areas of the town, modernity (in its more profound sense, involving vision and perception) did not take root. However, as happens in vari-ous non-Western contexts in which there are figures whose differences cannot be listed here (the *hijra* in India (Nanda 1998); the so called *berdache* or *two spirits* in Native American cultures (Roscoe 2000); the *sarin'ampela* in Madagascar (Astuti 1998); the *xanith* in Oman (Wikan 1977)), even in the Neapolitan cultural tradition, the hybrid, liminal, double identity of the *femminielli*, makes them good-luck givers and somehow sacred. These characteristics are connected to specific activities that they perform, such as giving the numbers for the lottery, drawing lots for the tombola,[11] and also interpreting dreams. All these capabilities attributed to them are related to the particular relationship that, in gen-eral, liminal figures establish with the supernatural world.

What appeared very clear during my fieldwork is that the *femmin-ielli* consider themselves to be women, showing no doubt whatsoever of their gender identity. They use the feminine version of the term *fem-miniello* 'femminella' (sing.), if they refer to themselves, and when they talk to each other the form they use is always the feminine. They do not expect 'others' (heterosexual or cisgender people) to refer to them as female; in this case, indeed, the feminine might sound strange to them (Mauriello 2014).

Not surprisingly, one of the most interesting aspects of their gen-der notion concerns the self-perception of their sexual orientation: they do not consider themselves 'gay' because, since they believe they are women, they like to have sex with 'real' men, and not with gay men. Having a sexual or intimate relationship with a gay man is just unthinkable (if not disgusting) for them. In regard to sexuality, being a *femminiello* means playing a passive role (women are considered to be passive in sex, as they are penetrated) during sexual intercourse with 'heterosexual' men who are not considered homosexuals since they are 'active' in sex. In the past, these men were considered to be doubly male, being willing to have sex with both women and men (Pini 2011).[12]

This way of considering sex roles reproduces the idea that 'sexual specificity itself is constructed at once as "difference" and as erotic by the eroticisation of dominance and submission' (De Lauretis 1990). The *femminielli* are repositories of tradition even in the sense that they share the same cultural values as the underclass. On the one hand, a love and sex relationship must occur between a 'man' and a 'woman' (at least in their gender configuration); on the other hand, the family is a sacred place to be protected and respected. The older people I met in the course of my ethnographic investigation, people between 70 and 80 years of age who have always lived in the Spanish Quarters, reported that traditional *femminielli* (of whom very few remain nowadays), have always been very respectful of family values and traditions, which is one of the reasons why they have long been welcomed by families. These informants underlined the difference between this traditional figure and 'new', contemporary representatives of the transgender experience, even though they did not know, nor did they understand, the difference between gay and trans people.

Concerning the latter, the *femminielli* think of themselves as neither gay nor trans (they make no differentiation between 'transgender' and 'transsexual', they use the term 'trans' for both categories); the refusal of the 'gay' category lies in a different choice of sexual partner,[13] but also because of the denial, in the gay community, of femininity in all its aspects—from body attitude to clothing.[14]

In the late 1970s and early 1980s, some of the *femminielli* started to change their bodies through cosmetic surgery and hormonal therapy— frequently without medical control and even illegally. This still happens today. Prostitution became more widespread in the community, on account of the fact that they could easily earn a substantial amount of money in order to pay for cosmetic surgery (Romano 2013). In relation to these changes, Neapolitans started to replace or alternate the term *femminiello* with the term 'travestito' (male transvestite), indicating people who fully dressed as women, especially at night, as sex workers.[15] They actually appeared more 'womanly' than a woman, showing off their hyperfemininity through sophisticated postures and clothing, with heavy makeup and perfect hairstyles. The term 'travestito' originated fundamentally to indicate the status of transgender sex workers in Naples.[16]

As many scholars claim, the traditional figure of the *femminiello* is on the verge of disappearing. The reasons for this relate—in part, at least— to the changes that have occurred in Naples in the past thirty years, as an effect of economic and cultural globalisation and the spread of new media (Valerio-Zito 2010; Zito-Valerio 2013), together with the crumbling of traditional community rules and values. These cultural and social transformations have involved the Neapolitan underclass too, a social category or a real microcosm where, if changes have occurred, they have been so small and few as to be barely visible.

This might be one of the reasons why medical technology and, more broadly, 'modernity', have not affected the *femminiellis'* vision and self-perception of their identity for a long time:

> There is often evidence in the lives of transgendered persons living in various historical and cultural settings that in the absence of modern Western medicine and technology, their lived gender identities were less subject to rigid institutional scrutiny and more freely allowed individual autonomy. (Barnes 2001, n.p.)

To some extent, 'Western culture' in the sense of a modern, globalised vision of the world, had not reached the Neapolitan lower classes until very recently. In the meantime, paradoxically, a place that has been historically considered a symbol of archaism (Niola 2006; Teti 2013) was also the place where 'gender fluidity' was contemplated and not condemned. In some ways, some areas of Naples represented a postmodern place before becoming a modern one. During interviews, some of the few, maybe the last—according to sources—representatives of the *femminielli* talk about themselves as being at risk of extinction; in the meantime, it is also clear that they have a profound consciousness of who they are:

> The interesting thing about this gender category is its vision and conception of beauty and the Self. If in the past objective difficulties might have occurred in surgical interventions, even today many of them refuse to take on a female appearance through cosmetic surgery or hormonal treatment. (Mauriello 2014, p. 445)

Furthermore, during interviews, they repeatedly underline the difference between them and other transgender categories, since their identity is made up of, and performed through, specific symbols, gestures, actions, and religious practices (Mauriello 2014).[17]

A documentary film directed by Massimo Andrei in 2007 and entitled *Cerasella, ovvero l'estinizione della femminella*, is about the last *femminielli*, where the disappearance of this figure is considered tied to a broader 'modernity', with the *femminielli* as representative of 'antiquity'.[18] Their category seems to belong to the past and is somehow seen as not appropriate to the present, where it is necessary 'to be or not to be': to be homosexual, but as a 'full' man or woman with a defined gender identity, which is considered, once and for all, separated from sexuality (Mauriello 2014). A homosexual man, since he is a man nevertheless, must be dressed and act *like a man*. Effeminate men are, in fact, often alienated and, in the worst cases, victims of violence and discrimination by other 'macho' gays (Mauriello 2012). For lesbians, if in the past there was a positive eroticisation of the masculine woman (the so-called 'butch' in English that in the Neapolitan dialect becomes *tatore*, from *Salvatore*, a typical Neapolitan male name), in recent interviews it looks as if this category is no longer appreciated but, instead, alienated. Furthermore, it seems that, despite the fluidity of the contemporary, postmodern world, the tendency towards what is perceived as a 'normalisation process' in relation to identities, is still unconsciously present in people's minds and behaviour, and in some cases even in those of the LGBTQI community (Mauriello 2012, 2013).

Thus it is not surprising that among the transgender community in Naples there is a kind of internal discrimination, or, at least, the need to highlight the differences between categories. In this respect, during my fieldwork many transsexuals claimed their willingness to be considered transsexuals but absolutely not *femminielli*, since to be included in this category means not only to be 'ancient' but also to be considered members of the underclass. In the vision of many contemporary transsexuals and transgenders, the *femminiello* is always 'inappropriate' insofar as body language is concerned, often considered exaggerated and sometimes vulgar. On the other hand, some of the 'old' Neapolitan trans women (mtf transgenders) are thought to have inherited the *'femminiello* style', since they have 'adopted' similar behaviours (gestures, and ways of walking and talking, for example).

Michel Foucault underlined how the lower-class strata were not involved in the 'dispositive of sexuality' (2006 [1976]), which of course includes a certain body vision. In relation to the figure of the *femminielli*, this could be one of the reasons they have lasted over time, in the sense that their condition has not been problematised until what I would call 'the new interpretative apparatus' intervened. The gradual disappearance of this figure is due to several changes in the social context of the Neapolitan underprivileged class. If in the past, as we have seen, this cultural and social microcosm created specific spaces of inclusion for these subjects embodying gender variance, medical technology and medicalisation have also contributed significantly in modifying the way individuals live their body experience. In this respect, it is clear that the body has replaced dress, becoming the real object upon which to rewrite one's own identity (Le Breton 2007 [1990]).

## POST-*LITTERAM* TRANSGENDER: YOU ARE WHAT YOU (DO NOT) HAVE (ANYMORE)

To be different, especially through a 'different' body, is what represents the central discourse on transgender experience and the idea of beauty, as it is profoundly related to the idea of monstrosity, once again in Mary Douglas's sense of something out of place (Douglas 1966). The proof of this need for 'identity clarity' is the path to SRS, whose aim, for transsexuals, is a clear definition of identity status; in this instance, one's ('abnormal') body must conform to one's brain, through a definite change (removal and reconstruction) of what is visible and considered the quintessence of gender—the genitals (Mauriello 2013):

> The transsexual body is not an absolute insignia of anything. Yet it makes the referent ('man' or 'woman') seem knowable. Paradoxically, it is to transsexuals and transvestites that we need to look if we want to understand what gender categories mean. For transsexuals and transvestites are *more* concerned with maleness and femaleness than people who are neither transvestite nor transsexual. They are emphatically not interested in 'unisex' or 'androgyny' as erotic styles, but rather in gender-marked and gender-coded identity structures. (Garber 1997 [1992], p. 110)

Some feminists ascribe to mtf transsexuals the responsibility for reinforcing sexual stereotypes that maintain women in a state of submission. More than that, and concerning the physical aspect and the attention paid to the body, some transsexuals tend to consider women as *simply women*, accusing them of total conformity (Vitelli–Valerio 2012). Some of them claim to know more than a biological woman what a 'real' woman is and what men's true desires and needs are, both in the sense of sexual satisfaction and of attention to physical appearance. According to Garber, nothing more than a similar perspective reinforces the idea of gender as performative (1992):

> Transsexuals, in these accounts, represent the dupes of the sex/gender system, even more than traditional heterosexual couples, insofar as they are subjects willing to alter their bodies in order to conform to established codes of gender appropriate sensibility and behaviour. (Hausman 1992, pp. 273–74)

During my fieldwork, transsexual people talked about SRS as an opportunity to realise the dream of being the person they have always imagined themselves to be; in many cases, sexuality is involved in this process of self-realisation, since there is the shame of not being a 'complete woman' during sexual intercourse with partners. As Hausman observes, 'that is due to the gender fixed dichotomy and binary logics of heterosexual matrix, where the sexual practices are often reduced to vaginal penetration' (1992, pp. 273–74).

Donna Haraway asserts that the 'proper state for a Western person is to have ownership of the self, to have and hold a core identity as if it were a possession' (Haraway 1991, p. 135) . If one's gender is brought back to the body, to its genital part, then not to have a compliant body means 'not to have property in the self', that is, not to possess a definite identity, not to be a subject, 'and so not to have agency' (Haraway 1991, p. 135). This is one of the reasons why in many cases trans people need someone from the outside (with medical knowledge) to define their identity status, and also the reason for the need to have a sex (gender) that overcomes ambiguity (Mauriello 2013). In this sense, the branch of biomedicine, that 'created' the transsexual phenomenon but not gender variances, served to confirm the 'normality' of a binary system in relation to the body and its genitals (Mauriello 2014).

The vagina is considered the definitive sign of femininity; it is the organ to be penetrated that *makes* a woman. Many transsexuals feel incomplete if they do not realise the dream of having a 'normal' body. In 2012 I interviewed Paola, 23 years old, who, was finally about to undergo SRS after almost four years of pursuing the obligatory path for it[19]; at the time of the interview, she was satisfied when she looked at herself and happy to be about to realise what used to be a dream for her: 'to feel good with myself'. Then she said:

> Today I still do not feel good with myself. I will not be satisfied until I undergo surgery. When you are with the person you love, you feel like... you feel ashamed and insecure when you take off your clothes in front of

your partner. He tells me 'don't be afraid, I know who you are', but I will not be OK until I am a complete woman, when I am able to take off my clothes and say 'today I am a woman, I am Paola'. For the Italian State I am not Paola, I am still Salvatore. I am a woman, there is only that one 'piece' that does not allow me to be 'she'. (Mauriello 2013)

There are many reasons why transgender people may not want to change their genitalia, as we have seen, not least because, as some of them said during the interviews, their perception of femininity is not related to the body: femininity, as some of the interviewees declared, is 'what you have inside, you have it or you do not' (Mauriello 2013). For some mtf transgenders, to be beautiful is not to be a *complete* woman, which means being physically aligned to the opposite gender (the significantly so-called *realignment*), and to embody femininity through a different body. Sara, a transgender woman of 40, affirmed during her interview that the main reason why she had decided to change her facial features (nose and lips) was to remove her father's memory from her face. She did not want to associate herself with that specific male image. After cosmetic surgery, however, she reported liking herself less than before (Mauriello 2013).

As Hausman asserts:

> a significant number of transsexual women request further refinements of their feminine appearance with rhinoplastic surgery, removal of the Adam's apple, facial reconstruction and the like. These additional requests for surgery may indicate the extent to which transsexual women try to live up to an idealized vision of the 'real' woman whose youthful femininity radiates from every pore of her body. Alternatively, the request for surgery might simply represent the desire of these subjects to appear different from (and unrelated to) their former selves. (1992, p. 298)

During fieldwork, from an emic perspective, transsexual women say that it is worth modifying the body only if the person already looks physically 'close' to the other gender—which for mtfs means having delicate features and a 'feminine' appearance. They assert that plastic surgery must have a 'good base' to start from, otherwise the 'final result' will be ridiculous. In order to be a nice-looking trans woman, which means appearing *more* feminine, a biological man has to reproduce the ideal of femininity, which necessarily goes beyond female beauty standards, even before starting hormonal therapy.

Therefore, the idea of 'beauty' appears as irrevocably tied to the 'unambiguity' of the body: in the case of transsexual individuals, the more the body conforms to the 'other' gender, the more the idea of beauty and the Self is realised. In this respect, a transsexual body internalises the heteronormative, neo-patriarchal, socio-cultural patterns and expectations that are what Pierre Bourdieu defined as the embodiment of naturalised classifications (Bourdieu 1998).

If it is true that biomedicine and cosmetic surgery represent a real chance for people embodying gender variance to realise the dream of becoming the person they have always imagined themselves to be, it is also true that this picture is culturally constructed and shot through with heteronormativity. In actual fact, what emerges is that mtf transsexuals develop a male hegemonic perspective in defining the female body and in imagining what a 'woman' must be like in order to attract and satisfy a male gaze. Therefore, there is an internalisation of heterosexual male perspectives concerning the female model of 'ideal beauty'. An mtf transsexual body is one which, in its transformation, develops and reinforces naturalised ideals of female beauty and identity as they are imagined, and constructed, by men.

## NOTES

1. Incidentally, even though it is clear that physicians—following the protests of worldwide activists of the Lesbian, Gay, Bisexual, Trans, Queer, Intersex (LGBTQI) community—are developing an attitude toward the depathologisation of transsexualism, it is still considered an anomaly, and 'gender dysphoria' is still present in the *Diagnostic and Statistical Manual of Mental Disorders* (DSM).
2. Here I am using the world 'transgender' to indicate the vast category of subjects embodying a gender variance, whom I had the chance to meet and observe.
3. In this research I am referring specifically to mtf (male to female) transgender.
4. I report their own words here.
5. In 2012 I was invited to a wedding close to Salerno (one of the five provinces in the Region of Campania), in a small town called Angri. The bride was a *femminiello*, the groom was a transsexual man who was about to undergo SRS. The former girlfriend of the groom played the role of his mother. The real groom's mother was also present, together with her husband and all their relatives.

6. The ceremony of the *figliata* is fully described in Curzio Malaparte's novel *La pelle*, first published in 1949. The movie director Liliana Cavani made the film of the same name in 1981, based on this novel.

7. This is what one of my informants told me during the interview.

8. Of the Neapolitan music and theatre tradition.

9. What they say about themselves is that people want to spend time with them since they are fun, joyful and amusing.

10. Concerning definitions, Patricia Bianchi, investigating the linguistic aspect of the term *femminiello*, finds that the suffix *-iello/-ielli* (sing. and pl.) would not have, in the Neapolitan language, any negative or diminutive sense, but it would rather indicate a different category of individuals (Bianchi 2013, pp. 55–74). In the common usage and sense, the term *femminiello* describes a homosexual, an effeminate man who acts like a woman—or, in a Goffmanian (1959) but also Butlerian (1990, 2004) perspective, *plays a female role*.

11. The *tombola napoletana* is a kind of bingo, traditionally played on Mondays exclusively by women (and *femminielli*) who live in the Neapolitan ground floor dwellings (*bassi* or *vasci*). The *tombola* is also the Christmas play par excellence, and in this case it involves everyone in the family.

12. The myth of so-called 'Mediterranean bisexuality'.

13. As the *femminielli* say they want a 'real man', it is impossible for them to find a gay partner and in the meantime it is also highly unlikely that they will have a stable relationship with a heterosexual man.

14. In the Neapolitan gay community, several episodes of discrimination towards effeminate gay men are recorded. Significantly, these people are called 'femminella' or 'femminiello' in a scornful way. For further information, see Mauriello 2012.

15. The term *travestito* must not be confused with the term *travesti* used by Don Kulick in his work on the Brazilian transgendered sex workers. In fact, as the author explains in the book (*Travesti: Sex, Gender, and Culture among Brazilian Transgendered Prostitutes*, 1995), the *travestis*, despite 'feminine' body modifications and cosmetic surgery, do not self-identify as women.

16. Concerning the practice of transvestism, it is worth noting that in past centuries there was the widespread belief that male homosexuals never wanted to be or to act like women, and that they started to practise cross-dressing in order to be attractive for 'normal men', since sexual intercourse between two 'manly' men was impossible, in the sense of unthinkable (Valentine 2007; Garber 1997).

17. The *femminielli* are devotees to the Virgin Mary. A legend relates that, at the beginning of the thirteenth century, two young homosexuals were

driven out of town for obscene acts and tied to a tree on the Partenio Mountain, close to the municipality of Avellino, one of the five provinces in the Region of Campania. They would have died but the Madonna appeared and saved them. On the 2nd of February a religious festival to celebrate the Madonna of Montevergine takes place, and it consists of a procession to, and ascent of, the mountain. The *femminielli* are the main characters of the ceremony. They come mainly from Naples to meet in the churchyard and sing their gratitude to the Madonna. The festival in honour of this Madonna (known as 'Mamma Schiavona' because of her dark skin colour) is called 'Candelora' (Ceccarelli 2010). This Latin word for 'candle' is related to the blessing of candles. The ascent to the mountain recalls some pagan rituals but it also recalls the ascent that the Virgin Mary had to undertake in order to reach the temple forty days after Jesus Christ's birth. Even though the Candelora is the *femminiellis*' religious festival par excellence, nowadays the whole Neapolitan LGBTQI community actively participates in the festival. In other words, on that special occasion, everyone becomes a *femminiello*.

18. The documentary film has been produced by the University of Naples, Federico II, and is available in the archive of the SOFTel (Centro di Ateneo per l'Orientamento, la Formazione e la Teledidattica) of the same university.

19. According to Italian law (164/82), the path to SRS must last at least three years. At the time when the interviews were conducted, for the above-cited Italian law, trans people who wanted to change their identity on official documents had to undergo SRS. Even though the law in question was not that clear in itself, since to oblige people to undergo surgery is unconstitutional, almost all judges refused to change trans people's names and sex unless they followed the sanctioned path for SRS. In 2015, the Italian Constitutional Court declared that it was possible for a trans person to ask for a new identity on official documents without necessarily undergoing genital surgical intervention.

## REFERENCES

Astuti, R., 1998. '"It's a boy", "It's a girl!": Reflections on Sex and Gender in Madagascar and Beyond', in M. Lambek and A. Strathern, eds, *Bodies and Persons: Comparative Perspectives from Africa and Melanesia*. Cambridge: Cambridge University Press, pp. 29–52.

Barnes, W. 2001. 'The Medicalization of Transgenderism'. Available at: http://www. trans-health.com/2001/medicalization-of-transgenderism/ [accessed 01.01.17; online, not paginated].

Bianchi, P., 2013. 'Femminielli: storia di una parola tra gergalità e comunicazione antropologica', in E. Zito and P. Valerio, eds, *Genere: Femminielli. Esplorazioni antropologiche e psicologiche.* Napoli: Libreria Dante & Descartes, pp. 55–74.

Bourdieu, P., 1998. *La domination masculine.* Paris: Éditions de Seuil.

Butler, J., 1990. *Gender Trouble. Feminism and the Subversion of Identity.* London and New York: Routledge.

Butler, J., 2004. *Undoing Gender.* London and New York: Routledge.

Carrano, G. and P. Simonelli, 2013 [1983]. 'Un matrimonio nella baia di Napoli?', in E. Zito and P. Valerio, eds, *Genere: Femminielli. Esplorazioni antropologiche e psicologiche.* Napoli: Libreria Dante & Descartes, pp. 163–170 (orig. edit.: 'Un marriage dans la ville de Naples?', *Masques. Revue des Homosexualites.* 18, 1983, pp. 105–115).

Ceccarelli, M., 2010. *Mamma Schiavona. La Madonna di Montevergine e la Candelora.* Perugia: Gramma.

Chiland, C., 2011. *Changer de sexe. Illusion et réalité.* Paris: Odile Jacob.

De Lauretis, T., 1990. 'Eccentric Subjects. Feminist Theory and Historical Consciousness'. *Feminist Studies*, 16 (1), pp. 115–150.

Douglas, M., 1966. *Purity and Danger: An Analysis of Concepts of Pollution and Taboo.* London: Routledge and Kegan Paul.

Ekins, R., 2005. 'Science, Politics and Clinical Intervention: Harry Benjamin, Transsexualism and the Problem of Heteronormativity'. *Sexualities*, 8 (3). London: SAGE. pp. 306–328.

Etcoff, N., 2010. *Survival of the Prettiest. The Science of Beauty.* New York: Anchor Books.

Feinberg, L., 1996. *Transgender Warriors: Making History from Joan of Arc to Dennis Rodman.* Boston: Beacon Press.

Foucault, M., 2006 [1976]. *Storia della sessualità. Vol. 1. La volontà di sapere.* Milano: Feltrinelli [orig. edit.: Histoire de la sexualité, vol. 1: *La volonté de savoir*, Paris, Gallimard, 1976].

Garber, M., 1997 [1992]. *Vested Interests. Cross-dressing and Cultural Anxiety.* 2nd ed., New York: Routledge, Chapman and Hall.

Goffman, E., 1959. *The Presentation of Self in Everyday Life.* New York: Doubleday Anchor.

Halberstam, J., 1991. 'Automating Gender: Postmodern Feminism in the Age of the Intelligent Machine'. *Feminist Studies*, 17 (3), pp. 439–460.

Haraway, D., 1991. *Simians, Cyborgs, and Women. The Reinvention of Nature.* New York, NY: Routledge.

Hausman, B. L., 1992. 'Transsexualism, Medicine, and the Technologies of Gender'. *Journal of the History of Sexuality*, 3 (2), pp. 270–302.

Kulick, D., 1998. *Travesti: Sex, Gender and Culture among Brazilian Transgendered Prostitutes.* Chicago and London: University of Chicago Press.

Laqueur, T., 1990. *Making Sex. Body and Gender from Greeks to Freud.* London: Harvard University Press.

Le Breton, D., 2007 [1990]. *Antropologia del corpo e modernità.* [orig. edit.: *Anthropologie du corps et modernité,* PUF, 1990].

Mauriello, M., 2012. 'Se sei gay non puoi essere femminiello! Note a margine su sessualità e genere nel mondo gay napoletano', in A. Simone, ed., *Sessismo democratico. L'uso strumentale delle donne nel neoliberismo,* 1st ed. Milano: Mimesis, 97–109.

Mauriello, M., 2013. 'La medicalizzazione dell'esperienza Trans nel percorso per la "riassegnazione chirurgica del sesso". Una ricerca etnografica nella Città di Napoli'. *AM - Rivista della Società di Antropologia Medica,* 35–36, pp. 279–308.

Mauriello, M., 2014. 'In corpore trans. Dinamiche di inclusione/esclusione nel processo di medicalizzazione delle identità transgender: una ricerca etnografica nella città di Napoli'. *AM - Rivista della Società di Antropologia Medica,* 38, pp. 437–456.

Nanda, S., 1998. *Neither Man nor Woman: The Hijras of India.* 2nd ed., Belmont (CA): Wadsworth.

Niola, M., 2006. 'L'invenzione del Mediterraneo'. *Littérature et Anthropologie. Société française de littérature générale et comparée.* Paris: Lucie éditions, pp. 153–172.

Pini, A., 2011. *Quando eravamo froci. Gli omosessuali nell'Italia di una volta.* Milano: Il Saggiatore.

Romano, G., 2013. *La Tarantina e la sua dolce vita. Il racconto autobiografico di un femminiello napoletano.* Verona: Ombre Corte.

Roscoe, W., 2000. *Changing Ones. Third and Fourth Genders in Native North America.* New York: St. Martin's Griffin.

Senelick, L., 2000. *The Changing Room: Sex, Drag and Theatre.* London: Routledge.

Simone, A., ed., 2012. *Sessismo democratico. L'uso strumentale delle donne nel neoliberismo.* Milano: Mimesis.

Stryker, S., 2008. *Transgender History.* Berkeley: Seal Studies.

Teti, V., 2013. *Maledetto Sud.* Torino: Einaudi.

Valentine, D., 2007. *Imagining Transgender. An Ethnography of a Category.* Durham: Duke University Press.

Valerio, P. and Zito, E., 2010. *Corpi sull'uscio, identità possibili, Il fenomeno dei femminielli a Napoli.* Napoli: Ed. Filema.

Vitelli, R. and Valerio, P., eds, 2012. *Sesso e genere. Uno sguardo tra storia e nuove prospettive.* Napoli: Liguori Editore.

Wikan, U., 1977. 'Man Becomes Woman. Transsexualism in Oman as a Key to Gender Roles'. *Man,* 12 (2), pp. 304–319.

Zito, E. and Valerio, P., eds, 2013. *Genere: Femminielli. Esplorazioni antropologiche e psicologiche.* Napoli: Libreria Dante & Descartes.

# CHAPTER 5

# Tattoos: An Embodiment of Desire

*Nina Nyman*

Two favourite issues of feminists are women's rights to express themselves and women's rights to their own bodies. Women's tattoos can be seen as an expression of both of these rights. In my chapter I will analyse women's decisions to get tattooed and women's relations to their tattooed bodies. The material for this chapter consists of interviews I undertook in 2011–12 with seven tattooed women. I will focus on the women's descriptions of their tattoos, and of their bodies as tattooed. I will analyse these stories through earlier feminist research about tattoos (Caplan 2000; Inckle 2007; Neville 2005; Pitts 2003; Sanders 1989) and through feminist theories concerning embodiment as a process (Braidotti 1991; 2002; Butler 1990; 2005; Butler 2007) and desire as productive (Braidotti 1991; 2002; Deleuze and Guattari 1987; Grosz 1995; 2010; Hickey-Moody and Rasmussen 2009; Nigianni and Storr 2009). My analysis focuses on the possibility of thinking about embodiment through an understanding of desire as productive, which in short means that desire creates rather than lacks. Thinking about an active process of embodiment through a productive desire shows ways in which one can change or relate to one's own body.

N. Nyman (✉)
Åbo Akademi University, Turku, Finland
e-mail: n.c.nyman@gmail.com

© The Author(s) 2017
E. Rees (ed.), *Talking Bodies*, DOI 10.1007/978-3-319-63778-5_5

My aim in this chapter is to understand how tattooed women understand their bodies *as tattooed*. I investigate how tattoos are a part of women's processes of embodiment and how an understanding of desire as productive, as opposed to desire as lack, can add to the understanding of women's decisions to get a tattoo. Feminist theory offers many tools for understanding why women choose to get tattoos, and is rich in offering understandings of women's embodiment and women's bodies. And this process also works the other way around: research about tattoos can give feminist theory examples of the active choices women make regarding their bodies; an agency that, historically, is in many ways new for women.

Understanding desire as productive opens up the possibility of viewing the body in a new way. And that in turn opens up possibilities of viewing sex and gender in other ways. Desire has a history of being understood as exclusively male, with male desire defining women's bodies from an outside perspective. In this chapter I analyse embodiment as a process of becoming where the driving force is a productive desire that constantly produces (creates) new possibilities instead of old limitations. I argue for an understanding of bodies and identities grounded in agency (see Braidotti 2002; Shildrick 2009). 'Embodiment' in this context is understood as the way tattoos become merged with women's bodies, and with women's understanding of their bodies and themselves. Embodiment is a part of a person's history and future that can be understood through the tattooing process: my analysis is an attempt to examine a renegotiation of desire and bodies through the active agency of tattooing.

## Method and Material

I interviewed seven women, with different numbers of tattoos, about their relationship with their tattoos and their bodies as tattooed. The interviewees were between 21 and 50 years old and they were from Denmark, Finland, Spain, Sweden and Wales. The interviews took place in Denmark, Finland and Sweden and we spoke Swedish, Danish and English. Because my Spanish is limited, one interviewee did not get to speak her mother tongue, but English was a language she used in her daily life and a language in which she was used to expressing feelings. All the other informants spoke in their mother tongue during the interviews.

The choice of informants was partly a strategic one; two of them were people I knew and three I found through a feminist e-mail list. Two of the informants I found through the snowball effect, they were friends of other informants and contacted me and asked to be part of the study. All informants were women, tattooed, and in some respect, feminist. I tried to get as varied tattoo-narratives as possible, mostly by interviewing women of different ages and with different numbers of tattoos. The representation of so many countries compared with the number of informants was not a goal of mine, but served to give the research bigger variation.

The interviews were semi-structured and thematically based. There was room for the informants to stray from the themes, which all of them at some point did. The interviews were qualitative and showed similarities with other studies (see Inckle 2007, Neville 2005). The informants themselves chose the places for the interviews. Some took place in cafés and some in the interviewees' homes. One interview was conducted in my own home. Every woman was interviewed once and the interviews took between one and one-and-a-half hours. I had imagined that some time would be necessary to establish the trust needed to talk about the themes, especially since I was the person who would analyse their stories, but this was not necessary: the informants had ready narratives regarding their bodies as tattooed and they were open to sharing them.

In hindsight I realise that the women, when volunteering for the study, knew that it was their bodies that would be discussed in the interviews and had naturally prepared for that before we met. About half of the women also had an academic background and were used to reflecting analytically and critically on the themes of the interviews. The fact that most of the informants defined themselves as feminists added to the openness of the interviews: all of them knew that I am a feminist.

Because I am interested in describing the women's feelings about their bodies, and not the way their bodies looked, I decided not to describe the tattoos themselves, even though some were mentioned during the interviews. Not describing the tattoos is a way of assuring anonymity for the women participating in this study. All the names of the women in this chapter are also changed and all quotations are translated into English further to guarantee anonymity.

Studies about tattoos have often been focused on the history of tattooing and the history of tattoos is often a narrative that places European tattoos on the arms of working or travelling men as symbols of masculinity. The main focus was on sailors and crusaders and in some cases research also addressed the development of techniques of tattooing. Tattoos became popular in Europe around 1700, but the art of tattooing had existed long before that, and on both men and women (Caplan 2000, p. xviii). I do not, like many (see Gelder 2007; Goode and Vail 2008), analyse tattoos as a part of a subculture: some of my informants might be said to belong to some kind of subculture, but it was not a subculture that they all shared. I could also have chosen to research body modifications that would include, for example, piercings (see Featherstone 2000; Pitts 2003). But focusing on tattoos emphasised the permanent aspect of the change in one's body. Tattoos are a choice one makes based on the understanding of oneself as a sum of numerous situations in one's life. It is not a temporary choice, for the moment, for some years, or just for specific situations.

## THE FIRST TATTOO

The informants had different reasons for getting tattooed, but for everyone getting the first tattoo was an important event. The women I interviewed had clear narratives describing the process of becoming tattooed. Some of the women had been contemplating a particular motif for years; others had been looking forward to getting a tattoo regardless of its motif. Among the women I talked with, only one, Sofie (27), had had the tattoo spontaneously:

Sofie:    Yes. Well, to me [having the tattoo] was a sign of something that would change in my life; that I was turning 18. So it was a birthday present from a friend when I turned 18. And it was something to do, to mark that moment. So I got a tattoo, I got drunk, I got in a plane, and I went to have a crazy weekend in London. All together. At the same time.

Nina:    So you had it done in London?

Sofie:    No, no! I had it in my home town, but it was like... (gesturing with hands)

Nina:    Getting prepared?

Sofie:    Yeah! Getting prepared to do like [...] all the things that I wanted to do. So the tattoo was a souvenir of turning 18, and becoming an adult with responsibilities and decisions and blah blah.

For Sofie, the act of getting tattooed related to becoming an adult, and marked the possibility of making her own decisions regarding her body. For her it was a sign of being a free subject, capable and willing to make her own decisions. She continues:

Sofie:  […] But I think that is the meaning for me of a tattoo, making your body yours and something that you have sort of chosen and you are. Because we are born with a whole body, hopefully, in ideal cases, and you don't get to choose anything about it.

Nina:   So you feel it makes your body more…

Sofie:  Mine. Yes. Absolutely mine, yes.

The feminist theorist and philosopher Elizabeth Grosz (2010, p. 144) describes free actions as expressions of the whole subject, actions that start in the subject without outside forces. Further, she writes that these actions not only express the will of the subject, but that they are fundamental to what the subject is: 'they not only originate in the or through a subject, they express all of the subject. In other words, they are integral to who or what the subject is'. In other words, the actions are fundamental to the subject. The subject is what the subject does. It is the repetitive and ritualised actions in individual humans that make them into agents and subjects (Coole and Frost 2010a, b, p.34; Nyman 2012, p. 15).

Yet the idea of getting a tattoo was not Sofie's own. In her case, it was a friend who suggested the tattoo and she let herself be influenced. But still the actual decision was Sofie's. The fact that somebody else was involved in the decision-making did not lessen Sofie's feeling that the tattoo strengthened her position as an active subject. To be independent and at the same time be affected; or in fact to be independent by being affected and relate through that, is essential to a posthumanist understanding of subjects. Where subjects used to be viewed as independent through their ability to remain unaffected, posthumanist theory views the subjects' ability to be affected and formed through affection as essential to the subjects' existence (Braidotti 2002, p. 207). Rosi Braidotti (2002, pp. 229–30) describes subjects as both embodied and embodying. She argues for an understanding of the subject that she calls Deleuzian which is neither an inner essence nor only created from outside. Braidotti describes the forming of the subject as simultaneous processes of taking in outside stimuli and acting out inner affects, and neither one of these has priority in shaping or making a subject.

This can be illustrated in becoming tattooed. The inner wish to become tattooed is manifested visibly on the flesh while the ink becomes a part of the inner structure of the skin, affecting how the body will be viewed in different social surroundings. A strong distinction between inner and outer becomes questionable.

## WOMEN AND TATTOOS

For Kay Inckle (2007, p. 96), femininity is built on the objectifying and dismissal of female bodies, for example natural occurrences such as body hair and menstruation are deemed shameful. If women's bodies are regulated by social rules, then making active decisions about those bodies makes embodiment an emancipatory act.[1] Inckle (2007, p. 102) argues that embodiment is an important tool when analysing women's experiences of their tattoos because tattoos are lived experience. Embodiment is a way of collecting experiences, and norms, to tie them together, and to live with them. Braidotti (2002, p. 21) defines embodiment as a process dependent on time and space, and the body as a complex assembly of the structures where we also find our identities. Braidotti (1991) further argues that the institutions that form our bodies are both material (for example school, family and so on) and discursive (for example laws). These serve to form bodies as embodied expressions of subjects. Bodies are, in other words, not natural or self-evident in their expressions. With this definition it is easy to see that tattoos are a form of embodiment. Through tattooing, the place in which one is located is embodied, both physically and mentally. This is a constant process where the body and the interpretation of the body are constantly formed by its inhibitor and spectators of the body, together with the surroundings of the body and its history (Makiko 2005).

Not a single woman I interviewed said that the way other people might view their bodies had an impact on their decision to tattoo themselves. But in terms of the placement and size of the tattoo, some of the women negotiated with real or imagined others. Nathalie (21) expressed her lack of concern for the possible judgment of others by saying that: 'It is more the fact that I have one; the motif probably doesn't matter to people who don't like tattoos'.

Inckle (2007, p. 186) interprets the resistance with which tattooing is sometimes met as a reaction to the taboo against shedding blood. The taboo is connected to an idea of pollution and infection, but may be due mostly to a fear surrounding the transgression of borders between self/other and inner/outer. In terms of the notion of shedding blood, Inckle refers to the blood lost when the tattoo needle punctures the skin to inject ink: the blood becomes a symbol of transgression and an opening of the natural border of the skin. The ink embodies this moment and makes the transgression into a permanent mark. Resistance against tattoos can, in other words, be viewed as a fear of a disruption of the social norm of the border of the skin. Judith Butler (2007, p. 209) writes that the borders that symbolise taboos, for example the skin, frame the social hegemony which is rendered vulnerable precisely at the point of the border. Tattooing as a puncturing of the skin is, therefore, surrounded by social taboos, especially since a permanent mark is left of the defying of the border.

Even if the tattoo signals a disruption of the social norm, there are still differences in terms of what kinds of tattoos are visible. The motif of the tattoo might provoke different reactions, affecting how the tattooed person is 'read'. Vera (33) gives an example of this when I ask her about placement and motif of the tattoo, especially regarding other people's potential reactions:

Vera:   I have [tattoos] on my arms. Just positive reactions really. I have 'nice' tattoos on my arms […] it is not like skulls and torn up corpses.

Nina:   Did you think about it when you chose a location? How visible they are and what motif is visible?

Vera:   Yes, actually a little bit.

Vera sees the motif of her tattoos as a possible reason for the (positive) reactions she gets. The reactions are then something that she, through her actions, has taken part in creating and influencing. Victoria Pitts (2003, p. 62) argues that even though tattoos might break some norms, women who choose to get tattoos are conscious of context. They play with, and renegotiate, borders (Pitts 2003, p. 62). Their actions signify embodiment (Butler 1990, 2005, 2007). According to Judith Butler (2007, p. 272) embodiment is the manifest form of the possibilities the body has, or does not have. But this is not to suggest that bodies are fully formed through conscious decisions, since those same decisions are always grounded in a context with a history that limits and regulates what is possible (Parisi 2009). Other people's possible reactions could, for some of the informants, be a source of uneasiness in the decision to get a tattoo. All of the women I interviewed had counted on getting reactions, and for the most part the reactions they got were positive. But the nature of the reactions did not always correspond to the women's own understanding of their tattoos. Julia's (50) and Tina's (26) stories exemplify that:

> Tina:    And I like that, I like that they are statements, I like that people are so [...] And it is something I have noticed during this short time I have had this tattoo on my hand. Everyone is like: 'Oh! It's a bit hardcore to have tattoos on your fingers!'. And for me it's like: 'What? This is just a [motif] It is the wimpiest tattoo'. But apparently it is still something.

> Julia:    Mmm, there were many people who thought that it would be possible to wash it off. That I couldn't possibly have done it for real. And even [a work colleague] commented on it. That he would never get a tattoo in such a visible place. But...

> Nina:    How did that feel?

> Julia:    Well, I'd really thought the decision through. So I was a bit surprised by comments like that, but I was enough of an adult when I got the tattoo that I knew what I was doing. And I had thought it through so it was OK. I could stand behind my choice and know why I did it. [...] Most times I get really positive feedback and everyone thinks it's a beautiful tattoo.

Of all the women I interviewed, Julia and Tina had the most visible tattoos. Our conversations revealed that both of them were conscious about the decisions they made, even though the reactions sometimes took them by surprise. In Tina's case, the tattoo on her hand was mostly an aesthetic choice. It was one among many tattoos and she had had them for different reasons. In Julia's case, the tattoo was her first, and so far her only one. She has chosen to have it as a carefully thought through symbol for a balance she had found through different life events. The high visibility factor of the tattoos was, in neither Tina's nor Julia's case, a conscious provocation, nor an expression of a desire for reactions. Both of them dealt with reactions through referring to the meaning the tattoo held for them personally. Inckle (2007, p. 121) describes similar situations among the women she has interviewed. She calls the situation a 'balance between visibility and acceptance' and describes it as something one does within existing norms. Further reactions can be seen as reflections on the idea that a tattoo makes visible something new about the tattooed person, something that the viewer might not have known and that now can be seen as exposed. The inner is made outer.

## PRODUCTIVE DESIRE

Deciding to get a tattoo means deciding to change one's body. The women who chose to get tattoos had an understanding of themselves in relation to their bodies. But the relationship of body and identity is not a simple one where actions have clear consequences. The relation can be understood through Gilles Deleuze's and Felix Guattari's concept of *becoming*. According to Deleuze and Guattari the self is involved in a constant process of becoming something other than it is, and this process involves both material, bodily, and psychological changes (Hickey-Moody and Rasmussen 2009, p. 43). Anna Hickey-Moody and Mary Lou Rasmussen (2009, p. 43) argue that the human body within the Deleuzian frame of thought is a consequence of its own movements and processes. The body does not precede the flow of time in which its becoming is created, but is in a constant process of becoming, where according to Hickey-Moody and Rasmussen (2009), it is realised as one of many exciting potentialities.

Becomings are thus not conscious choices, but processes of change in which potential is realised and made again and again; processes without an end. In other words, becomings are not only, or even mostly, physical events, and becomings are open-ended. You never finally become the becoming in which you are involved. Becomings are thus not teleological (Weinstein 2008). Tattoos can be understood as processes of becoming since tattoos are part of the body's past and future *at the same time*. Tattoos rarely have stable definitions in regard to the relationship between identity and body. They rather serve the constant transformation of this relationship. In some cases, the tattoo can, for example, help a woman like her body better, as Vera reported:

Vera:   Regarding my body and skin, I have noticed that it has become easier to accept it. When I was younger I had more complexes regarding my body. With tattoos and piercings, I have become better friends with it. I like my stomach better after I pierced my navel. Then I focused on that and not the size of it. It was a way for me to like myself better. It is the exact same thing as cosmetic surgery. [...] It is really difficult to know what you yourself want, what really comes from the inside, and what are the reactions against, or with, others.

Grosz (1995, p. 175) describes the problem with women's bodies, and desire, as that of making something constructed as passive into something active. Further, she places two traditions of understanding desire against each other. One of them Grosz dates back to Plato: a tradition of defining desire as an unfulfillable lack. This tradition lives on in Freudian psychoanalysis. Grosz links the other tradition to Spinoza. According to that tradition, desire is a force that creates connections, produces something new, and requires interaction. Grosz (1995, p. 179) writes that, according to Spinoza, as opposed to Freud, desire is not limited by meeting reality. On the contrary, reality is produced by desire. Further, Grosz writes that desire as production does not give one, or many, directions, models or goals. Instead it experiments and creates (Grosz 1995, p. 180). According to Grosz, the understanding of desire as productive is an important tool in understanding women's desires. In the Freudian understanding of desire, women have been understood as lack. The lack of lack in an understanding of desire as productive allows for women to avoid this position.

Understanding desire this way shatters the understanding of entities where something can be one element missing another, with desire as the third piece existing between the two first elements. Dualisms and hierarchies are in this way drastically impeded since, as Grosz (1995, p. 182) writes, there are no more ready-made erogenous zones; everything has the possibility to act as such. Desire reorganises and deorganises bodies in a way that does not lock them, or desire itself, to claims. In this way the important thing is what desire does, not was desire is.

But desire often, sadly, creates what it is said to represent, namely sex (gender). Grosz describes desire as the link between two parts that do not necessarily need to be erogenous zones in a psychoanalytical sense.

According to Grosz, it is the meeting itself that creates the desire. Where a classic psychoanalytical understanding of desire limits and defines bodies that then serve a hierarchal understanding of gender, by contrast, a Deleuzian understanding of desire as productive opens up possibilities of bodies becoming, and can disrupt the power structures of desire. Desire, then, is no longer only a sexual desire, but desire becomes a force that opens up the possibility for new kinds of actions, and interpretations of these actions, through the disruption of the borders of bodies. Tattoos can here be viewed as an example of the 'deorganising' of the borders of bodies.

Viewing desire as productive shows that tattoos are not a way of organising bodies. To organise the body is, according to Deleuze and Guattari (1987, pp. 175–176), a phallic pleasure that is connected to organs and then only becomes the pleasure of the organ. In this way the organ organises the body. For both Deleuze and Guattari, desire is an ontological reorganisation and *de*organisation of bodies. When the needle and the ink are injected into the skin there is a reorganisation of that skin. This is partly physical (the structure of the skin is changed), and partly social (the skin now has a different meaning through a new sign, the tattoo). The skin as an organised organ is for a moment disrupted and a possibility for something new is created. To understand bodies through a desire-perspective is to shift the zones of the body and their use; it is to see new openings where earlier there were none. It is to desire change, to desire a picture; it is a feeling of pleasure outside the organisation of sex and gender.

Claire Colebrook (2009) describes two main points central to Deleuze's understanding of an active subject. In Colebrook's interpretation of Deleuze there is one construction of the self that just repeats, and so has a passive relation to the world. This leads to repetitions defining the subject without a choice being made. Colebrook names this type of self 'pre-individual' and she opposes it to an active subject. The active subject is not a coherent subject, but is made up of 'a thousand tiny egos, each effected from an encounter' (Colebrook 2009, p. 16). In other words, there is not a conflict between dependence and independence. On the contrary, the acting subject is highly dependent on meetings with others, maybe even more so than a self that passively repeats. Important in Colebrook's understanding of the definition is also the fragmented subject, the schizophrenic subject that results in a myriad of conditions and meetings at the same time. This is the opposite of the coherent, acting, and consciously controllable subject of the enlightenment. To act is, then, not to have a clear direction; it is not a teleological movement and it does not have a goal. To act is something different than to reproduce. The action can thus seemingly have one direction and at the same time be influenced. And to be influenced does not necessarily signify a lack of goal. This is illustrated by Tina's description of how her feeling about her body changes when she has tattoos:

Nina:  Do you think your view of yourself, your nakedness and such, has changed by you tattooing yourself?

Tina:  Yes, it really has. Because I notice that I look at the tattoos and focus more than I did before. I might have stood and thought 'Oh, my stomach looks so boring', but now I think: 'Oh, this is a good surface to make something cool on!' And it can also give me the feeling that [tattoos] would give me good-looking legs. And that's interesting.

Nina:  So you first choose a spot, and then you find it more beautiful after tattooing it? You don't tattoo spots you find beautiful?

Tina:  No, not at all. On the contrary, I think the tattoo is beautifying. That it simply makes you more beautiful. And the small 'hang-ups' especially become less noticeable; instead you look at something else.

Once Tina started getting tattooed she started seeing new possibilities for her body, and her skin has, through the injection of ink, become a potential surface for something new. Colebrook (2009, p. 17) writes that every meeting, every event, is a realisation of the potentialities buried in it. The event is a potential to become that is created at every moment. This of course ties together with the shattering of the subject and the many acting forces within the subject. Not to allow oneself to react to the possibilities that these forces open is what creates passive repetition. The active subject Colebrook describes, inspired by Deleuze, is thus not active through the mode of action, but rather through relating to the *potential* of actions. What creates and changes the subject is a productive desire that can be, but is not always, sexual.

## THE TATTOOS OF OTHERS

One aspect of desire in tattoos is how one views other people's tattoos. I asked the women I interviewed if they noticed a difference in how they look at other people's tattoos after they themselves got tattoos. Most of them had noticed a difference. Tina told me that she had started looking more at other people's tattoos. For Tina, having a tattoo could make a person better-looking. At the same time, there were tattoos that she definitely did not find attractive, even though she realised she could have had tattoos like them herself:

> Tina:   Yes, I look a lot at other people's tattoos. A lot. Partly in an arrogant way: 'Oh my god, that one wasn't well done!', but mostly because they make me envious. And I can feel that a person becomes really good-looking because of their tattoos. [...] Because I think they are really cool. And that is what it's about; they are cool. They are rock and roll: not to give a damn about anything. I guess that's what I find attractive. So I look a lot at others and I judge harshly people who have Asian signs and tribals and such. At the same time I know it could have been me (*laughter*).

When Julia looked at other people's tattoos she thought about the situations they might have been in when they chose to have them done. Julia has a daughter who very much wanted to get a tattoo at some point and who at the time of the interview was not yet of age. Julia then contemplated other people's tattoos from the perspective of her having some power to influence if, or when, another person tattooed herself. For Julia, then, the most important thing was that the other person knew what they were doing when they got tattooed:

> Julia:   And then I feel like this: you have to be fully mature, and mentally. If you ever become that. But you have to be at a certain stage so that [...] so that you on some level know what you want.

Julia underlines the importance of knowing what you want when you get a tattoo. This she calls being fully developed mentally. At the same time, she raises doubts about this being a fixed point one reaches. Vera, on the other hand, had realised that her contemplating her own reasons for changing her body had changed her view of other people's body transformations. And not only regarding tattoos:

Vera:   I have started to think differently about things like cosmetic surgery and such. I was previously totally against them. But it's the
same thing. The tragic thing is that you often, but not always, try
to fit into a norm. But that's also the case for many who tattoo
themselves; it is also a norm. Especially people who get [...], well,
readymade motifs. There are many people with motifs that thou-
sands of other people have: they just want a tattoo. Like I said,
in the beginning, I wanted a tattoo, of what didn't matter; I just
wanted a tattoo. And that's also a norm. And is it a tragic norm just
because more people conform to it? I think so. But it's not with my
mind; it's with my heart that I think so.

These stories have in common that the women draw on their own
experiences when they consider other people's tattoos. All of them are
conscious of their minds having changed at some point, which means
that they might change again. In all three cases they refer to feelings;
to finding tattoos appealing; to feel that you know what you want; to
think with the heart and not with the head. What they do is describe an
affective relation to tattoos; a relation open to change, to contradictions,
based in the body, and dependent on feelings. Affectivity, according to
Braidotti (2002, p. 70), regulates the truth-value of an idea. Braidotti
describes affectivity as the opposite to phallogocentrism, where phallogocentrism represents linear thinking. She links affectivity to Deleuze's
concept of the 'rhizomatic'. Rhizomes can, put simply, be described as
structures without centres, with an unlimited number of openings and
a potential for even more (Deleuze and Guattari 1987). An affective
knowledge-model, or truth-value, is thus not hierarchic or dualistic,
but open to change. Braidotti (2002, p. 100) describes the affective as
happening in the meeting between different embodied subjects that are
united in the sameness of the forces that drive them. Affectivity is, then,
not an inner state of a subject, but a situation and a meeting.

The informants found tattoos desirable on themselves and on others,
but that was not the most important reason to get a tattoo. Even though
the women I interviewed clearly found tattooed bodies desirable, tattoos did not matter much in their choice of partner. Of the informants
that were in a relationship, only one, Julia, had a partner with a tattoo.
And in that case he had had the tattoo once they had been married for
over 15 years. Two of the informants, Tina and Amanda, had partners
who did not appreciate that they continued to tattoo themselves. But in

neither case had the partners managed to changes the informant's attitude to tattoos or wish to get new tattoos.

Tina:   the next one is going to be a big one. I will get it on my thigh. It's going to be a [...motif] on my thigh.

Nina:   Wow! (*both laugh*)

Tina:   And my girlfriend doesn't like the look of it. She's asking me not to do it, but...

Nina:   Because it's on the thigh or..?

Tina:   Yes, she thinks it's ugly. She thinks it's shabby to get a tattoo on the thigh. A bit white trash. And that's why I like it!

Vera mentions that the man she lives with does not have tattoos, and that not having tattoos is something that stands out among their friends:

Vera:   The man I live with doesn't have a single one.

Nina:   He doesn't?

Vera:   No.

Nina:   And he hasn't thought of getting one?

Vera:   No. He did in the beginning, but then he noticed that... And it's a bit different not to have one. 99 percent of the people around us have tattoos, so it's a bit special *not* to have one.

For the informants, finding tattoos desirable did not prompt their choice of partner. And when their partners did not find tattoos desirable it did not change the informants' views on tattoos or choices about getting new tattoos. The attraction tattoos hold is connected far more with an individual's own body than with the bodies (or opinions) of others. The informants found tattoos attractive, but that their partners do not have tattoos does not affect them. And neither does it matter if their partner does not find tattoos attractive.

So what does desire consist of? Desire, viewed as productive and not only sexual, can be seen as a way of creating the body, as a becoming. Margrit Shildrick (2009, p. 125) argues that 'becoming entails an inherent transgression of boundaries that turns the pleasures—sexual or otherwise—of the embodied person away from dominant notions of human subjectivity'. Braidotti (2002, p. 77) describes desire as something other than lack, as a passion-driven network of impersonal or machinelike connections. Desire is movement and its goal is not to fill or compensate for a void, but to create. It is, according to Braidotti, an understanding of the subject as passion driven but at the same time linked to machinelike connections outside it. Machines in this sense do not need to be what one automatically might think of as a machine, for example a machine to make tattoos with. Rather, machines are entities that do not have to be physical, but can be social situations; they work together to create a new, temporary entity. In other words, machines are alliances that are bound in, and reflect, a specific time and space. A single tattoo can be interpreted in different ways in different settings, and the passion behind the tattoo continues to exist, but not unaffected. The productive desire is in interaction with the embodiment and it is affecting the understanding of women's bodies as tattooed.

## BECOMING TATTOOED

Becoming tattooed changes the status of the body. It is a way of manifesting one's relation to one's body. Getting one's first tattoo was an important moment for all the women I interviewed. At the same time, tattooing was also a way of forming one's subject through forming one's body in an irreversible way, and thus changing other people's perceptions of it.

The reactions the women got to the tattoos varied and were, in some cases, surprising. By getting tattoos the women could not directly affect how their bodies would be read, but the tattoos were changes they stood behind and were happy about. The tattoos were a way of tying together their bodies and their own feelings about their bodies and this did not end when the tattooing process was over, but continued in new situations and new meetings. Feminist theory has shown how women's bodies are defined and limited both materially, and discursively; tattooing can work as a way of taking back some of the power over one's own body. Inckle (2007) writes that surroundings influence a person's processes of embodiment, but actively to relate to these surroundings, and the agency that that entails, is an important part of the process of becoming tattooed.

Most of the informants were very interested in other people's tattoos and considered them in the light of their own tattoos and processes of becoming tattooed. The informants had an emotional, affective way of understanding other people's tattoos. The affective dimension of their relation to tattoos also showed in their relation to their own tattoos. The tattoos often had a deeper meaning to them, rather than being 'just' embellishments. Some tattoos had been done during difficult times, for example, when a loved one had died. Some had been chosen to symbolise important moments in life, like becoming an adult. However, some really were 'only' embellishments and their aesthetic dimensions were probably always taken into account in some way.

The choice to become tattooed was grounded in a feeling of taking decisions about one's own body. But does every single tattoo have a history for the person who takes it (embodies it)? For the women I interviewed every new tattoo was a production of something new, not a *reproduction* of the first decision to become tattooed. The interviews gave many examples of this, with the women having different narratives surrounding each tattoo they had done. They described getting tattooed together with friends, because they found a tattoo artist they really liked; some had them because a new chapter in their life was starting, or because they were leaving an old city, and so on. Even though many tattoos had deep personal significance, not all did. And some women underlined the fact that they found being tattooed the important thing—not the style, placement or picture of the tattoo. Vera, especially, argued that for her the tattoo was a way of relating to her body by not taking it too seriously, but at the same time using the tattoo to feel better about her body. One might argue that the importance of getting tattooed and the importance of an individual tattoo are rarely the same thing.

Women are to a larger extent than men defined by their bodies (see Davies 1997). Their actions and statements regarding their bodies to a large extent influence how they are viewed as people, and how they themselves feel they are viewed. Some of the women I interviewed felt people's reaction to their tattoos were linked to their gender, that being a woman and being tattooed challenged what a woman should be. While not one of the women I interviewed said that this affected their choice in getting a tattoo, all of the women I interviewed at some point expressed some kind of view on tattoos linked to gender. Tattoos illustrate a practice that used to be linked to masculinity, but they have become common among women as well, and views of the practice have changed.

My interviews show that the milieu of the tattooed person affects how gendered the practice of tattooing was thought to be. Only a few of the women I interviewed had, interestingly, a partner who shared their feelings about tattoos. Only one had a tattooed partner and two of them even had partners who would have preferred that they did not continue to tattoo themselves.

For the women I interviewed there was a difference between having and not having a tattoo. To get a tattoo changed feelings about, and relations to, the body, and influenced how others viewed the body. Even though my study was a qualitative one, with women of different ages and nationalities, there were many similarities between them as this chapter has shown. The biggest difference between them was what kind of tattoos they found beautiful. They all found tattoos beautiful in general, but the motif and style differed greatly. They might not have liked each other's tattoos if they had met. The narratives and reasons for getting new tattoos also varied among the women. Their stories also varied when they told me about the possible fears they might have had before getting tattoos. Their stories were more similar after getting a tattoo than when they told me about the time before getting it. The women felt that tattoos could give them a sense of being in charge of their own bodies, and feminist theory confirms this feeling. Tattoos could be used as a feminist strategy to take charge of one's own body through actively taking the decision to change it. A tattoo often exists in thoughts before it is manifested physically on the skin. Further, once engraved in the skin, the tattoo stays there. For the women I interviewed, tattoos embody a productive desire through which the body exists in a state of constant becoming.

## NOTE

1. When I use the term 'embodiment' I aim at describing a social process where bodies relate to their surroundings in their shaping, hence both sex and gender are part of the process of embodiment.

## REFERENCES

Braidotti, R., 1991. *Patterns of Dissonance*. Cambridge: Polity Press.
Braidotti, R., 2002. *Metamorphoses. Towards a Materialist Theory of Becoming*. Cambridge: Polity Press.

Butler, J., 1990. 'Performative Acts and Gender Constitution: An Essay in Phenomenology and Feminist Theory', in Case, S–E. ed., *Performing Feminisms, Feminist Critical Theory and Theatre*. Baltimore: Johns Hopkins University Press.

Butler, J., 2005. *Könet briner*. Köping: Natur och kultur.

Butler, J., 2007. *Genustrubbel. Feminism och identitetens subversion*. Göteborg: Daidalos.

Caplan, J., ed., 2000. *Written on the Body: the Tattoo in European and American History*. London: Reaktion.

Colebrook, C., 2009. 'On the Very Possibility of Queer Theory', in Nigianni, C. and Storr, M., eds. *Deleuze and Queer Theory*. Edinburgh: Edinburgh University Press.

Coole, D. and Frost, S., eds., 2010a. *New Materialism. Ontology, Agency and Politics*. Durham & London: Duke University Press.

Coole, D. and Frost, S., 2010b. 'Introducing the New Materialisms', in Coole, D. and Frost, S., eds. *New Materialism. Ontology, Agency and Politics*. Durham & London: Duke University Press.

Davies, K., 1997. *Embodied Practices on the Body*. London: Sage.

Deleuze, G. and Guattari, F., 1987. *A Thousand Plateaus*. London and New York: Continuum.

Featherstone, M., ed., 2000. *Body Modification*. London: Sage Publications.

Gelder, K., 2007. *Subcultures: Cultural Histories and Social Practice*. New York: Routledge.

Goode, E. and Vail, D. A., 2008. *Extreme Deviance*. Los Angeles Pine Forge Press, an imprint of Sage Publications, Inc.

Grosz, E., 1995. *Space, Time, and Perversion: Essays on the Politics of Bodies*. New York: Routledge.

Grosz, E., 2010. 'Feminism, Materialism, and Freedom', in Coole, D. and Frost, S., eds. *New Materialism. Ontology, Agency and Politics*. Durham & London: Duke University Press.

Hickey-Moody, A. and Rasmussen, M L., 2009. 'The Sexed Subject in-between Deleuze and Butler', in Nigianni, C. and Storr, M., eds. *Deleuze and Queer Theory*. Edinburgh: Edinburgh University Press.

Inckle, K., 2007. *Writing on the Body? Thinking Through Gendered Embodiment and Marked Flesh*. Newcastle: Cambridge Scholars Publishing.

Makiko, K., 2005. *Tattoo: An Anthropology*. Oxford and New York: Berg.

Neville, H., 2005. 'Marking Gender: Women and Tattoos, Practice and Representation'. *Philament* 7, pp. 42–63.

Nigianni, C. and Storr, M., eds., 2009. *Deleuze and Queer Theory*. Edinburgh: Edinburgh University Press.

Nyman, N., 2012. *Tatuerade kvinnor - ett förkroppsligande av begär*.

Parisi, L., 2009. 'The Adventures of a Sex', in Nigianni, C. and Storr, M., eds. *Deleuze and Queer Theory*. Edinburgh: Edinburgh University Press.

Pitts, V., 2003. *In the Flesh: The Cultural Politics of Body Modification*. New York: Palgrave Macmillan.

Sanders, C., 1989. *Customizing the Body: the Art and Culture of Tattooing*. Philadelphia: Temple University Press.

Shildrick, M., 2009. 'Prostetic Performativity', in Nigianni, C. and Storr, M., eds. *Deleuze and Queer Theory*. Edinburgh: Edinburgh University Press.

Weinstein, J., 2008. 'Introduction', in Colebrook, C. and Weinstein, J., eds. *Deleuze and Gender*. Edinburgh: Edinburgh University Press.

# CHAPTER 6

# Learning Womanhood: Body Modification, Girls and Identity

## *Abigail Tazzyman*

In Western popular imagination appearance is equated with identity, and this association is noticeably gendered (Goffman 1963; Lindemann 1997; Lawler 2008; Jackson and Scott 2010). It is almost impossible in Western cultures to avoid being a constant witness to images of modified bodies and body modification methods. We are besieged by cultural imperatives constantly to think about the body and to see it as a project to work on. Women (and to a lesser degree men) are endlessly assailed by exhortations to manipulate their bodies to fit in with certain body norms. This emphasis on bodily appearance is overt in the popular media and highly gendered. Women's appearance is inspected and critiqued (Denham 2014; O'Carroll 2014; Rose 2014); TV shows are dedicated to the topic (*Secret Eaters*, 2012–2014; *SuperSize vs SuperSkinny*, 2008–2014; *How to Look Good Naked*, 2006–2008); pages in women's magazines are devoted to body modification; and, despite the economic climate, the cosmetic/beauty/fitness industries are growing (The Leisure Database Company, 2012; Mintel 2013). The high visibility of issues surrounding body modification is indicative of the importance it holds

A. Tazzyman (✉)
Manchester Business School, Manchester, UK
e-mail: abigail.tazzyman@gmail.com

© The Author(s) 2017
E. Rees (ed.), *Talking Bodies*, DOI 10.1007/978-3-319-63778-5_6

and the extent to which its enactment permeates society. The attribute viewed as the most important aspect of a woman is her appearance (Wolf 1991; Bordo 2004 [1993]; Jeffreys 2005).[1] Body modification is the tool which enables us to create the self-image we wish to display to others. It is a highly normative and gendered practice which for the most part goes unquestioned. As appearance is culturally so central for women's identity and perceived value, it is important to understand their decisions and practices in shaping it.

This chapter is based on research which investigates female body modification, and on data collected from in-depth life history interviews with thirty university-educated British women, aged between eighteen and twenty five.[2] In this chapter I analyse what initial and early body modification engagement meant and means for these young women's identities. In this I consider their reasons for commencing body modification, and their experience of it during their school years.

Analysing initial engagement with, and early use of, body modification practices offers an explanation of why and how these practices were begun. It makes visible how my participants, when non-practitioners of body modification, understood these practices and how they and others read their bodies and selves before and after they began to engage in body modification. This was a period marked by both the point of participants' first engagement with body modification and the point of no return. After this stage not modifying one's body was no longer understood as a valid option and engagement with body modification became a constant feature of daily lives and practices of self. Research on body modification has suggested that the life stage of youth may have significance for women's relationships to their bodies and the practices they engage with to alter them (Bordo 2004; Frost 2005). Young women are frequently positioned, in both academia and the media, as at heightened vulnerability to pressures which result in body modification. Frost, for example, argues that 'it is between fourteen and eighteen years that most, and the most extreme, forms of body-hatred are manifest, and mainly in girls, which indicates that the dimension 'youth' may have significance' (2005, p. 74). Body modification is viewed as the result of this body hatred. Simultaneously, and in stark contrast, young women have been positioned in third wave feminism as particularly able to deconstruct and elude social pressures of acceptable femininity (Crane 1999; Davis 1991, 1999; Stoller 1999). Body modification from this perspective is seen as a free choice of self-expression (Duits and van Zoonen 2006). This chapter addresses this debate and calls into question the notion of free choice.

My participants' decisions around body modification were based on how they assumed the practice and the appearance it produced would be read by others. Lindemann's (1997) work on bodily distinction is a useful conceptual starting point for explaining the impact of the objectification of the body upon body modification decisions and their significance for embodied identity. She presented a three-fold differentiation of the body based on its phenomenology. The first level of the body is the objectified body, the body as a visible and concrete gestalt. The second level is the experiencing body, the body which lives in sensory and practical reference to the environment. The third level is the experienced body, one's own body distinguished to the extent that it is experienced. If these last two levels cannot be distinguished from one another they are referred to as 'living body'.

The objectified body and the living body, Lindemann argues, have been assumed to have an increasingly reflexive relationship as the cultural formation of the living body is seen to orient itself more and more towards the construction of the objectified body (1997, p. 83). The objectified body becomes a prominent sign, modelling to the living body how it should act. Dissatisfaction with body occurs when it becomes objectified; when others comment on it; and when individuals come to see their own body in comparisons to others. For an individual's embodied identity then, appearance is critical. Appearance is, however, always measured against others. The limit of Lindemann's theory here becomes apparent. In her three-fold conception there is no body of comparison against which the objectified body is held up. This dimension is absent.

I argue that there is a fourth external and objectified body, the ideal body, against which all others are compared and judged. This is both the ideal and unattainable body of popular culture and the ideal image of any specific identity. If one cannot be recognised as having an objectified body that sits with the identity one wishes to embody then from this perspective it is not possible fully to embody that identity. The four-fold distinction established here enables one to examine the impact of external influence and the objectification of the body, without this relationship being reduced in conception to mind/body dualism at the expense of embodied experience. How my participants saw and experienced the objectified female body, both their own and that of others, formed their decisions of body appearance and so their engagement with body modification. Sociality was intrinsic to the practices in which they engaged and the appearances they presented.

First engagement with body modification was reported by my participants as being interpreted as a sign of becoming a woman. This was an understanding held by both themselves and others around them. Here I want to place emphasis on the *becoming*. It was not age, or stage of physical development that was the cultural barometer or defining factor of where along the line of transition from girl to woman my participants saw themselves as situated, but their engagement with specific forms of body modification. This perception of the link between body modification and identity transition was evident on two levels: participants' recollections of how they conceived their initiation into body modification at the time and the reactions of parents and guardians to their engagement in these practices.

Participants' understanding of body modification as part of growing up was consistently apparent in their narratives, as demonstrated in the following excerpts:

Phoebe:   It is something you haven't done before, it makes you feel all grown up, so for me it was part of the growing up stage.

Natasha:  [It] seemed important that I have that [makeup] because other girls had it and it was a signifier of maturity.

Kerry:    I remember being really little and shaving my legs, like probably before I even had hair on my legs like in the bath when I was really little but that is because you see your mum doing it so you think that, that is like what being a grown up is.

Body modification is here positioned as a sign and means of growing up, of becoming a woman. Even when the participants' bodies had not developed enough for certain practices to be required, as in Kerry's case, engagement in them was still seen to offer this identity transition. For them, as is articulated by Peggy in the following quotation, body modification was experienced as 'the real transition between like a child and a woman [...] it is a changing attitude in how you are going to portray yourself to people'. Body modification was seen as significant for identity because of how it portrays the doer to others, in this case because it was assumed to be read specifically as a sign of womanhood. To be a woman in this view was to be perceived as one. It was the judgement of the viewer that had precedence in this identity categorisation. Body modification became the means to signal particular identities to others. Objectification of the self was given precedence.

The identity of womanhood in my participants' conception was not just about appearance or bodily materiality but about actions. As Shelley Budgeon (2003) has argued, identity is an embodied event. The existence of normative perceptions of womanhood, of 'regulatory ideals', meant that initial and early body modification was experienced almost identically by all my participants. To have the identity of a woman and to be perceived as feminine was not just about a bodily appearance but also about the actions undertaken and the practices engaged in.

To take on or embody an identity involves more than merely looking 'right'. Engagement in the normative practices associated with an identity is necessary for it to be embedded and for an individual to be perceived as embodying it. The problems and limitations of conceptualising the body in mind/body dualistic terms are apparent here. The body is not an object simply acted upon; it is inseparable from embodied experience. For my participants both the act of specific forms of body modification and the image these provided were intrinsic to the feminine identity into which they wished to transition. If hair removal is taken as an example here, both the image of hairlessness as an ideal body and the act of removing this hair, were held as paramount in achieving an acceptable female identity. To be a woman and not engage in hair removal was not regarded as an option by my participants at this age. The ideal of hairlessness was so intrinsic to the identity of womanhood and my participants' embodiment of it, that both the practice and the image were necessary.

Even less conventional forms of body modification were motivated by the notion that visible body modification would make the individual appear older. This was clearly the case for Samantha, who attributed her desire to be perceived as older as the motivation behind the facial piercings she had undertaken when at school:

> ... we thought if we had like piercings and stuff that we would look older and I don't know why but when you are fifteen and stuff, that seems important. You can go out and get served and stuff.

Samantha understood body modification, in this case specifically piercings, to be read as a sign of maturity. Her desire to look older was, however, not just for its own sake. Samantha wished to appear older because of what she believed it would enable her to *do*. Being perceived as older in this instance meant that she and her friends would be able to go out and drink (alcohol) while underage because their appearance would enable them to get served. Samantha desired a particular image for the opportunities of the identity it signalled.

The manner in which participants' parents and guardians reacted to and understood body modification reinforced the view of these practices as signs of womanhood and maturity. Parents' reactions to their daughters' engagement with body modification, while not consistent, were evidently based on the assumption that these practices meant a girl was developing or transitioning into being a woman. Reported parental reactions to body modification fell into two camps: parents who discouraged these practices, and parents who encouraged them.

Parents' conception of body modification as a sign of development meant its prohibition was understood as a means to stop or slow down the transition of their daughters from girls to women. Natasha's explanation of why her parents prevented her from wearing makeup clearly exemplifies this:

> I was quite young when I decided that I wanted to wear makeup [...] I was still at primary school and I wasn't allowed to wear it and I was told by my parents that I was too young to wear it, only older girls wear it [...] I remember my dad saying, 'you don't need to be doing that, that's, you know', I think my dad had a lot of anxieties about me engaging in beautifying practices at too young an age [...] he was anxious that I would grow up too fast.

Perceptions of the age appropriateness of body modification practices were echoed in Kerry's recollection of her grandparents' reaction to the first time she shaved: 'I remember my grandparents being like, "no you are too young to shave", and made me grow it all back'. This grand/parental anxiety around daughters' engagement in body modification practices centred on the fear that they would grow up 'too quickly'. Though not defined in the previous examples, I take the phrase 'growing up too quickly' to denote sexual activity. My assumption of the meaning of this phrase is based both on its use in popular culture and the context in which the term was used by my participants. Sexual activity is deemed not suitable for those at a school age in both popular culture and in law.[3] In popular thought, it is correlated with a loss of innocence and 'childhood' and often reported as something from which girls in particular need protection. Preventing girls from engagement in these practices was conceptualised as a means of delaying their growing up, because engagement in them was seen as part of 'becoming' a woman.

In contrast to the former group of parents, some parents actively encouraged their daughters to engage in body modification. However, this reaction still demonstrated an understanding of body modification as a sign of womanhood. This group understood their daughters to be growing up and deemed these practices necessary. Andrea's description of her mother's reaction to her developing body illustrates this:

> When I was little I remember telling my mum I had started getting under-arm hair and she just gave me a razor immediately and sort of just that was what was expected I think.

Andrea's mother's reaction to her revelation of the physical development she was experiencing projected the message that bodily development requires the use of body modification. Her becoming 'a woman' necessitated that she engage in these specific and gendered practices. This was also evident in Sara's narrative. When explaining how she first came to engage in body modification she said:

> It is something my mum got me into, my mum told me to do and introduced me to different methods and stuff like that.

Sara's mother's input and instruction are very evident. In her narrative it is her mother whom Sarah attributed as instigating her engagement with these practices.

Those parents who encouraged body modification did so because they saw these practices as essential attributes of the identity into which their daughters were transitioning. Their views were informed by certain social norms of adult femininity. Parental encouragement was to ensure their daughters adapted to and fitted into the prescribed norms of this identity. Budgeon (2003), considering body modification practices, argues that 'transformation in the meaning of embodiment can be effected through an engagement in processes and practices in ways that destabilize the subject/object binary' (p. 43). It is not just in the appearance provided by these practices, but in the doing of them, that girls were perceived to and experienced the beginning of their identity transition. Prevention or enforcement of body modification was understood as an effective way of determining identities because, as Budgeon argues, as embodied acts they were seen not just to alter appearance but also to result in participants' identity transitions from girl to women. My participants' social interactions at this life stage confirmed to them that to be a woman meant engaging in body modification.

Body modification practices, as a generic category, were attached to this identity of womanhood in my participants' narratives. Individually however, these practices signalled different identities or different aspects of a woman's identity. All aspects of a girl's self-presentation were taken to indicate facets of her identity. For example, while body hair removal was viewed as necessary for acceptable femininity, pubic hair removal was usually specifically situated as a separate practice from the hair removal of other body parts. It very rarely featured as part of their daily or regular body hair removal regime, instead being engaged in as a separate practice. Much of the discourse encountered among peers and in popular culture on the topic presented this practice as part of active heteronormative female sexuality. For example, Natasha said that she 'associate[d] it with a healthy sexual relationship' while Stephanie directly attributed the practice to the acquisition of a partner: 'Most women in a relationship would probably think of shaving their pubic hair'. As these quotations demonstrate, most of my participants began to remove their pubic hair when they became, or intended to become, sexually active. This was usually based on the belief that hairlessness or neat pubic hair was the appearance men would prefer and expect. Some partners of participants had directly instructed them to remove their pubic hair at this time, reinforcing the women's assumptions of male expectations. Carla, for example, described her first boyfriend's opinion and instructions on pubic hair removal as the reason she first practised it:

> [I] didn't really think anything of it until I had my first boyfriend and it was him rather unhealthily, he was a lot older than me, and it was him who rather unhealthily I think suggested that I shave my pubic area. That was the first time that I had even considered doing that, and I did, I shaved all my pubic hair.

Carla's motivation for this practice was to be visually pleasing to her partner, who clearly felt he had the right to dictate his own preferences to her. The importance of pleasing the male gaze was frequent and substantial in explanations given for taking up this practice.

It was not just sexual activity, but also sexuality, which was believed to be identifiable through appearance. Susanna, for example, noted that if a girl did not present herself in a conventional manner then her identity as acceptably feminine and heteronormative would be questioned:

> When you are even younger sort of high school people say 'oh she is a lesbian'. It makes absolutely no sense whatsoever, but if you are not interested in putting makeup on or looking a certain way then people will say ridiculous things because that is not normal. You should be conscious of the way you look if you are a young girl and then if you are not then that is a bit weird.

An individual's sexuality is assumed to be reflected entirely in their appearance. Sexual identities do not exist equally in contemporary Britain in terms of acceptance and positive reception (Jackson and Scott 2010; Rubin 1992 [1982]). This is significant in the school context, as given the prevalence of homophobia, having one's sexuality questioned and labelled as 'different' is likely to be unwanted because of the associated stigma. Fear of being perceived as a lesbian could be seen as pressure to engage in normative body modification practices (Brackenridge et al. 2007; DePalma and Jennett 2010; Morris-Roberts 2004).

Appearance was also deemed a significant indicator of gendered identity. Many practices of body modification featured in my participants' narratives as integral to a feminine identity. Stephanie, for example, described how she had perceived facial hair as at odds with this identity:

> One of my teachers had facial hair and I couldn't understand it [...] you assume a person with a moustache is a man, so I remember saying to my mum, 'mum my teacher has a moustache but she says she is a woman' [...] my mum was like 'no, she is a woman, Stephanie', and I am like 'she has got a moustache she must be a man'.

In this case, hairlessness is perceived as intrinsic to believable womanhood. As Toerien and Wilkinson (2003) argue: 'the hairlessness norm is [a] taken-for-granted social practice. Strongly normative, and unquestioned across a range of contexts, women's hair removal symbolically demarcates the feminine from the masculine' (p. 342). Hair removal is therefore necessary in order to ensure that gender is not confused or seen as damaged.

Even body modifications which may appear less pervasive and normalised were seen frequently as intrinsic to a convincing feminine identity:

Jessica:      My sister that made me get my ears pierced she was like 'you will look like a boy if you don't get your ears pierced'.

Stephanie:   My mum was like 'you have to go and get your ears pierced you're a girl, come you have to go and get it done'. And I remember thinking it was really weird, I was like why isn't my brother getting it done, and she was like 'he isn't getting it done, it is not the thing'.

Both Jessica and Stephanie explain how they were taken to have their ears pierced because of concerns of meeting expected gendered norms of appearance. Engagement in body modification in these instances was not the choice of participants but enforced by family members who taught them through these gendered norms.

Appearance was also explained as significant for group affiliation. While an ideal femininity was always referred back to, participants' more nuanced decisions of self-presentation were made to ensure they fitted in with the appearance of the group with which they wished to be identified. Nicola exemplified this when she stated that she began to wear makeup because she 'started a new friendship group' and that was the norm of the girls within it. She needed to wear it to be accepted as part of the group. Similarly, when explaining why she had had multiple piercings while at school Samantha noted that it was 'to be part of a specific group'. Body modification was an act which signalled group affiliation. A shared group identity was believed to necessitate matching appearances and body modification practices.

Body modification practices and tools were also experienced by my participants as significant for social status and popularity at school. Betty, for example, when explaining why she had decided to get her belly button pierced, said it was because she 'thought it was really cool, all my friends did it, it was when like Britney Spears and Beyoncé had it […] I did think it was going to make me sexy'. Betty had wanted this piercing because of the identity she saw as attached to it and the positive perception of this practice among her peers.

Hair straightening was a form of body modification where bodily appearance was not the limit of its significance for identity.[4] The owning of straighteners themselves was desirable and gave one kudos, and specific brands were more desirable than others. When speaking to me about this product many participants used a particular brand name instead of a generic description. This brand was fashionable and expensive, contributing to the social positioning of my participants. Costing around one hundred pounds, these straighteners were out of the financial reach of most at this age without significant aid from their parents. This hefty price tag was part of the product's appeal. Products are important for this age group because 'commercial values now occupy a critical place in the formation of the categories of youthful femininity' (McRobbie 2008, p. 532). Consumption and ownership of this product was reported as being as desirable as the appearance it provided, which the following excerpt from Amanda exemplifies:

> Do you remember when GHDs became a big thing? I was really young when that happened but I was using all sorts of really bad straighteners [...] then my mum was like, 'oh' like, my brother was getting something or something and my mum was like, 'do you want GHDs or do you want money?' I was like, 'yeah, I will get the GHDs' [...] But it was kind of then that people were like, 'ooh GHDs!'

Amanda was specific in her consumption choices. Her previous ownership of another brand of straighteners did not provide the positive associations which accompanied the GHD brand. Product awareness and identity attachment to consumption has repeatedly been found in girls at this life cycle stage, leading McRobbie (2008) to suggest that when

> magazines like *Bliss* and *Sugar* imagine a very young female consumer into being [... they] activate the subject by mobilizing her as a consumer; she is called upon to play a key role in deciding what she likes and what suits her such that she participates 'in the world of goods' and comes to recognize herself and be recognized by others by means of this 'political economy of subjectification'. (p. 545)

The perceived and embodied identity of an individual is altered by the consumption of certain products because the products themselves are associated with certain identities. What is also illustrated here is the impact of economic status on body modification practices. Even at this young age when one's personal disposable income was likely to be small, displaying wealth still created a positive social image and provided status. A lack of spending power was limiting to an individual's capacity to engage in body modification and therefore how socially acceptable individuals could make their appearance. Through her assertion that '"(good) looks" are a form of "cultural capital" for young people, especially girls' Frost argues that 'the all-important group memberships of young people may increasingly be understood as predicated on the cultural capital and potential weapons of exclusion that "doing looks" can encompass' (2005, p. 76).

My participants engaged specifically in those practices they saw as necessary to fit in with their peers and that would enable them to portray a chosen identity. Participants' practices at this time, then, were not diverse or random. On the whole they conformed to the normalised peer image they encountered, and generally assimilated in their practices towards their closest group of friends. Among them a shared appearance and body modification regime was understood to signify a shared identity and belonging to that group. The importance of social and group acceptance during this life stage has been explored extensively in childhood development studies (Evans et al. 1992; Pellegrini 1999; Sheriff 2007; Veenstra et al. 2010). Evans et al. (1992) and Nakajima (2007), for example, demonstrated in their research how peer behaviour informed individual behaviour and practices. Similarly, peer preference was also found to inform consumption practices (Cotterel 2007; Narayan et al. 2011). Sherriff (2007), when looking at masculine identity, asserted the importance of peer constructions and perceptions of an identity for individual behaviour and identity construction. Peer perceptions of appearances and identities informed my participants' own understandings of them.

External perceptions of an individual's appearance was the most influential factor in participants' body modification decisions. The objectified body was crucial in the formation and experience of identity. The significance of participants' understanding that appearance is taken to signal identity was intrinsic to their decisions to begin these practices. Participants pointed to their social situation, the school context, as the main catalyst for beginning body modification because the appearance deemed acceptable there required female body modification. When recalling why she initially began to wear makeup, Charlotte, for example, stated that: 'It wasn't because I wanted to start wearing it, it was because I saw other people doing it and it's like, oh why is she doing that, I want to do that'. Charlotte acknowledges that her personal preferences were not key. Her decision was defined by what she saw as normative in her social environment, informed by the actions and appearance of her peers. She argues that without this influence she would not have begun to wear makeup at this point. Peer pressure was also visible in Anouk's explanation of why she began to shave:

> I started shaving my legs first when I was in year seven because when I was in the changing room with the other girls, they were allowed to shave and whether they could tell that I couldn't shave or just knew I wasn't allowed to, they said that I had very hairy legs, so that is when I started doing that.

As in this example, time and time again, the P.E. changing room setting was pinpointed as significant. Seeing peers' bodies provided the opportunity for bodily comparison. An individual's objectified body is compared to the ideal, and not meeting this ideal was problematic. The importance placed on peer norms by Charlotte and Anouk was not unique.

Participants' decisions about self-presentation were based on how they believed ultimately these appearances would be read and received by those with whom they interacted. In social interaction 'appearance may be taken to refer to those stimuli which function at the time to tell us of the performer's social statuses' (Goffman 1990 [1959], p. 34). Social status here refers to class, race, gender, occupation and personality. Different appearances are attached to different identities and classifications. As Goffman argued 'a given social front tends to become institutionalised in terms of the abstract stereotyped expectations to which it gives rise' (Goffman 1990 [1959], p. 37). The objectified body is equated with one's identity. The importance of appearance for character assumptions lies in the fact that 'the impressions that others give tend to be treated as claims and promises they have implicitly made, and claims and promises tend to have a moral character' (Goffman 1990 [1959], p. 242). We present ourselves so as to signal to others our identity and role. This impacts upon the embodied experience because,

> to be a given kind of person, then, is not merely to possess the required attributes, but also to sustain the standards of conduct and appearance that one's social grouping attaches thereto [...] A status, a position, a social place, is not a material thing to be possessed and then displayed; it is a pattern of appropriate conduct, coherent, established and well articulated. (Goffman 1990 [1959], p. 81)

Individuals at school know the associated norms of roles, and when they take on a role they tend to adhere to these associated norms both to feel they fully embody that identity and as a signal to others that they identify with it. Participants' internalisation of this meant that their body modification decisions were not free choices but ones made in the constraints of social expectations: they were determined by sociality.

Individuals try to approximate the image they want to establish for themselves but there are limits to how much this can be controlled. Identity is subject to external judgement and affirmation. As Ann Branaman notes in her discussion of Goffman:

> The sense of self arises as a result of publicly validated performances [...] even though individuals play an active role in fashioning these self-indicating performances, they are generally constrained to present images of themselves that can be socially supported in the context of a given status hierarchy. Thus, the self is a social production in the sense that it depends upon validation awarded and withheld in accordance with the norms of a stratified society. (Branaman 1997, p. xlvi)

Identity is validated by external acknowledgment. An individual has limited control in determining this. The objectified body thus influences how the lived body is experienced. Because identity assignment is reliant upon the perception of others, it is unsurprising that my interviewees' concern for acceptance was focused on others' perceptions of them.

Those who did not conform to normative body modification or who failed to meet the required appearance of their desired identity experienced bullying and ostracism. Previous research into girls' body modifications uncovered similar findings (Walter 2010). Being perceived to have an unacceptable appearance was problematic and resulted in stigma. Goffman (1963) defines the process of stigmatisation as 'a special discrepancy between virtual and actual identity' (p. 3). Being perceived with the wrong appearance can result in what he terms 'identity damage'. This reinforces Lindemann's and my own argument of the impact of the objectified body upon the living body. The objectification and categorisation of the body act to pressurise people in relation to body modification, so that the gap between the ideal and objectified body can be reduced as a means of achieving social approbation. The inseparability of appearance, and perceived and embodied identity that participants learnt at this life stage, can also be seen through the changes that occurred in their body modification practices.

The topic of change in the narratives I collected was inseparable from distinctions made between the past and the present self. My participants had a strong historicised sense of self, of a stage history. They understood their practices as defined and developed by their context, a context which changed as they progressed through their life cycle. 'Self' was, for my participants, a project undergoing continuous revisions. Change in body modification and appearance featured in participants' narratives as a means to illustrate identity changes. The school years were the lifecycle stage most clearly contoured in my participants' histories. Their school self was the identity they most wished to distance themselves from and they did so by highlighting the difference in their self-presentation at this time and at the time of the interview.

Participants' distancing of themselves from their school identity began as soon as they left the school context. As my participants moved into the sixth form or college environment, their initial disposition while at school to be 'the same' was replaced by a preference for socially acceptable uniqueness, being the same but different. My participants still very much wanted to fit in, to be perceived as socially acceptable and part of the 'gang', but in addition they also wanted to be seen as 'unique'. This trope was reiterated by almost all. This image of individuality was strongly linked to an idea of maturity, of no longer needing to follow the crowd, even though in wanting to be perceived as different they were indeed following a trend. In this social context 'difference' (though in an acceptable form) was valued more highly than sameness and so this is what was aimed at by most. My participants' relation to body modification and their practices altered, as Ellie illustrates: 'I guess it changed from like not wanting to be left out to then like having a bit of fun and now I have gone a bit more toned down cos I'm a bit more boring'. Body modification was not a static regime or experience. To embody a more mature identity and detach themselves from their school identity participants aimed to be viewed as 'individual'.

Paramount to the idea of a historicised self and a developing regime of body modification was participants' gradual acquisition of knowledge and skills of these practices. Participants emphasised that body modification skills were not innate but gradually learnt. This contrasts somewhat with popular understandings of body modification as a 'natural' part of female identity, not a learnt practice. My interviewees positioned their younger selves as unskilled and still in the process of learning, illuminated by stories of past mistakes. A practice which illustrated this well was the use of makeup. While a constant in participants' body modification regimes following their first engagement with it, it was a practice that saw much change as my participants' lives developed. This change included style, products, frequency and aim. My participants made evident the contrast between their initial engagement with makeup and their present, acknowledging the changes in their situation that had occurred as their practices developed. A clear distancing of their contemporary persona from their younger selves was apparent as change was highlighted. This is illustrated in Ellie's description of her younger self:

> I remember experimenting with it and looking quite hideous. Sometimes I used to go like blue eye shadow and, you know, really pink lip gloss and also cos my mum didn't wear much makeup I never knew how to do it properly.

Ellie's use of the past tense ensures that the mistakes she discusses are distanced from her contemporary practices. Taste is what she primarily situates as at fault in this narrative. Cait echoed this when she said: 'What you used to think looked good is actually horrific'. A narrative of progress frequently featured which demonstrated the participants' developing skill and seemingly improving tastes. 'Good' taste, and competence in carrying out body modification practices, were assets, and developing them became a signifier of maturity in becoming a woman. The development of a body modification regime was experienced by my participants as being a symptom of their changing identities.

## CONCLUSION

In this chapter I have focused on women's first and early engagement with body modification. This analysis has revealed three main points: the importance of context and sociality in determining individuals' engagement with body modification; the role of the objectified body for the impact of the social; and the meanings of body modification in this context.

The dominant motivation of my participants to begin body modification was peer behaviour and gendered norms. The actions of peers were assimilated in order to ensure participants fitted in within the school context and avoided negative social ramifications and ostracism.

Presiding over this desire to fit in and avoidance of a negative social reception was the meaning attributed to body modification and its importance for gender normativity. In the school context, participants learnt that appearance and the practices employed to achieve it are equated to identity, and, crucially, that identity is validated by external acknowledgment.

Participants' narratives illustrated that their interpretation of body modification practices at this stage in their life was a sign of womanhood and the means of transition from girl to woman. The forms of body modification begun at this stage were, unsurprisingly given this, highly gendered and normative. Participants' narratives showed that in this period they believed that in order to be a woman they needed to engage in these very specific forms of body modification. Body modification was inseparable from the identity of acceptable adult femininity.

The importance and workings of external perceptions, the objectified body, on body modification decisions and identity formation were demonstrated through the expansion of Lindemann's (1997) three-fold bodily distinction with the addition of a fourth level, the ideal body. Comparison was the critical aspect of the experience of the objectified body which triggered feelings of lack in one's own body and initiation into body modification. The embodied experience of objectification was explored through Budgeon's (2003) conceptualisation of identity as an embodied event. Body modification was not just something done to the body but something which a living body engaged in as an embodied practice. Identity was intrinsically linked to appearance and to the practices and consumption employed to achieve it. At a young age where identity and acceptance was sought, body modification practices were a way of composing an identity and embodying it.

Once begun, body modification became a constant feature of my participants' daily lives and self-presentation. Girls' first encounters with, and participation in, body modification practices signalled their entering into a relationship and dialogue with the identity of womanhood and certain forms of femininity. Unanimously my participants explained their body modification decisions at this life stage as determined by how they believed others would perceive their identity; these practices were not, then, about free choice or personal preference but about social acceptance. Sociality was key, and, in learning body modification, girls were learning womanhood.

## NOTES

1. For men, appearance holds less prominence in terms of cultural perceptions of value. Instead, a wide range of attributes and abilities contribute to judgements of men's worth (Burton et al. 1995; Davis 2002; Norman 2011). While it has been acknowledged that men now face more pressure in relation to their appearance, particularly in masculinity studies, this pressure has been understood as both less than, and different from, that faced by women. Appearance and body modification are less associated with the masculine but are viewed as intrinsic to the feminine (Davis 2002; Wright et al. 2006).
2. Twenty seven of my participants identified as white British, one as white British and French, one as British Pakistani and one as of white British Italian and black British Caribbean descent.
3. The age of consent in Britain is sixteen.
4. All of my participants spoke of this practice in very similar ways. Differences in hair type and ethnicity were not reported as resulting in a difference in girls' experience of this practice and understanding of it.

## REFERENCES

Bordo, Susan, 1993 [2004]. *Unbearable Weight*. London: University of California Press.

Brackenridge, Celia, Ian Rivers, Brendon Gough and Karen Llewellyn, 2007. 'Driving Down Participation: Homophobic Bullying as a Deterrent to Doing Sport', in Aitchison, Cara, ed., *Sport and Gender Identities: Masculinities, Femininities and Sexualities*. Oxon: Routledge. pp. 122–39.

Branaman, Ann, 1997. *The Goffman Reader*. Oxford: Blackwell.

Budgeon, Sally, 2003. 'Identity as an Embodied Event'. *Body & Society*, 9 (1), 35–55.

Burton, Scot, Richard Netemeyer and Donald Lichtenstein, 1995. 'Gender Differences for Appearance-Related Attitudes and Behaviours: Implications for Consumer Welfare'. *Journal of Public Policy & Marketing*, 14 (1), 60–75.

Cotterell, John, 2007. *Social Networks in Youth and Adolescence*. Hove: Routledge.

Crane, Diana, 1999. 'Gender and Hegemony in Fashion Magazines: Women's Interpretations of Fashion Photographs'. *The Sociological Quarterly*, 40 (4), 541–63.

Davis, Kathy, 1991. 'Remaking the She Devil: A Critical Look at Feminist Approaches to Beauty'. *Hypatia*, 6 (2), 22–43.

Davis, Kathy, 1999. 'Cosmetic Surgery in a Different Voice: The Case of Madame Noel'. *Women's Studies International Forum*, 22 (5), 473–88.

6 LEARNING WOMANHOOD: BODY MODIFICATION ...   113

Davis, Kathy, 2002. 'A Dubious Equality: Men, Women and Cosmetic Surgery'. *Body & Society*, 8 (1), 49–65.

Denham, Jess, 2014. 'Sarah Millican Hits Back at Twitter Trolls Who Called Her "Fat and Ugly"'. *The Independent* (online). Available at: http://www.independent.co.uk/news/people/sarah-millican-hits-back-at-twitter-trolls-who-called-her-fat-and-ugly-with-brilliant-rant-9384011.html [Accessed 01.01.17].

DePalma, Renée and Mark Jennett, 2010. 'Homophobia, Transphobia and Culture: Deconstructing Heteronormativity in English Primary Schools'. *Intercultural Education*, 21 (1), 15–26.

Duits, Linda and Liesbet van Zoonen, 2006. 'Headscarves and Porno-Chic: Disciplining Girls' Bodies in the European Multicultural Society'. *European Journal of Women's Studies*, 13 (2), 103–17.

Evans, William, Wallace Oates and Robert Schwab, 1992. 'Measuring Peer Group Effects: A Study of Teenage Behaviour'. *Journal of Political Economy*, 100 (5), 966–91.

Frost, Liz, 2005. 'Theorizing the Young Women in the Body'. *Body and Society*, 11 (1), 63–85.

Goffman, Erving, 1963. *Stigma: Notes on the Management of Spoiled Identity*. Englewood Cliffs, NJ: Prentice-Hall.

Goffman, Erving, 1959 [1990]. *The Presentation of Self in Everyday Life*. London: Penguin.

*How to Look Good Naked*. (2008). Channel 4, 27 June 2006–8 April 2008. Available at: http://www.channel4.com/programmes/how-to-look-good-naked [Accessed 01.01.17].

Jackson, Stevi and Sue Scott. 2010. *Theorizing Sexuality*. Maidenhead: Open University Press.

Jeffreys, Sheila, 2005. *Beauty and Misogyny*. Abingdon: Routledge.

Lawler, Steph, 2008. *Identity: Sociological Perspectives*. Cambridge: Polity Press.

Lindemann, Gesa, 1997. 'The Body of Gender Difference', in Davis, Kathy, ed. *Embodied Practices: Feminist Perspectives on the Body*. London: Sage Publications, pp. 73–92.

McRobbie, Angela, 2008. 'Young Women and Consumer Culture'. *Cultural Studies*, 22 (5), 531–50.

Mintel. (2013). British Make-up Market Hits the 1 Billion Mark. Available at: http://www.marketresearchworld.net/index.php?option=com_content&task=view&id=972 [Accessed 01.01.17].

Morris-Roberts, Kathryn, 2004. 'Colluding in "Compulsory Heterosexuality"? Doing Research with Young Women at School', in Harris, Anita, ed. *All About the Girl: Culture, Power and Identity*. Oxon: Routledge, pp, 219–31.

Nakajima, Ryo, 2007. 'Measuring Peer Effects on Youth Smoking Behaviour'. *The Review of Economic Studies*, 74 (3), 897–935.

Narayan, Vishal, Vithala R. Roa and Carolyne Saunders. 2011. 'How Peer Influence Affects Attribute Preferences: A Bayesian Updating Mechanism'. *Marketing Science*, 30 (2), 368–384.

Norman, Moss, 2011. 'Embodying the Double-Bind of Masculinity: Young Men and Discourses of Normalcy, Health, Heterosexuality, and Individualism'. *Men and Masculinities*, 14 (4), 430–49.

O'Carroll, Lisa, 2014. 'John Inverdale's Marion Bartoli Comments "Wrong" Says BBC New Chief'. *The Guardian* (online). Available at: https://www.theguardian.com/media/2013/jul/09/john-inverdale-marion-bartoli-bbc [Accessed 01.01.17].

Pellegrini, Anthony, 1999. 'School Bullies, Victims and Aggressive Victims: Factors Relating to Group Affiliation and Victimization in Early Adolescence'. *Journal of Education Psychology*, 91 (2), 216–24.

Rose, Hilary, 2014. 'Golden Globes: Best and Worst Dressed'. *The Times* (online). Available at: http://www.thetimes.co.uk/tto/life/fashion/article3974342.ece [Accessed 01.01.17].

Rubin, Gayle, 1984 [1992]. 'Thinking Sex: Notes for a Radical Theory of the Politics of Sexuality', in Vance, Carol, ed. *Pleasure and Danger: Exploring Female Sexuality*. London: Pandora Press, pp. 267–78.

*Secret Eaters*. (2014). Channel 4, 16 May 2012–23 April 2014. Available at: http://www.channel4.com/programmes/secret-eaters [Accessed 01.01.17].

Sherriff, Nigel, 2007. 'An Integrated Approach to Understanding Masculinities'. *British Educational Research Journal*, 33 (3), 349–70.

Stoller, Debbie, 1999. 'Sex and the Thinking Girl', in Karp, Marcella and Debbie Stoller, eds. *The Bust Guide to the New Girl Order*. London: Penguin, pp. 75–84.

*Supersize v Superskinny*. (2014). Channel 4, 22 January 2008–9 January 2014. Available at: http://www.channel4.com/programmes/supersize-vs-superskinny [Accessed 01.01.17].

The Leisure Database Company, 2012. 'The 2013 State of the UK Fitness Industry Report'. Available at: http://www.exerciseregister.org/1400-uk-fitness-industry-worth-3-86bn [Accessed 01.01.17].

Toerien, Merran and Sue Wilkinson, 2003. 'Gender and Body Hair: Constructing the Feminine Woman'. *Women's Studies International Forum*, 26 (4), 333–44.

Veenstra, René, Siegwart Lindenberg, Anke Munniksma, et al., 2010. 'The Complex Relation Between Bullying, Victimization, Acceptance, and Rejection: Giving Special Attention to Status, Affection, and Sex Differences'. *Child Development*. 81 (2), 480–86.

Walter, Natasha, 2010. *Living Dolls: The Return of Sexism*. London: Virago Press.

Wolf, Naomi, 1991. *The Beauty Myth*. London: Vintage.

Wright, Jan, Gabrielle O'Flynn, and Doune Macdonald, 2006. 'Being Fit and Looking Healthy: Young Women's and Men's Constructions of Health and Fitness'. *Sex Roles*, 54 (9), 707–16.

# CHAPTER 7

# The Construction of a Personal Norm of Physical and Psychological 'Well-Being' in Female Discourse

*Maria Krebber*

## INTRODUCTION

The body is a crucial element in individual identity construction. We are who we are to a great extent because of how we look and there is little doubt that this is still more true for women than for men: women are still frequently evaluated based on their looks, their body shape, the way they dress, their hair, their makeup and so on. Because of this centrality of the body, especially in female identity construction, when I was putting together the interview script for the data collection for this chapter, among questions regarding the present situation of women in Portuguese society, gender equality, maternity and family relations, I decided to include one question about my interviewees' relationship with their (female) bodies. I intended to explore how this relationship was constructed and what influence the female body had on these women's lives. It turned out to be the most difficult question to ask, as it can be a particularly personal and intimate one. Depending on the focus

M. Krebber (✉)
Independent Scholar, Lisbon, Portugal
e-mail: mariakrebber@gmail.com

E. Rees (ed.), *Talking Bodies*, DOI 10.1007/978-3-319-63778-5_7

115

the interviewee decides to give, it can touch on topics such as body (dis) satisfaction, menstruation, menopause, ageing or the physical aspects of maternity. Usually, people do not easily talk about these topics in an interview situation and particularly with a person they've never met before.

Maybe to soften the intimacy of the question, most women directed their answer to the topic of body (dis)satisfaction, this being one to which, it would seem, every woman can relate without revealing too much of herself. Apart from the choice of the topic, I was particularly surprised by the large number of women replying that the important thing about a woman's relationship with her body was for her to feel 'well' with it. On the face of it, such an answer seems to reject the normative character of thinness and beauty ideals operating in Western societies. In this chapter I will argue that this is not necessarily the case and that on the contrary, in many of the answers, physical and psychological well-being is closely linked to these ideals and even helps to reinforce them. Furthermore, the interviewees have very clear perceptions of what is 'correct' behaviour to achieve that well-being and about potentially transgressive behaviour. The analysis draws on a corpus of 16 interviews, which were analysed based on the theoretical-methodological assumptions of critical discourse analysis.

In the first section of the chapter I seek to situate the analysis within the field of body image studies and to introduce some crucial theoretical concepts such as body image norms, body (dis)satisfaction, monitoring processes and disciplinary practices. The second section is dedicated to the linguistic aspects of norm construction, and in it I reflect on some relevant aspects of the theoretical framework of critical discourse analysis. After some remarks on the data in the third section, in the next section I analyse and critically discuss constructions of physical and psychological well-being and their interplay with the concepts introduced in the first section.

## BODY IMAGE NORMS, MONITORING PROCESSES, BODY DISSATISFACTION, THE IMPORTANCE OF PHYSICAL APPEARANCE, AND DISCIPLINARY PRACTICES

This section looks at body image norms from a socio-cultural perspective. In other words, I assume that body image norms circulate in Western societies in the form of beauty ideals. In these societies, the beauty ideal can be described as 'young, tall, long-legged, large-eyed, moderately large-breasted, tanned but not too tanned, and clear-skinned' (Tiggemann 2011, p. 13). To this list we have to add that the ideal woman is usually white and—most importantly—thin. This body ideal is constantly transmitted by the media, in particular by fashion magazines, advertising and popular television programmes, but also by other socio-cultural agents such as parents and peers, and it is subsequently internalised by the individual. One's own body is constantly compared to the internalised ideal and inevitably found deficient in some or several aspects (cf. Tiggemann 2011). Feminist theory highlights that women especially are judged and evaluated in terms of how their bodies do or do not fit the norm. From an early age, the very process of judgement and evaluation is internalised by girls, together with the norm itself, and in order to avoid negative judgement from the outside girls start to monitor their appearance and continue to do so when they are adult (McKinley 2011). This bodily self-scrutiny expresses a feminine dependence on the judgement of others that has often been criticised by feminists (McKinley 2011). And that potentially spreads to other aspects of women's lives. Complying with the norm is usually socially rewarded (girls and women frequently receive comments on how they look and are complimented on their appearance), while not accepting the normativity of the established body image holds a series of threats for the feminine identity, as Bartky (1997) points out: by abandoning the beauty project women risk losing their sense of a secure female identity and becoming desexualised. Since women are still mostly defined by their body and appearance, *in extremis* a woman who does not engage in the project of femininity may simply cease to exist to the outside world (Bartky 1997).

Depending on the individual's perception of whether his/her body meets the norm or not, (s)he will experience body satisfaction or dissatisfaction, with dissatisfaction being the more likely reaction, since for the majority of women the ideal body is totally impossible to achieve. The impossibility of most women conforming to the thinness ideal in particular makes body dissatisfaction a normal or normative attitude (ex. Rodin et al. 2016). Women are *expected* to be dissatisfied with their bodies; a woman stating that she considers her body perfect and without physical fault is a rare exception and she would most likely risk being regarded as arrogant and overconfident by the people that surround her.

Different studies have shown that this dissatisfaction remains relatively stable throughout one's life span. Stevens and Tiggemann (1998) found that dissatisfaction with one's own body is hardly ever influenced by age, or by other variables such as marital/relational status, educational level or occupational status. This is surprising, if we consider that the physical changing processes associated with ageing take the body further away from the ideal every year. We might expect women to become increasingly dissatisfied. But the main focus (weight loss), and areas of the body that cause concern, remain the same as women age. Grogan (2011) refers to several studies that indicate that older women often have a more positive body image than younger women. She also indicates two possible reasons for this:

1. Older women have internalised different and more realistic body shape ideals than younger women, so that the discrepancy between the real and the ideal body is not actually increasing as the woman gets older;
2. as they achieve self-esteem by other means, for example through their role in relation to the family, their professional career and the community, older women do not attribute so much importance to appearance as their younger counterparts do. (Grogan 2011; Tiggemann 2004)

These factors potentially reduce the individual's vulnerability to sociocultural pressures. As not all women suffer from body dissatisfaction, they can probably be found to be mediating younger women's relationship with their bodies as well, thus shielding them from the influence of unrealistic ideals.

As most people's bodies do not correspond to their internalised norm, they are expected (and expect themselves) to do something to transform the supposedly deficient body. In order to do so, they engage in what Bartky called disciplinary practices (DPs). The author accounts for three different categories of DPs:

1. DPs that aim to produce a body of a certain size and general configuration;
2. DPs 'that bring forth from this body a specific repertoire of gestures, postures and movements';
3. DPs 'directed towards the display of this body as an ornamented surface'. (Bartky 1997, p. 132)

The second and third types of DPs show that having the perfect youthful and thin body at which the first type aims, is not enough. The body has to be displayed in socially prescribed ways and it has to be 'decorated' correctly, which includes clothing, hair care, makeup and so on. These and other 'feminizing practices' (Lazar 2009, p. 379) 'produce a body which in gesture and appearance is recognizably feminine' (Bartky 1997, p. 132), that is, they produce a feminine body out of a female one.

Disciplinary feminising practices give women the idea of a fixed and secure female identity (Bartky 1997) as they are working towards a specific feminine ideal, a kind of prototype of femininity so to speak, as opposed to what is considered masculine appearance and bodily behaviour. The result is a binary system where masculine and feminine body characteristics complement one another (strong vs. fragile etc.). The complementariness is only ensured in a heterosexual relationship, while all other imaginable combinations are condemned to deficiency. In addition to dictating to women what they should look like, body image norms also reinforce the normativity of the heterosexual order.

Feminist theory has criticised the fact that women's body dissatisfaction is often considered an individual issue, a psychological problem of individual women (McKinley 2011). The individual internalisation of social body image norms obscures their social as well as their normative character making them look like individual desires and goals and making any intervention on a higher level difficult to justify. The first step towards social change is to raise awareness in women that they are *not* free to desire their body any way they like. In fact, their supposed personal ideals are not an expression of individuality but the result of social context and social pressures. Due to the kind of body image figuring as the norm in Western societies, these ideals leave women in an unfavourable position. In my analysis I will show that even when women try to distance themselves from body image norms such as thinness and beauty, stressing that they value physical and psychological well-being instead, evidence emerges of monitoring processes, body dissatisfaction, the importance of physical appearance and disciplinary practices. My analysis focuses on the interaction and correlation of these processes.

## THE DISCURSIVE CONSTRUCTION OF NORMS

This section focuses on the linguistic representation of body image norms and the speakers' discursive positioning in view of these norms. Languages have a huge repertoire of grammatical and semantic tools that allow their speakers to construct all kinds of norms. The following paragraphs present some examples; the list does not claim to be exhaustive.

One possible way to construct a norm is by the use of attitudinal lexis. Martin and White (2005) developed a complex system to ascertain analytically the evaluative meaning of texts: the appraisal system. For the purpose of the present analysis, the most fruitful category of appraisal is the category of *judgement*: 'judgement categories represent a resource for evaluating someone's behavior (verbal, mental or physical) as either conforming to or transgressing the speaker's social norms' (Eggins and Slade 1997, p. 30). In order to judge someone's behaviour, we can use *judgement* devices of positive social esteem and simply tag that behaviour as 'normal', which marks all deviant behaviour negatively. The use of lexical items that indicate absoluteness has the same effect. To say that 'everybody' does something evaluates all different behaviour negatively; to say that 'nobody' does something marks the one that does as non-conformist and, therefore, potentially negatively.

Apart from *judgement, affect* resources can also serve to construct normative behaviour. There are emotions that in a specific culture and time are understood as good (positive) and others that are understood as bad (negative). Individuals are expected to pursue what triggers positive feelings, for example to feel good about themselves or to like/love themselves instead of feeling bad about, and/or being dissatisfied with, their body. A norm is indirectly constructed in what comes along with positive feelings.

Another even more indirect way of norm construction is simply to describe one's own behaviour. An interview situation can be understood as a social encounter in which one of the communicative goals of the interviewee is to construct a positive impression. If not explicitly indicated otherwise, the interviewee's behaviour will be constructed as correct and normal.

Last but not least, modality devices can construct acts or facts as norms, for example by indicating that an act is mandatory or obligatory. Different kinds of modality account for different strengths of the invoked norm and different degrees of urgency to correspond to it. High modality is a powerful device, as it indicates strict obligation to correspond. The use of high modality (for example 'must') leaves no room for argument or for deviating opinions on the matter in question. A little less demanding is the use of 'should' which comes across as a piece of advice to engage in the suggested behaviour. In the end the threat of social sanction attributed to a deviant behaviour is the same in both cases. The obligation can be softened by a projection clause such as 'I think (that)', indicating that the constructed norm is a personal one and other opinions may be possible.

I have used these and other grammatical devices to analyse my data critically. In doing so, I follow the theoretical assumptions of critical discourse analysis (CDA) (Fairclough 1992, 2003). This approach assumes that there is a dialectical relationship between language and social life. Texts[1] are influenced by, and influence, social life. They do not merely represent or reflect an unchangeable 'reality', but they actively construct it. A certain set of 'facts' can be discursively constructed in many different ways, depending on the producer's goal and other variables. (S)he constructs a personal temporary version of reality by choosing from among the words, grammatical structures, meanings, discourses and so on at his/her disposal. His/her choice is neither totally free nor fully constrained. The resulting version only acquires its full meaning potential in the light of all the other versions that the speaker/writer did *not* choose to construct.

Another important aspect to bear in mind is that textual representations and constructions of social life are ideological in the sense that they transport particular worldviews in the service of particular social groups and thereby establish, maintain or change social reality, including power relations. The same is true for the analysis of texts. In particular, a critical analysis inevitably carries the ideological orientations of the analyst. One of the main objectives of CDA is, in fact, to uncover textual manifestations of societal power asymmetries and hierarchies that maintain/establish social domination of one social group over another (Benwell and Stokoe 2006; Martin 2000; Fairclough 1992).

DATA

My analysis is based on 16 interviews with Portuguese women from two generations (8 mothers and their respective daughters). These interviews were selected from a larger corpus of a total of 40 interviews. Tables 7.1 and 7.2 show the socio-cultural variables of the sixteen selected women:

**Table 7.1**   Socio-cultural characteristics of the daughters

| ID[a] | Year of birth | Highest level of education | Family status | No of children |
|------|---------------|---------------------------|---------------|----------------|
| F01 | 1971 | 12th grade | married | 1 |
| F02 | 1972 | 11th grade | divorced/living together | 0 |
| F03 | 1974 | 12th grade | living together | 0 |
| F06 | 1969 | 12th grade | single | 1 |
| F07 | 1971 | 12th grade | living together | 1 |
| F08 | 1970 | 12th grade | married (2nd) | 2 |
| F09 | 1974 | 12th grade | married (2nd) | 1 |
| F10 | 1968 | 12th grade | married | 3 |

[a]I am using a combination of numbers and letters to identify the interviewees for two reasons. First, these identifications allow me to ensure the anonymity that I guaranteed my interviewees. This anonymity was very important for some women. Second, this form of identification is an attempt to go beyond the strictly personal level. Without losing sight of the singularity of the answers, I would like to emphasise their social character. That means, without forgetting that the answers have been produced by individual women, identifiable by name, each of them with their very individual life story that in the end made them present themselves the way they do in the specific interview situation, the answers are also the result of social dynamics, drawing on discourses that are circulating in society and that are available to women (and men) in general. More than individual disclosures, the answers of these women represent possibilities of identity construction available in Portuguese society

**Table 7.2**   Socio-cultural characteristics of the mothers

| ID | Year of birth | Highest level of education | Family status | No of children |
|----|---------------|---------------------------|---------------|----------------|
| M01 | 1950 | 4th grade | married | 2 |
| M02 | 1948 | 9th grade | married | 2 |
| M03 | 1952 | 11th grade | separated (2nd) | 1 |
| M06 | 1932 | 4th grade | divorced | 1 |
| M07 | 1940 | 9th grade | widowed | 3 |
| M08 | 1948 | 9th grade | married | 1 |
| M09 | 1953 | 9th grade | married | 2 |
| M10 | 1944 | 4th grade | divorced | 2 |

Five of the daughters (F01, F02, F03, F07 and F10) and three of the mothers (M01, M03 and M09) proceed to construct a norm of well-being at some point in their answer to the following question:

Q5: Many women like to care about their body, they go to spas; they have their hair done; do manicures, pedicures, have massages [...] Do you think the body is important for a woman?[2]

My main interest lay in the last part of the question, but in the pre-test interviews the first part turned out to be a necessary preamble. The introductory part obviously influences the answer suggesting possible topics for the answer. In fact none of the women expanded much beyond these specific feminising practices. The most important topics that were not alluded to by the question were weight and health, which indicates their importance in the relationship of women with their bodies.

## 'WOMEN NEED TO FEEL GOOD ABOUT THEIR BODIES': THE NORM OF PHYSICAL AND PSYCHOLOGICAL WELL-BEING

The norm of well-being is constructed throughout the corpus as a personal norm, as opposed to the social norms of thinness and beauty. It manifested itself in eight of the sixteen interviews. The social norm, on the other hand, is what the interviewees construct as beliefs circulating in society that tell women how they should look and behave. It represents the ideal female body and conduct. As I am analysing representations in discourse, all women could—in theory—construct different social norms. But although they focus on different aspects of the ideal, taken as a whole these different aspects form a body image like those we see in fashion magazines or advertising. The 'ideal' woman is thin, uses makeup and beauty products, wears feminine clothes, shoes and accessories, and has beautiful hair, and nice nails. This social norm is constructed directly as well as indirectly. Direct constructions usually make use of phrases such as 'society demands that ...' or 'in our society...'.

Throughout the corpus, social norms are more frequently constructed indirectly. They are presumed, but not explicitly expressed. For example: 'I am like this but I don't worry'. The verb 'to worry' only makes sense if we interpret the speaker's way of 'being' as usually being considered a reason to be worried. The speaker constructs a social norm of being, different from her being, and a social norm of mental behaviour (to worry) in the case of non-correspondence to that norm. Her own behaviour (*not* to worry) can be understood as the speaker's personal norm, that is, what she constructs as desirable and correct behaviour for herself and people in general and as differing from the social norm. Personal and social norms are usually only constructed explicitly when there is a discrepancy between them. In this case the first serves to criticise the second. When there is no clear distinction made between them, we can assume that the social norm became—at least for the moment of the interview—the personal. In this case, the speaker internalised the demands of society and took them on as her personal goals.

The norm of well-being constructs body satisfaction as a goal and thereby contradicts the idea of normative dissatisfaction. It is based on an idea of harmony between body and mind in which the mind accepts the body, independent from its appearance. In the present corpus the relation of the mind with the body is mostly represented as an emotive process of 'liking'. In the following sections I analyse what determines this positive mind-body relationship, that is, what is necessary in order for the mind to be able to 'like' the body.

## No Well-Being Without 'Taking Care'

The following excerpt shows one example of how well-being can be constructed as a norm to which one conforms:

1. F02: but I think that it is essential that a woman takes care [...] I think it would be good, that it is good if people do a little bit of exercise, take care of the body to feel better, because sometimes people end up unhappy because 'I don't like this or that about my body' but they resign themselves to it.[3]

In this excerpt, F02 justifies the taking up of disciplinary practices using evaluative language. 'Doing exercise' and 'taking care of oneself' are judged as 'good' and 'essential' and their ultimate goal is to make the person 'feel better'. Opposed to these positive values is 'unhappiness' as a clearly negative value which ought to be avoided. The monitoring of one's own body reveals a discrepancy between the concrete female body and the way the woman pictures its ideal form and shape. The logical consequence is bodily dissatisfaction: the woman is unhappy because she does not like certain aspects of her body. In a situation in which this discrepancy occurs, F02 constructs two possibilities of (non)action: (1) the woman can become resigned to it, but due to the negative value of the resulting unhappiness, that is not really an option. The only real option for the woman is (2) to do something to fight her dissatisfaction by making her body assume a certain shape that corresponds to the personal (and social) norm.

Compliance with the norm or the process of pursuing it are a source of happiness and well-being. Interestingly, this is portrayed as only true for other women, while F02 presents herself as someone who does not attribute any importance to her physical appearance. Monitoring processes, body dissatisfaction and disciplinary practices are normative for other women; they do not describe F02's own relationship with her body.

It has to be emphasised that the appropriateness of the dissatisfaction itself is not called into question by F02, who characterises this feeling as a perfectly normal and understandable one for a woman. Furthermore, for F02 the dissatisfaction is not a permanent issue, but one that can be fought and ended by disciplinary practices. F02 uses what I would call a 'discourse of free transformability', constantly suggested by the media, telling individuals that total or partial transformation of the body (and the mind) is within their power. Or, in other words: 'Popular culture does not apply any brakes to these fantasies of rearrangement and self-transformation. Rather, we are constantly told that we can "choose" our own bodies' (Bordo 1993, p. 247). The consequence of this discourse, which is supported by a 'rhetoric of choice and self-determination' (Bordo 1993, p. 247) is that dissatisfaction is also represented as the result of choice: individuals are dissatisfied only if they want to be so, as they are considered to have full agency over their bodies.

That there is no physical and psychological well-being for a woman without 'taking care', without disciplinary practices, is shown a little later in the same interview:

2. F02: even on a relationship level 'well now I'm married I don't give a damn if I am fat or skinny or whatever'. I don't think that way at all! I think one should always take care of oneself! Always! If only for one's physical well-being. Physical and psychological.[4]

Using modality devices and the adverb 'sempre' (always), F02 shows that in her opinion taking care of appearance is a lifelong obligation for women, not restricted to periods of dating. 'Taking care' means body surveillance at all times in order to intervene if necessary. The lack of surveillance is evaluated negatively by the use of '*borrifar*' (not to give a damn); the choice of the word clearly indicates carelessness and negligence. But disciplinary practices that go beyond the purpose of well-being are also negatively evaluated and construed as frivolous in this interview, as the following example shows:

3. F02: I love going to the gym, why because—well! I don't go there just to have a great body, just to have it, even because I don't do gymnastics, I don't have the patience.[5]

Aiming for physical beauty alone, 'just to have it', is not enough. This creates a clear distinction between women who do just that and F02. The goal of the former is regarded as frivolous while F02's practices are presented as a necessity, the prerequisite for the greater goal of well-being and directed towards the positive influence that physical activity potentially has on one's state of mind.

## OBSESSED, NEGLIGENT OR NORMAL?

Another woman, F10, divides the female population into three categories: (1) materialist/obsessed women; (2) negligent women; and (3) normal women. Her choice of words marks clearly what she considers correct and incorrect behaviour. Women in the first category, she says, have serious mental health problems, which lead to pathologies such as anorexia, because the individuals in question are not in harmony with themselves. The attitude of the second category—those women who do not care about their appearance—is neither clearly praised nor condemned. It could, in theory, be considered a positive exception if these women were considered to feel 'well' anyway or if their attitude was positively evaluated otherwise. This is not the case, however. There can be no doubt their attitude is not an example to follow if we consider that these women are not part of the 'normal' category. 'Normal' is to want to feel good, which is impossible for a woman when she gains weight or when she is heavier than the norm permits:

4. F10: a person when she gains weight, it affects that person, (s)he doesn't feel good, I am speaking for myself. When (s)he has put on

weight, the clothes don't seem to fit me well, I don't feel good, it seems that I can't move, I feel more tired, I feel heavier and so on. [...] Normally a woman, every woman, nobody, no woman likes to—with the possible exception of someone with a few extra pounds who is all 'whatever, I don't care' but well, normally, as a rule, a person that has a little pride and that likes herself, also likes to—likes to feel good.[6]

The norm of thinness is directly expressed by the use of '*por norma*' ('normally') and by the use of absolute categories ('nobody', 'every woman', etc.) in the second half of the excerpt. Apart from that, every interlocutor would naturally like to be included in the group of people 'with a little pride', who 'like themselves', which we can consider positive values and feelings. In order to belong to that group, you have to aspire to well-being: women cannot exceed the correct weight, because that would prevent them from being 'well'.

There is no clear distinction between social and personal 'norms' in this interview. This indicates a complete internalisation of the social norm by the interviewee. F10 constructs her personal norm of well-being as depending directly (although not necessarily exclusively) on the individual's capacity to fulfil the social norm of thinness. Aspects of well-being, in the form of clothes fitting well, the person being able to move, and so on, depend on that thinness. Neither F10 nor F02 account for body image as a social phenomenon. Body dissatisfaction and disciplinary practices are construed as merely individual issues; the wish to correspond to a certain body image as an exclusively individual desire. Furthermore the body project is interiorised, so she engages in it 'for herself', for the sake of re-establishing her own well-being:

5. F10: if I put on weight and then, and if I want to lose weight, I'll do it for me, not to show the others. it is for me to feel better, to feel healthier.[7]

The fact that disciplinary practices can bring about not only well-being but also good health makes engagement even more urgent. With the apparent easiness of the sequence: identifying the problem—wanting to resolve it—actually resolving it, F10 presents herself as being in control of her body. Dieting and other disciplinary practices chasing the intangible ideal of body image give women a sense of empowerment.

The greater the difficulty in achieving the ideal, the more empowered the women feel (McKinley 2011). The domain of empowerment, perpetuating the traditional association of women and the body, becomes problematic if it is the only one in which women are constructed as having power.

## 'As Long As I Look in the Mirror and Like What I See'

One interviewee of the older generation, M03, constructs a personal norm which implies harmony of body and mind brought about by a positive emotional relation of the mind with the body: the mind has to *like* the body. In theory this leaves space for possible transgressions of a supposed social norm and allows for bodies that do not fit the thinness ideal or those who do not undergo feminising practices to be liked by the mind. A closer analysis makes it clear that this is, however, only partially true:

> 6. M03: I have always been a bit chubby. So nowadays I am definitely fatter. No doubt at all. But I have always been more—I have—I am broader, but I never worried a lot about this [as long as] I look in the mirror and like what I see. [...] It's just there is another problem. It's that the country itself is a bit disapproving, and if I go maybe to answer a job advert and there is another person who has a different body type, even when I was younger maybe that person would have got the job not me. It's also important to remember this. that the people think the obese, well, a little discrimi- they still discriminate a bit.[8]

M03 is clearly aware of the social norm of thinness and body surveillance has shown her that her own body does not fit the ideal ('I have always been a bit chubby'). But the discrepancy does not result in body dissatisfaction, as the interviewee attributes reduced importance to her weight. Consequently she does not engage in disciplinary practices of type 1 that would bring about a body of the correct shape and size. Instead, M03 criticises the social norm as discriminatory.

Things are presented in a very different way when it comes to those disciplinary practices of type 3 that aim at the presentation of the body as an ornamented surface:

7. M03: I think that a woman also has to make an effort without going
   overboard [...] putting on lipstick [...] styling her hair for sure [...]
   makes one feel nice. It's like I said, if—we look in the mirror and say
   'these clothes don't look bad!', 'look my hair isn't OK, I have to get
   it trimmed', and things like that. Well, if one does not feel good about
   one's—with what one sees, one starts to get a bit [...] it's part of being
   a woman as well, being a bit—one needs to pay attention—make the
   best of what one's got. If you've got beautiful eyes [...] let's put on
   a bit of makeup, accentuate them, one has to take advantage of these
   things, not—now one cannot start to be sloppy! Not that! No way!
   Then we would go back to like my grandmother's day.[9]

Surveillance practices are clearly evident in the representation of M03's
sermons in front of the mirror; the surveillance advice *par excellence*.
The use of cosmetics, choice of clothes, hair care and so on, are constructed as obligatory and not negotiable mostly by the frequent use of
high modality ('have to...'). Even more, they are part of being a woman,
of the project of femininity; they are part of what defines a feminine individual. Without them, female identity is called into question.

On the other hand, these practices are constructed as something that
pleases the female self, as an intrinsic desire independent from the outside world. They apparently contradict the feminist critique of women's
constant search for external approval. The engagement itself becomes a
sensual experience (Lazar 2009 )—something that makes women feel
good. As in the other interviews I've discussed, the fact that this desire
is not a genuine one but the result of social pressures is hidden behind a
post-feminist neoliberal discourse telling women that they are free agents
in the project of femininity; that they should confidently embrace feminine practices, 'claim leisure and pleasure as women's entitlement, along
with the celebration of all things feminine' (Lazar 2009, p. 374). In the
last sentence of example (7) M03 even links the project of femininity to
modernity and civilising progress, as a negligence of feminising practices
like hair care and makeup encourages society to fall back into the age of
M03's grandmother.

By positioning herself differently in relation to different practices
(type 1 is optional, type 3 is not), M03 shows that the lack of the ideal
body shape—potentially a source of body dissatisfaction—can be com-
pensated for by the correct ornamenting practices. In the case of the

individual being unwilling or unable to conform to the body shape norm, well-being can be brought about by a positive emotional relationship between mind and body and by conforming to another social norm, that of taking care of one's appearance in terms of makeup or hair, for example. The distinct impact that the different practices have on the life of an individual is certainly an issue here. While transforming body shape is a long-term engagement which includes changing deeply-rooted habits, putting on makeup has an immediate effect. While the latter can be considered a source of pleasure itself, the former implies quite the opposite as disciplinary practices aiming at 'correcting' the body's shape (dieting, exercise) force the individual to renounce pleasures with an often more than uncertain outcome. In M03's words it is acceptable not to be willing (or able) to make the sacrifices necessary to lose weight, as long as one gains pleasure and success from other practices.

## BODY-MIND DUALISM

In her initial statement M09 accepts all kinds of appearances, on condition that the person feels at ease with herself.

> 8. M09: I think that every person has their choice, has their way of being, so if that person feels good and gets on well [...] OK. That's their choice. Then there is the role of society, that deep down demands a bit more—the person has to be very well dressed [...] in my case, for example, it is much more important what the person is, than what she is making herself out to be. So if the person is educated, if she is friendly, if she is loyal, if she is honest, for me that is much more important than how the person goes about—of course nobody likes to see a person that is badly dressed, that's obvious, right?[10]

After establishing that everything is acceptable as long as well-being is assured, she criticises society for demanding a kind of normative dress code. The respective construction is interesting, as it attributes an active role of 'demanding' to the abstract entity 'society' and positions herself somehow outside of that entity by criticising it. This construction creates the illusion that the individual speaker is free of any responsibility for society demanding whatever it is it demands and ignores any possibility of agency or power of the individual over society.

M09 criticises 'society's' focus on physical appearance in favour of the mind: values such as honesty, loyalty, education, and friendship are more important to her, she says, than the way people look. These values represent what the person 'is', while the body represents what the person 'makes itself out to be', which defines the former as a kind of 'essential/genuine self', while the latter appears to be artificially put on. This distinction between an outside and an inside self—the emphasis on the latter—was identified by Clark (2008) as a strategy to negotiate the loss of physical attractiveness in later life as well as the outcome of a 'socialization in which the Cartesian perspective predominates and the women have been taught to value character over appearance' (Clark 2008, p. 468). The internalisation of this Cartesian perspective represents an interesting instrument that shields women from social pressures aiming at physical attractiveness and therefore preventing body dissatisfaction. That this is not quite the case with M09 becomes clear at the end of interview, when she agrees with the previously criticised social norm of dressing well and establishes a level of minimal care which requires that the individual attributes importance to his/her appearance, monitors her body in order to make sure that it conforms to the norm of dressing (reasonably) well, and engages in disciplinary practices of the third kind if it does not. The lexical choices that frame the norm, '*claro*' ('of course') and '*é lógico, não é?*' ('that's obvious, right?'), leave no doubt that this is a universally-accepted way of thinking. In contrast to the other cases discussed above, M09 does not construe conformity to the social dress code as a source of well-being for the individual who engages in the respective disciplinary practices. She discursively assumes the position of the judging other who either approves, or does not, of a woman's appearance and of whom women need to be aware and aim to please. The individual's freedom to set their own priorities regarding physical appearance as long as they feel at ease is clearly limited here by an internalised social norm which M09 applies in her judgement.

## SUMMING UP

I have shown in my analysis that the norm of physical and psychological well-being, that apparently liberalises women's relationship with their bodies, depends (in many cases) on the fulfilment of very clear social norms of body image. Beauty and the 'correct' body shape/weight are often understood as the source of that well-being and the imprisoning cycle of self-surveillance and disciplinary action over the body is exactly the same as if one sought to comply with a 'simple' body image norm such as thinness. In many cases, well-being seems simply to add another body image norm without replacing the others. The kind of necessary minimal action over the body that ensures well-being differs from interview to interview but all construct some kind of disciplinary practices as mandatory: two interviewees understand disciplinary practices directed at body shape as obligatory (F02: doing exercise; F10: dieting); two construct beauty practices as a must (M03: makeup, hair care etc.; M09: dressing well). Although generalisations are impossible to make due to the small corpus, it is interesting to note that the younger women's disciplinary practices are directed towards body shape, the older women's towards some kind of ornamentation. One explanation could be the greater difficulty in successfully shaping an older body and therefore it could be an example for Tiggemann's (2004) argument that the body ideal accompanies the evolution of the ageing body. More data needs to be analysed in order to test the appropriateness of that claim.

In all interviews, well-being is construed as being within the reach of the individual; the transformation of the body that allows the individual to achieve well-being is possible for everybody and therefore the individual is only not well, if he or she *chooses* not to be. Being able to meet beauty standards is often interpreted simply as an individual issue, ignoring the social dimension of these standards and the pressure to meet them, as has been frequently criticised by feminist theory. In these cases (F02, F10, M03), there is no accounting for possible social restraints in the interviews. The social norm is internalised to the extent that it is no longer separable from the personal norm. In other cases (M03, M09), a part of the norm is criticised as discriminatory or as irrelevant and as opposed to a more liberal personal norm while other parts remain unchallenged.

The main objective of this chapter has been to show that the construction of a norm of well-being, which apparently contradicts the normative dissatisfaction of women with their bodies and the need to meet socially established norms of thinness and beauty, is in most cases tied to these very social norms of physical appearance. This chapter does not pretend to be representative: it does not claim to have identified a very frequent discursive figure or one that is typical for Portuguese women or for women that share certain characteristics. The small corpus does not allow for such generalisations or conclusions. Therefore my objective has been to create awareness of the fact that compliance with the social norm is often seen as a source of well-being, and that even when an apparently liberal discourse rejects social norms, these very norms operate 'under the surface', constructed as consensual and normalised by linguistic features.

## NOTES

1. The term 'text' is used in the broader sense, referring to 'any instance of language in any medium that makes sense to someone that understands the (respective) language' (Halliday and Matthiessen 2004, p. 3).

2. My translation of the Portuguese original: *Muitas mulheres gostam de cuidar do seu corpo: vão a SPAs, ao cabeleireiro, à manicura, pédicure e fazem massagens [...] Acha que o corpo é importante para a mulher?*

3. My translation of the Portuguese original: *F02: mas acho que é essencial uma mulher tr- tratar de-- [...] eu acho que era bom acho que é bom as pessoas fazerem um[:] pouco de exercício, tratarem do corpo para se sentirem melhor. porque as vezes as pessoas acabam por ser infelizes porque 'não gosto disto o daquilo no meu corpo' mas acomodam-se.*

4. My translation of the Portuguese original: *F02: até a nível de relacionamento 'olha agora já estou casada já me estou a borrifar se sou gorda se sou magra se não sei quê' acho que não! acho que se devia cuidar sempre! sempre! até para o[2:] bem-estar físico. físico e psicológico.*

5. My translation of the Portuguese original: *F02: eu adoro ir ao ginásio, porquê porque-- é assim! não vou lá, para ter um corpus bel só por ter até porque não faço ginástica não tenho paciência.*

6. My translation of the Portuguese original: *F10: a pessoa quando está mais gordinha, mexe com a pessoa, não se sente bem, eu falo por mim. se é mais gordinha a roupa parece que não me assenta bem, eu não me sinto bem, parece que não me consigo mexer, fico mais cansada, sinto mais peso e não sei o quê [...] normalmente a mulher, toda a mulher, ninguém, nenhuma mulher gosta-- tirando uma ou outra que é gordinha 'ah, não quero saber' mas pronto. normalmente por norma uma pessoa que tem um bocadinho de brio e que gosta dela própria, também gosta de -- gosta de se sentir bem.*

7. My translation of the Portuguese original: *F10: se estiver mais gordinha e depois, e se quiser emagrecer, vou fazer isto por mim, não é para mostrar aos outros. é para me sentir bem, para me sentir mais saudável.*

8. My translation of the Portuguese original: *M03: eu sempre fui mais para o cheio. portanto hoje em dia estou mais[2:] gorda. não há dúvida nenhuma. mas sempre fui mais-- tenho-- sou larga, mas nunca me preocupei muito com essa [xxx] [desde] que olho para o espelho e me gosto de ver. [...] e depois tem*

*outro problema. é que o próprio (.) ã: país condena um pouco, e se eu se cal-*
*har se eu chegar para a responder a um anúncio e chegar outra pessoa que*
*tem outra fisionomia, mesmo quando eu era mais nova se calhar ela ficava*
*e eu não ficava. porque isso também é importante. que as pessoas ã: acham*
*o[:2] obeso pronto, ã: um pouco descrim- ã: descriminam um pouco ainda.*

9. My translation of the Portuguese original: *M03: e acho que a mulher tam-*
*bém tem que se produzir um pouco. não cair no exagero. [...] o pintar os*
*lábios, [...] arranjar o cabelo com certeza, [...] a pessoa também se sente*
*bem. é como digo se-- a gente gosta de olhar para o espelho e dizer 'esta roupa*
*até não está mal! olha lá o cabelo não está bem tenho que o cortar um bocado*
*e tal'. pronto quando a pessoa não se sente bem cons-- co-- com aquilo que vê,*
*a pessoa começa a ficar um bo—[...] faz parte da[:] mulher também s-- ser*
*um pouco-- a pessoa tem que ã: aju-- puxar um pouco os atributos que tem.*
*se tem uns olhos bonitos [...] vamos pintar um pouco vamos realçar qualquer*
*coisa, tem que aproveitar estas[:] coisas, não-- agora não pode entrar no*
*desleixo! isso não! de maneira nenhuma! então voltamos ao tempo se calhar*
*da nem da minha avó.*

10. My translation of the Portuguese original: *M09: eu acho que cada pessoa ã:*
*tem a sua opção, tem a sua maneira de ser, portanto, se a pessoa se sente bem*
*a dar bem [...] tudo bem, é uma opção dela. ã: depois, há a parte da socie-*
*dade em si. que no fundo exige um bocado-- aquele rótulo de-- a pessoa tem*
*que andar muito bem vestida [...] para o meu caso, por exemplo, ã: é muito*
*mais importante ã: o que a pessoa é, do que a pessoa que ele demonstra ser,*
*portanto, se a pessoa é educada, se é[2:2], amiga, se é leal, se é honesta, para*
*mim é muito mais importante do que se a pessoa fo-- andar-- claro, que*
*ninguém gosta de ver uma pessoa mal vestida, é lógico, não é?*

## REFERENCES

Bartky, S., 1997. 'Foucault, Femininity, and Modernization of Patriarchal Power'. In: K. Conboy, N. Medina and S. Stanbury, eds. *Writing on the Body: Female Embodiment and Feminist Theory.* New York: Columbia University Press, pp. 129–151.

Benwell, B., and E Stokoe, 2006. *Discourse and Identity.* Edinburgh: Edinburgh University Press.

Bordo, S., 1993. *Unbearable Weight.* Berkeley: University of California Press.

Clark, L, 2008. 'Older Women's Bodies and the Self: The Construction of Identity in Later Life'. *Canadian Review of Sociology/Revue canadienne de sociologie.* 38 (4), pp. 441–464.

Eggins, S. and D Slade, 1997. *Analysing Casual Conversation.* London: Cassell.

Fairclough, N., 2003. *Analysing Discourse.* London: Routledge.

Fairclough, N., 1992. *Discourse and Social Change*. Cambridge: Polity.

Grogan, S., 2011. 'Body Image Development in Adulthood', in: T. Cash and L. Smolak, eds. *Body Image. A Handbook of Science, Practice and Prevention.* New York: The Guilford Press, pp. 93–100.

Halliday, M. and C Matthiessen, 2004. *An Introduction to Functional Grammar.* London: Arnold.

Lazar, M., 2009. 'Entitled to Consume: Postfeminist Femininity and a Culture of Post-Critique'. *Discourse & Communication*, 3 (4), pp. 371–400.

Martin, J., 2000. 'Close Reading: Functional Linguistics as a Tool for Critical Discourse Analysis', in L. Unsworth, ed., *Researching Language in Schools and Communities. Functional Linguistic Perspectives.* London: Cassel, pp. 275–302.

Martin, J. and P. White, 2005. *The Language of Evaluation*. Basingstoke: Palgrave Macmillan.

McKinley, N., 2011. 'Feminist Perspectives on Body Image', in T. Cash and L. Smolak, eds. *Body Image. A Handbook of Science, Practice and Prevention.* New York: The Guilford Press, pp. 39–47.

Rodin, J., R. Silverstein and L. Striegel-Moore, 2016. 'Women and Weight: A Normative Discontent', in T. Sondregger, ed., *Psychology and Gender.* Lincoln: University of Nebraska Press, pp. 267–307.

Stevens, C. and M Tiggemann, 1998. 'Women's Body Figure Preferences across the Life Span'. *The Journal of Genetic Psychology*, 159 (1), pp. 94–102.

Tiggemann, M., 2011. 'Sociocultural Perspectives on Human Appearance', in Cash and Smolak, eds, *Body Image. A Handbook of Science, Practice and Prevention.* New York: The Guilford Press, pp. 12–19.

Tiggemann, M., 2004. 'Body Image across the Adult Life Span: Stability and Change'. *Body Image*, 1 (1), pp. 29–41.

# CHAPTER 8

# No Body, No Crime? (Representations of) Sexual Violence Online

*Jemma Tosh*

Sexual violence is an ever-increasing feature of online culture, with rape the central aim of 'stalking simulators' as well as the violence directed towards avatar sex workers in the *Grand Theft Auto* franchise (Martinez and Manolovitz 2010). This is in addition to the word 'rape' being commandeered and redefined by online gaming communities to refer to murder, humiliation, and destruction (Hernandez 2012) while simultaneously being ridiculed in online rape 'jokes' (Kramer 2011). Using discourse analysis (Parker 2014), this chapter examines discussions from online forums about the use of the word 'rape' to refer to instances of sexual violence in online spaces. It interrogates the debate around whether these occurrences are forms of sexual violence, or representations of sexual violence based on the presence/absence of an embodied material experience. The implications of this complex construction of rape online are considered in relation to the increasing use of communication technology in sexual victimisation (Hughes 2000). This chapter

J. Tosh (✉)
Chartered Academic Psychologist, The Psygentra Institute,
Vancouver, Canada
e-mail: jtosh@psygentra.com

© The Author(s) 2017
E. Rees (ed.), *Talking Bodies*, DOI 10.1007/978-3-319-63778-5_8

argues that while such developments should not be ignored, they are not new (e.g. Mystique 1982) and campaigns that focus on the novelty of the technology detract attention from long-standing issues of gender and sexual inequality.

## New Technologies, Changing Relationships

Changes in social communication provide new possibilities for sexuality, such as moving beyond physical boundaries (Cooper et al. 2000; Doring 2009, 2000). Cybersex and cyberflirting occur within a variety of online contexts, including metaworlds like Second Life (SL) and World of Warcraft (Eklund 2011). SL enables users to purchase genital attachments, which permits sexual activity between avatars. Users are also able to alter the avatars' arousal level from 'no arousal' to 'orgasm'. Sexual activities are initiated using 'pose balls' that provide a variety of behaviours, such as 'stroke penis' (Brookey and Cannon 2009). Once an individual has selected an option, the onscreen avatar performs the action. Pose balls for sexual activities are available throughout SL and enable a variety of sexual activities to be performed by avatars, while being controlled by offline users (Brookey and Cannon 2009). SL also provides opportunities for virtual weddings (Reid 1995) and erotica, with virtual pornography and avatar strippers as popular features (Wajcman 2006).

While users often described these acts as 'virtual', they have the potential for intense subjective experiences (Reid 1995). Furthermore, this cybersexuality does not occur exclusively online, particularly as the difference between online and offline has blurred (Jones 1995; Kendall 1999; Morahan-Martin 2000); individuals are part of both realities simultaneously. For example, dating websites illustrate the role of technology within sexual or romantic relationships as involving both online and offline interactions (Doring 2000; Sprecher et al. 2008). In addition, romantic communication is cited as a popular motivation for people to use Social Networking Sites (SNS) where the online profile is a virtual representation of the individual's offline life (Dong et al. 2008).

This incorporation of technology into sexual relationships also enables opportunities to redefine sexual experience or intervene in public discourses of sexuality. For example, online blogs are used to describe personal sexual experiences and desires that are publically shared. As Muise stated:

Blogs provide a forum for expression that can be anonymous and flexible and a virtual space that allows individuals to explore their sexuality beyond social prescriptions (e.g. Ross 2005). Blogs have also been described as one potential 'safe space' for women to articulate missing discourses (Harris 2005: 39) and a place where women can engage in a 'process of regaining control over information about sexuality' (Wood 2008: 480). (Muise 2011, p. 412)

Like Haraway's (1991) cyborg metaphor then, technology has become completely entwined in sexual relationships. This includes the initiation of relationships between individuals, how those relationships are maintained through communication, and how sexuality is defined and experienced.

## Technological and Violent Advancement

While advances in technology have provided benefits in relation to communication, they have often been used further to oppress women and gender minorities, or to develop existing methods of abuse. The intertwining of the sex and technology industries in a 'Technocapitalist' venture has led to increasing feminist awareness of the uses of global communication tools to expand human trafficking networks (Wajcman 2006). As Hughes stated:

> Communications technology is the significant factor in the globalization of sexual exploitation. The Internet and other types of telecommunication, such as satellite transmission, provide the sex industry new ways of marketing and delivering women and children as sexual commodities to male buyers (Hughes 1999). As a rule, when a new technology is introduced into a system of exploitation, it enables those with power to intensify the harm and expand the exploitation. (Hughes 2000, p. 36)

The interactive relationship between technology and offline abuse is illustrated by forums being used to feed back and advise on purchasing non-consensual sex. Websites such as 'Rape Camp' advertise their services to visitors to Cambodia and build on previous racial discrimination and victimisation. Hughes (2000) concludes that such aspects of this industry are an example of negative consequences of technological advancement, which has combined with sexual exploitation to produce a globalised industry of abuse.

The extent of technology in developing forms of violence goes beyond organised human trafficking to include individual encounters within communities. For example, reports of rapes being filmed or pictures being taken during an assault that are then subsequently distributed over the Internet provide an additional form of public humiliation to sexual coercion (e.g. 'Emailed Rave Rape Pictures Earn Teen Probation', 2012; 'Gang Rape Photos on Facebook' 2010; 'Steubenville Ohio School Footballers Guilty of Rape' 2013), with increasing examples of slut-shaming on a global scale when women's public sexuality is filmed and uploaded to the Internet (e.g. Wiseman 2013) and the emotional consequences of this mass abuse documented in the suicides of young women (e.g. White 2014). This is in addition to the mocking or trivialisation of rape in many online spaces. The proliferation of Facebook pages and groups dedicated to rape 'jokes' (e.g. 'It's not rape if you yell "Surprise!"') instigated an online activist response by several feminist groups (Tosh n.d.). Furthermore, Kramer's analysis of 'online rape jokes' identified a variety of media being used to promote 'rape humour', including,

> a viral video featuring Will Ferrell in which a group of overzealous environmentalists (the 'Green Team') go to extreme and violent lengths to protect the environment, including gang-raping a woman who pollutes the air by smoking; a newspaper comic strip in which an elderly man makes fun of his elderly female companion for carrying mace, telling her that she is too old to have to worry; a statement made by comedian Jerry Seinfeld upon the debut of his 'Bee Movie' ('Bees have the only perfect society on Earth. They have no crime, they have no drugs, they have no rape. A little rape, but it's not that bad'); t-shirts with statements like 'Stop Rape, Say Yes' written on them; and several traditional scripted jokes with a set-up and a punchline. (Kramer 2011, pp. 139–140)

This mimics the backlash to second wave campaigns to stop rape (Ehrlich and King 1992) but is able to reach a wider audience.

## VIRTUAL VIOLENCE

The first documented online experience labelled as 'virtual rape' occurred in the MOO (a Multi User Dimension (MUD) that is object-oriented) 'LambdaMOO' (Dibbell 1998), where a user called 'Mr Bungle' used a subprogram of computer code (referred to as a 'voodoo doll' in the MOO) to take control of other users' characters. This then enabled Mr Bungle to make those characters perform particular sex acts, which were described in textual descriptions sent to every computer of every character that was within the MOO 'room'. Also, in 2007, discussions arose regarding virtual rape in SL. Virtual rape within this context also utilised computer code to take control of another user's avatar within the form of pose balls. Rape is argued to be impossible in SL, as the other user has to agree to accept the object therefore indicating consent, but this code can be disguised as anything (Duranske 2007). Also, just because a user accepts one part of the object (such as agreeing to 'love' for sex) it does not necessarily mean that they will consent to everything that happens after, such as the behaviours that can be purchased in SL, including choking and slapping, for example. Furthermore, while avatars can usually stop an action, Brookey and Cannon (2009) note that once an avatar has committed to an action in which they are the passive recipient, they are usually unable to stop the action until the dominant avatar has finished. They also observe that sexual pose balls often have active and passive sexual actions distributed between male and female pose balls (coloured blue for men and pink for women), with the passive options more likely to be listed as options for female avatars.

Since these isolated events, sexual violence has become much more mainstream and a normative aspect of online gaming. For example, the hugely popular game franchise *Grand Theft Auto* (Rockstar Games 1997) includes rewards for having sex with sex workers and assaulting them afterwards, which can include beating, being set on fire or running them over with a car (e.g. Houser et al. 2001). Martinez and Manolovitz (2010) argue that the use of sexual violence in *Grand Theft Auto* is to add entertainment value to the game, as many gamers find this amusing. Rape has also become a feature of many narratives of popular games, such as the rebranding of *Tomb Raider*'s highly sexualised character, Lara Croft, as a survivor of an attempted rape (Consalvo 2012). As Hamilton described:

Crystal Dynamics revealed a new, gritty version of Lara Croft's history – one that sees her bloodied, bruised, badly wounded, and forced to fight for her life against mercenaries, one of whom tries to rape her before she blows his head off. (Hamilton 2012, para. 1)

However, Martinez and Manolovitz (2010) also describe a range of 'niche' games where rape is either the sole purpose of the game, such as *RapeLay* (Illusion 2006), or a key part of the game's narrative. They describe the game franchise *Biko* (Illusion 1999, 2000, 2004):

> stalking simulators in which you follow one of five women, gather items, and try to remain unseen. After catching the girl, you will achieve a different ending depending on choices made throughout the game, one of which includes vivid scenes of sexual violence. (Martinez and Manolovitz 2010, p. 68)

Martinez and Manolovitz (2010) observe that similar games appear to include 'as many types of sexually violent acts as possible' (p. 68). However, they also highlight that while the technological advances have been able to portray these scenes in more realistic ways, rape within games is not new. For example, *Custer's Revenge* (Mystique 1982) included a rape of a Native American woman by General Custer.

Realistic images of violence and the ability to participate in violent acts are deemed a 'highly valued' part of online gaming (Herbst 2005). This violence is associated with inner animalistic desires, which draws on masculine discourses around sexuality (Hollway 1995). For example, Herbst (2005) quotes from the producer of the game *God of War* (Krawczyk et al. 2005), who states:

> I wanted there to be the vibe of letting your inner beast out to run free; letting the player just cut loose and run wild. That was my barometer. It was like: 'Is this element making the player feel strong and brutal?' If so, in it goes. And more often than not, violence was one of the tools that allowed us to give the player this feeling. (Herbst 2005, p. 315)

Gendered constructions of technology often portray 'high-tech' devices as masculine and important and 'low-tech' or 'no-tech' as areas associated with femininity and feminine technological incompetence (Wajcman 2006, p. 15). The increasing focus on the sexual victimisation of women in online gaming culture therefore reflects the continued influence of hegemonic constructions of masculinity in technology and entertainment.

## METHOD

Media reports of rape in online spaces have inspired discussions regarding how rape is defined, and whether it is possible within a virtual space. Material was collected from online forums following an extensive inquiry using search engines and keywords. These comments were not originally intended for research purposes, however they can also be considered an online version of naturally occurring data (Giles 2006; Hookway 2008). I adopted a 'lurking' approach to data collection, with posters unaware of their participation (Sharf 1999). Two forum discussions were selected due to their specific debate regarding the possibility of virtual rape and its potential definition. The posts were made between 20th April 2007 and 11th June 2007. The forum discussions explicitly demonstrated the difficulty in applying terminology that was defined and developed prior to recent technological advancements. The debate, therefore, also demonstrates the transformation of the word 'rape' and its different meaning when used in online contexts.

The forums involved over 100 individuals, and included a wide variety of viewpoints. The discussions were analysed using discourse analysis (Parker 2014), drawing on feminist poststructuralist theory (Weedon 1996). Criteria from Parker (2014) were used to identify discourses from the comments posted in the forums. Texts construct versions of reality and each one has underlying assumptions about the objects and categories featured within (Potter and Wetherell 1987). Different versions have different social and political implications (Parker 2014). Posters had a range of definitions of 'rape', each emphasising and omitting certain aspects in each case. My aim was not to identify these different perspectives, but to interrogate the discourses being drawn on as well as examining the contradictions within them.

## ETHICS

Jones (1995) argues that offline methodologies are not necessarily directly applicable to online data. This is particularly relevant to discourse analysis, where quotations from texts are traditionally considered an imperative aspect of demonstrating/validating the discourses identified (e.g. Potter and Wetherell 1987), whereas over-quotation can risk summarising rather than analysing text (Antaki et al. 2003). However, this causes an ethical dilemma in relation to the analysis of forum discussions regarding emotive topics. By reporting direct quotations it becomes possible for those who posted on the website to be located through the use of online search engines. Such was the case for research completed by Finn and Lavitt (1994) who altered the names of participants from a sexual abuse support forum but reported the name of the website as well as the times that posts were made. Consequently, the participants could be identified despite the researchers ostensibly ensuring anonymity (King 1996; Sixsmith and Murray 2001).

The discursive analysis of online texts is therefore very different to those who quote from interview transcripts, as online data leaves participants exposed. This is why current Internet research guidelines state that direct quotations and website names should not be reported. Therefore, the details of the website analysed and quotations are not reported in this chapter. Only short general phrases, that are unidentifiable by searching online, are included. This is due to the forum discussions still being available online and thus individuals could be contacted following the publication of their comments, which were not originally intended for research purposes.

## Analysis

The purpose of the analysis was to identify discourses related to rape that were used when discussing the possibility of virtual rape. When deciding whether or not an incident would be classified as 'rape', individuals compared online events to a definition with related criteria. Therefore, while the contributors to the forum were discussing virtual rape, they were building on discourses and definitions of the offline equivalent. By analysing the debate of whether 'virtual rape' really was 'rape', I aimed to gain a better understanding of the changing definition of rape and the influence of technological development and communication in its transformation. The analysis identified four discourses: (1) never surrender; (2) it's not me, it's you; (3) fantasised absolution; and (4) committed to consent.

## 'Never Surrender' Discourse

The term 'never surrender' is often associated with military discourse, or a military strategy (Overgaard 1994) but it signifies resolve within a conflict situation. For example, Churchill's 1940 speech during World

War II used 'we shall never surrender' and the concept is well referenced within the Northern Ireland conflict, on both sides of the political divide. The Irish Republican Army (IRA) used the term during the 1970s campaign (Shanahan 2009) and loyalists popularised 'not an inch, no surrender' (White-McAuley 1999; Wilford 1996). The use of 'never' as opposed to 'no' is to denote the importance of time within the discourse. As will be demonstrated, resistance on its own is not enough; constant and continual resistance is required on the part of the victim. They must *never* surrender to the will of the rapist.

The declaration that virtual rape does not exist in online environments is based on the logic that some form of resistance was always available to the user. Most often, users described the possibility of 'TPing' (teleporting) to another part of the virtual world; muting the avatar that was causing offence; logging out of the software; or turning off the computer. However, this perspective neglected the events leading up to the 'escape'. For example, avatars being forced to the ground by a naked avatar and finding themselves unable to move; or the beginnings of sexual animation prior to the individual utilising one of the means of resistance. Therefore, the definition of this virtual rape as 'simply' not possible required completion of the act. Being forced into a non-consensual sexual encounter or the penetration of one avatar by another was not sufficient for the act to be deemed rape, if during the act the non-consenting individual somehow stopped the event. This implies that the rapist needs to 'finish' prior to an act being defined as 'rape'. Virtually, this would suggest that the sexual animation would need to run its course.

'Offline', it is more likely this would mean orgasm, due to the coital and orgasm imperatives within Western culture (Nicolson 1993; Potts 2002). However, it also defines the act by the power of the individual's ability to control their actions. For example, if the rapist is dominant and forces the victim to be subdued until they have 'finished', they control the situation and decide how and when it is completed. This would fulfil the definition of a 'successful rape' within this discourse. Due to the victims' ability to decide how and when the act is completed (e.g. through teleporting or turning off the computer) the act is not considered rape. It is not the act of forceful penetration that defines the act but the power to control the situation and have autonomy over its outcome, rather than its content. The victim always retained this power as they were perceived as being able to end the encounter at any time, despite still being described as a 'victim'. Therefore, to avoid being a rape victim, one has not to 'give in' or submit in any way.

This inability to be overpowered in your actions was reasoned to be why virtual rape did not exist. Ergo, the definition of (offline) rape is that it is 'inescapable'. Any possibility of autonomy, or resistance and the event is seen as undeserving of the label 'rape'. This places full responsibility on the victim, and requires not just evidence of resistance, but no evidence of potential sources of resistance not employed by the victim. Not to pursue a potential course of resistance deemed the act 'avoidable' and subsequently the victim became blameworthy. This was even the case when discussing sleeping avatars. The response was that the user should have had a 'security orb'. Therefore, by not using all possible avenues of resistance, including preventative ones, the act does not fulfil the definition of rape as 'inescapable'.

This precedence given to resistance replicates myths or discourses identified by second wave feminists, which assert that 'rape does not exist'. For example, Burt identified the myth that, 'any healthy woman can successfully resist a rapist if she really wants to' (Burt 1980, p. 223) and Schwendinger and Schwendinger described how, 'rape is impossible because it can easily be avoided by the woman's resistance' (Schwendinger and Schwendinger 1974, p. 20). Schwendinger and Schwendinger go on to describe examples from legal and medical professionals illustrating the alleged impossibility of rape. For example:

> The doctor said he didn't believe in rape if a girl really wanted to resist it. He performed a little trick with me holding a cup and showing that if I moved it around he couldn't put a stick in it. (Schwendinger and Schwendinger 1974, p. 20)

They concluded that 'the rape victim must act like a contender for a boxing title who does not let her fans down: it must be clearly demonstrated that she didn't throw the fight' (Schwendinger and Schwendinger 1974, p. 20). However, a difference between the second wave rape discourses and that of the never surrender discourse, is the role of the body. Within the 'rape is impossible' myth the strength of 'healthy' women is cited as a reason why they can stop a rape before it happens (Schwendinger and Schwendinger 1974), whereas it is precisely the lack of a physical body that equalises the conflict and enables rape to be seen as an impossibility online. Physical domination is considered the main difference between the impossibility of virtual rape, and the possibility of 'inescapable' (offline) rape within this discourse, which colludes with popularised constructions of violent 'stranger rape' as 'real rape' (Estrich 1987).

If resistance was unsuccessful, or inadequate (to stop the assault), the implication was that there was an 'unconscious' desire (or fantasy) to be raped. Burt described this myth as one in which, 'many women have an unconscious wish to be raped' (Burt 1980, p. 223). Therefore, when there is evidence of possible resistance not employed by the victim, the act is considered consensual. This also colludes with the construction of rape as almost inevitable if the opportunity arises. There is an implicit assumption that rape is normal or expected. The expectation that it would be safe to sleep in a public (offline) space and that rape would not occur is considered naïve. Within this logic, if exposing yourself to risk or vulnerability is likely to lead to sexual assault, then any actions increasing risk or vulnerability can be interpreted as 'asking for it' or in some way wanting/inviting the assault to occur.

## 'It's Not Me, It's You' Discourse

Within the 'never surrender' discourse, the victim's actions are thoroughly interrogated and evaluated, whereas the actions of the virtual rapists avoid any such scrutiny. This selective scrutiny continues within the 'it's not me, it's you' discourse. In contrast to the popularised 'It's not you, it's me' (Ranganath et al. 2009) justification for ending a relationship, the 'it's not me, it's you' discourse justifies the continued focus on the actions of victims at the expense of interrogating the rapists' behaviour and wider cultural constructs of hegemonic masculinity and heteronormative sexuality. However, it also goes beyond this by displacing the discussion of rape with discussions of rape victims' subjectivity. This fundamentally challenges the moral condemnation of sexually coercive or violent behaviour. In sum, it argues that sexual coercion is not the problem, but the overly emotional reaction to it is a problem. It subsequently deflects blame or responsibility for the problematic consequences of sexual violence onto victims rather than perpetrators. This changed the discussion from one of victimisation to one of feeling victimised. It is a subtle but effective redirection.

In directing blame for the negative consequences of rape onto victims, this discourse constructs the problem as an internal mental phenomenon. Therefore, it is not the actions of others, but the *interpretation* of those actions, which is problematic: the problem resides within the victim. The negation of discussion regarding the act of rape resulted in constructions of those who find rape upsetting as a specific category of people. This category does not describe individuals who have experienced rape, but targets people who find the general concept of rape distressing. While these two groups overlap, there is a broad consensus that an actual experience of rape is upsetting. Rather it argues that depictions, images, role-plays and performances of rape should not be upsetting.

Individuals differentiated between those who found representations of rape as a form of online harassment (or 'griefing') and those who were considered to be 'damaged' and thus were more distressed by such images. These 'damaged' folk were constructed as a pathologised minority, drawing on descriptions of diagnoses such as post-traumatic stress disorder (PTSD). The use of psychiatric discourse abnormalises those who find images, or experiences, of virtual rape upsetting. Consequently, it positions those who do not find these images disturbing, as 'normal'. This construction of normalcy as unperturbed by images of sexual violence is extremely problematic. This pathologising discourse was sympathetic to those who were distressed/'damaged', although it also extended this construction of rape victims as 'damaged' to offline victims as well.

In addition to sympathy, this category of individuals was considered worthy of pity, and in some way disadvantaged or 'beneath' those who discussed them. This construction of victims as 'damaged' as a result of rape was inescapable. A label of 'damaged' applied to a rape victim remained long after they might have become a survivor, as they will always have been raped and only a change in history would enable the removal of 'emotionally damaged'. While the label was lasting, in contrast to the 'never surrender' discourse, the duration of the experience was considered irrelevant, as any attempt to stop the encounter would be deemed too late since the individual was already 'damaged'.

The emphasis on the emotional experience following the threat of virtual rape, or witnessing images of rape, was emphasised both by those who considered an emotional reaction as relatively abnormal, and those who identified with highly emotional reactions. However, those who described this category as Others tended to pathologise this as a minority, whereas when the group self-represented, they constructed the experience of feeling distressed as normative and frequent in online spaces. This validation of fear and worry at experiencing a virtual rape was welcomed and appreciated.

In addition to people listing fear and worry, rage was also cited as a possible emotional reaction. This wide range of emotional reactions was considered justification for the use of the word 'rape', while those who pathologised the 'damaged' minority considered virtual rape solely as a depiction or representation that had a 'triggering' effect on survivors and victims. The presence of a physical body or physical dominance was not considered to be as important as the psychological trauma in defining rape. This is a particularly individualised perspective which considers the subjective experience of the victim as paramount.

Some highlighted how there was a real person on the other side of the avatar. This is another significant difference between those who constructed virtual rape as a depiction and those who considered it another form of sexual coercion or abuse; the disconnection between fantasy and reality. Those who could relate the reality of rape to the virtual 'depictions' described their experiences of distress at witnessing or experiencing virtual rape. Those that framed virtual rape as 'scenes' or 'depictions' were able completely to disconnect the online 'fantasy' from the 'reality' of rape. Much like the difference between those who find rape 'jokes' funny and those who do not, for those who have witnessed or experienced rape, it is 'inescapably realistic' (Kramer 2011, p. 143).

## Discourse of Fantasised Absolution

The disconnection of 'fantasy rape' from reality results in the absolution of guilt and responsibility (Sethna 1992). However, the reality of rape cannot be separated from depictions or other variations of abuse, such as virtual rape. As a representation of the real, it is intangibly connected to the real, or as Salih states, 'fantasy is essential to a real which itself turns out to be a construction established on the basis of its differentiation from fantasy' (Salih 2004, p. 184). Ergo, fantasy and reality are not mutually exclusive, and as Salih's description of Butler's paper 'The Force of Fantasy' shows (Butler 2004), the two are connected by their opposition. Therefore, the absolution of responsibility is also a fantasy. Whether it is described as 'griefing' or 'virtual rape', the responsibility for abusive actions remains. However, the discourse of fantasised absolution works in conjunction with the 'never surrender' and 'it's not me, it's you' discourses to shift responsibility from perpetrators onto victims. It is simultaneously used to justify or excuse any form of abusive action online as 'not real', despite the challenge that while the act is virtual it has the potential to produce real emotional reactions described within the 'it's not me, it's you' discourse.

Chayko states that, 'The frames we once used, conceptually, to set the real apart from the unreal are not as useful as they once were [...] we require new concepts and new understandings' (Chayko 1993, p. 178). There are those who define the online content in terms of non-corporeal entities, for example Benedikt (1991) argues that 'objects' in cyberspace are not physical (or representations of physical) objects but are 'pure information'. However, Jones (1995) cautions that 'information' can be too easily considered a physical entity rather than series of ones and zeros. Others argue that the content of online environments exists within the user, as a subjective and internal experience. Reid (1995) states that 'the illusion of reality lies not in the machinery itself but in the user's willingness to treat the manifestations of his or her imaginings as if they were real' (p. 166). Miah (2000) argues that human existence has 'always been mediated through the senses or some other media [and therefore] has always been virtual and that cyberspace is another media through which we experience the real' (p. 221). However, some argue that interactions between Internet users are more than a 'meeting of the minds' and resist an overemphasis of disembodiment. For example, Whitty (2003) describes the reconstruction of bodies online, particularly in relation to cybersex or cyberflirting relationships.

Other theorists place a greater emphasis on the blurring between the 'real' and the 'virtual' as well as on the superficiality of the wall between the two. For example, Chayko (1993) asserts that the 'real' should be considered in terms of 'degrees' of reality, whereas Whitty (2003) theorises that virtual experiences are more aligned to Winnicott's concept of 'potential space'. This is developed from Winnicott's object-relations theory regarding 'play', which argues that illusion that is separated from the 'real' is the foundation of play. Winnicott (1997) defines potential space as somewhere 'between the subjective object and the object objectively perceived' (p. 100), a bridge between the 'inner' and 'outer' worlds. Whitty (2003) summarises that 'The potential space is not pure fantasy, nor is it pure reality' (p. 878).

The constructions of online rape as 'a game' and devoid of reality often used humour or insults to mock the very assertion that virtual rape existed. The implication that online actions could be abusive or harmful was considered complete 'rubbish' and 'absurd'. While this minimised the potential emotional impact of online versions of rape, or virtual rape, it constructed offline rape as particularly serious and dangerous. Therefore, rather than trivialising rape, the mocking of virtual rape was actually reinforcing the seemingly indisputable seriousness of offline rape. The emotional reactions described by many on the forums were not considered deserving of the label 'rape', and like the 'it's not me, it's you' discourse, those who were distressed by such actions were framed as unusual.

The definition of (offline) rape was based on 'dangerousness'—although this definition of 'dangerous' excluded emotional trauma. Fundamentally, virtual rape did not fulfil the definition of (offline) rape as ultimately life-threatening or physically precarious, which contrasts with the 'it's not me, it's you' discourse by prioritising the role of embodied trauma and experience. Therefore, embodied experience is the difference between fantasy and reality within this discourse. However, rather than arguing that images of rape should not be distressing, this discourse did not consider virtual rape as any form of abuse (representational or otherwise) due to the negation of reality on the part of victims as well as the virtual act of rape. In other words, if avatars are not 'real people' then there is no victim.

The separation of the virtual representations of users of online metaworlds (avatars) from their offline user counterparts created the illusion that only the individual user was 'real'. This replicates traditional gaming formats, prior to the advent of online multiplayer games, where one player would play on a console and all the other characters were computer operated. This was further reaffirmed by some users' description of online environments as, 'just a game'. Without recognition of an individual behind the avatar there was no 'real' victim for any sexual abuse to be acted out online and subsequently no consequences. However, in online metaworlds all the avatars are connected to, and controlled by, offline users. Some individuals noted concern over the dismissal of other users that resulted in an uncompromising and self-centred online space.

Many denied this connection to offline reality, referring to 'fake' bodies but failing to acknowledge that any 'fake' genitalia were a representation of a 'real' body. The threat of sexual violence in an online environment is only threatening due to the (offline) meaning attributed to it. For example, a 'fake' body would be connected to a real user who would be producing a real threat. The threat may not be physical contact with a 'real' penis, but whether it is harassment or verbal abuse, it would still be a sexualised threat. This construction of online and offline experience as mutually exclusive can be a mechanism for reducing responsibility for abusive actions. For example, material collected from a forum for another project distinguished between viewing explicit sexual images of child abuse and molesting children by arguing that the former was not as harmful.

Similarly, this negated the harm done to children in the making of pornography. Another consequence of the intersection of technology and sexuality, then, is the removal of associated responsibility due to the abuse being viewed as a depiction of harm, rather than intrinsically harmful or abusive.

Offline threats relating to online sexual predation were recognised when victims were children. For example, users stated that resources to prevent virtual rape would be better used to protect children from 'paedophiles' who used the Internet to groom victims. The construction of sex with children was deemed immoral and children were automatically classed as victims regardless of the actions of the child or perpetrator. This incorporated a definition of rape that required the victim to be vulnerable or naive due to a lack of experience or relevant knowledge. Within the context of online gaming, 'newbies' or new users are childlike due to a lack of knowledge regarding the environment as well as being inexperienced in navigating their way through the online world and controlling their own (virtual) body. Nevertheless, the inevitability of sexual aggression, as well as an emphasis on (female) victim responsibility were reiterated with conclusions that women needed to be taught how to escape a violent encounter. As women were expected to resist sexual aggression (the 'never surrender' discourse), and understand the meaning of sexual activity, the online sexual threat was not recognised as a genuine (offline) threat to adult women.

## COMMITTED TO CONSENT DISCOURSE

The negation of online victims, through the disconnection between online abuse and offline users, replicated the construction of rape role-play as always fully consensual. Some individuals compared virtual rape to rape role-play based on the assumption that there were no victims, but this perspective had a problematic construction of 'consent'. Due to the sexualised content of some online areas and games, it was often assumed that by entering the area women were consenting to all possible forms of sexual activity with any present avatar. Within this discourse, 'consent' was synonymous with 'permission' and once permission had been given, it could not be retracted; hence the individual is committed to consent. The commitment of perpetrators to define rape based on this very restrictive notion of consent, resulted in the dismissal of any subsequent evidence of resistance.

There were a multitude of potential actions that could be interpreted as sexual consent, including being in a sexualised or violent area, even if unconscious (or 'afk' which means 'away from keyboard') within this area. Once others had observed this 'consent', it could not be retracted no matter how much the women never surrendered. This consent was framed as a 'binding' social contract, but neglected the continual process of sexual consent. Consent to a rape role-play does not necessarily mean that any potential variation of rape role-play is acceptable to both individuals; this is why consent and the discussion of boundaries and safe words have such importance within BDSM communities (Ritchie and Barker 2005). However, the trivialisation of resistance and the sole focus on 'permission' resolved the complex myth that 'sometimes "no" really means "yes"' for some users.

This construction of resistance and evidence of non-consent as untrustworthy provides no means for women to stop an unwanted sexual activity. The potential impact of such experiences was minimised as impolite, which was due to the construction of virtual rape as a breach of social contract or a lapse in social etiquette.

## Discussion

Virtual rapes within online environments could be argued to be more 'real' than other media descriptions of rape as the computer code required to produce a rape within an online game uses language to produce an action. Therefore, it is a performative utterance (Austin 1979); the production of the computer code does not simply replicate the code on the screen, but transforms it into a visual and social action that is enacted on to others who are connected to the screen. It is not simply an image, but the participation of individuals actively entering language to produce a meaningful act that is done to others. Moreover, separating the verbal from the embodied, or the threat of violence from violence, assumes a hierarchy where physical trauma is considered most serious and verbal/visual attacks are harmless, except to those who have already been 'damaged' by 'real' violence. This construction underestimates the power of 'virtual' violence, where 'virtual' is defined as occurring in essence but not necessarily present. As many feminists have argued, the body does not need to be physically touched in the context of sexual violence (e.g. Kelly 1988). The symbolic body can be manifested through sexual innuendo; sexual 'jokes'; staring at women's bodies; or commenting on them. Even enacting/simulating sexual acts near or around an individual without touching them, draws on sexual intimidation techniques that require no physical contact to be effective (Langelan 1993).

These tactics are effective because they occur within a larger context of gender inequality and sexual violence. Women have reason to fear retaliation if the harasser dislikes their reaction (Langelan 1993). In a culture where ('physical') rape is a frequent occurrence, and the threat of rape is continually communicated through all forms of media (newspaper reports, film depictions, novels, online games and so on) the virtual violence within online metaworlds is another reminder that women are vulnerable. This upturns the infamous radical feminist slogan that 'all men are potential rapists' into 'all women are potential victims'. This awareness of vulnerability can result in women restricting their movements (Kelly 1988; Stanko 1985, 1990), being hypervigilant or avoiding particular places in attempts to minimise risk. As Langelan states:

> Harassment colors women's decisions at every level so deeply internalized that it may be almost unconscious: what to wear, what routes to take, where to sit or walk or stand, how to get through the day at work, how to get past a construction site or maneuver around that gang of teenage boys in the parking lot. (Langelan 1993, p. 37)

While it is unsurprising that virtual rapes were relegated to the category of 'sexual harassment' by several individuals, this category of sexual violence was positioned as less serious than rape. This underestimates the power of sexual harassment to threaten and intimidate women, as well as the relationship between sexual harassment and rape. For example, Stanko uses a variety of terms to refer to sexual harassment, including 'little rapes' (Stanko 1990, p. 97) and 'psychological rape' (Stanko 1985, p. 61). Kelly's continuum of sexual violence also included sexual harassment (Kelly 1988), and more recent conceptualisations, such as the feminist activist network 'Hollaback', describes such harassment generally as 'gender-based violence' and a 'gateway crime' which suggests a connection to sexual assault and rape ('HollaBack' 2012, para. 1).

Feminist conceptualisations of sexual harassment and rape are interconnected as they both involve the abuse or 'doing' of (male) power (Langelan 1993; Wise and Stanley 1987). This perspective redefined sexual harassment, from justifications that such acts were a result of unwanted sexual advances, to a form of aggression. As Langelan argues, 'Any rational male, acting on a genuine desire to interest a possible sexual partner, would quickly come to the realization that his best bet is to abandon this disastrous approach' that has women 'react[ing] with disgust, not desire, with fear, not fascination' (Langelan 1993, p. 39). She concludes that, 'Like rape, sexual harassment is designed to coerce women, not to attract them' (Langelan 1993, p. 40).

This difference in power is a result of male privilege, particularly in certain male-dominated environments. Therefore, virtual rape and online harassment function to keep online environments male dominated, as Kendall says, and, while the Internet has the potential to challenge gender norms, it is often used to reproduce them (Kendall 1999). This is in addition to sexual harassment/violence (Kimmel and Mahler 2003; Robinson 2005) being viewed as a key aspect of hegemonic masculinity. Therefore, rather than instances of virtual rape representing an aberration of online experience, they are part of a wider environment where sexual harassment/violence is the 'norm', due to the transposing of these offline masculine norms (Stanko 1985, 1990). Langelan asserts that male privilege is the reason that instances of harassment are an abuse of power (Langelan 1993), therefore online events of virtual rape and online harassment are closely related to constructions of technology as 'masculine' (Wajcman 2006) and women as incompetent 'technophobes' (e.g. Brosnan 2010) that function to subjugate women in the realm of technology. Positioning of men as superior in technological environments not only excludes women from learning how to use and develop forms of technology, but also reinforces an environment where women remain vulnerable to male violence.

Virtual rape is a serious phenomenon that requires feminist attention, as it has the potential to restrict women's access to online spaces, in addition to their limited role in producing and designing online technology, which remains relatively male dominated in the UK and US (Othman and Latih, n.d.). Langelan (1993) classes these online harassers as 'strategic and territorial harassers' who 'apply sexual harassment as a way to exclude women and protect their turf' (Langelan 1993, p. 42). Online spaces therefore replicate the offline sexual harassment of women in public spaces by strangers. While there has been debate regarding whether or not rape (or sex) can occur 'online', this neglects the blurring boundaries between 'online' and 'offline', as well as the unclear (or superficial) distinction between 'sexual harassment' and 'sexual violence'. The focus should not be on the act in isolation, but on the interaction. Interactions that involve sexual harassment/violence online still contain an abuse of power between two individuals, only the bodies are spaced further apart. As a gamer in Downing's research stated, 'Real people are doing real things to real people when they do them in game […] The only difference is that when it's done online, there's more space between you and the person you're speaking with' (Downing 2010, para. 2). Thus it is neither the violence nor the act that the definition is based on, but the space; the space between bodies, and the space that is inhabited (and dominated) by men.

## Conclusions

Developments in technology incite debates and discussions regarding the potential consequences of 'new' media, devices and means of communicating. Fears of 'cyberstalking' and 'virtual rape' frame such events as unique phenomena, separate from offline forms of violence and harassment. However, discussions that centre on the medium and the difference between online and offline environments neglect to consider the important commonalities that centre on gender inequality and abuse of power. The technology is fairly irrelevant (Miah 2000), as it is the interaction between individuals/genders (Kelly 1988) that results in violence, albeit through a communication medium. Consequently, the focus should not be on the novelty of the medium, but on the (unequal) interaction and, as other research has shown (e.g. Hughes 2000), technology only develops existing forms of abuse. It is gender inequality that creates environments where sexual violence/harassment occur.

**Acknowledgements** This chapter is from my doctoral dissertation submitted to Manchester Metropolitan University, UK. The author would like to thank Professor Erica Burman, Dr Geoff Bunn and Dr Asiya Siddiquee for their helpful feedback on an earlier version of this chapter.

## References

Antaki, C., M. Billig, D. Edwards, and J. Potter, 2003. 'Discourse analysis means doing analysis: A critique of six analytic shortcomings'. *Discourse Analysis Online, 1*, 1–24.
Austin, J., 1979. *Philosophical papers.* Oxford: Oxford University Press.

Benedikt, M., 1991. 'Introduction', in Benedikt M., ed. *Cyberspace: First Steps.* Cambridge MA: The MIT Press, pp. 1–25.

Brookey, R., and K. Cannon, 2009. 'Sex lives in Second Life'. *Critical Studies in Media Communication, 26,* 145–64.

Brosnan, M., 2010. 'Technophobia: The psychological impact of information technology'. Presented at the *Cyberpsychology & Computer Psychology Conference,* University of Bolton, UK.

Burt, M., 1980. 'Cultural myths and supports for rape'. *Journal of Personality and Social Psychology, 38,* 217–30.

Butler, J., 2004. 'The force of fantasy: Feminism, Mapplethorpe, and discursive excess', in Butler, J., and S. Salih, eds. *The Judith Butler Reader.* Oxford: Blackwell Publishing, pp. 183–203.

Chayko, M., 1993. 'What is real in the age of virtual reality? "Reframing" frame analysis for a technological world'. *Symbolic Interaction, 16,* 171–81.

Consalvo, M., 2012. 'Confronting toxic gamer culture: A challenge for feminist game studies scholars'. *Ada: A Journal of Gender, New Media, and Technology,* 1 (online; not paginated).

Cooper, A., I. McLoughlin, and K. Campbell, 2000. 'Sexuality in cyberspace: Update for the 21st Century'. *Cyberpsychology & Behaviour, 3,* 521–36.

Dibbell, J., 1998. *My tiny life: Crime and passion in a virtual world.* New York: Henry Holt & Company.

Dong, O., M. Urista, and D. Gundrum, 2008. 'The impact of emotional intelligence, self esteem and self image on romantic communication over MySpace'. *Cyberpsychology & Behaviour,* 11, 577–78.

Doring, N., 2009. 'The Internet's impact on sexuality: A critical review'. *Computers in Human Behaviours,* 25, 1089–1101.

Doring, N., 2000. 'Feminist views on cybersex: Victimization, liberation, and empowerment'. *Cyberpsychology & Behaviour,* 3, 863–84.

Downing, S., 2010. 'Online gaming and the social construction of virtual victimization'. *Eludamos: Journal for Computer Game Culture,* 4, 287–301.

Duranske, B., 2007. 'Reader roundtable: "Virtual rape" claim brings Belgian police to Second Life'. Retrieved 01.01.17 from http://virtuallyblind. com/2007/04/24/open-roundtable-allegations-of-virtual-rape-bring-belgian-police-to-second-life/.

Ehrlich, S., and R. King, 1992. 'Gender-based language reform and the social construction of meaning'. *Discourse & Society,* 3, 151–66.

Eklund, L., 2011. 'Doing gender in cyberspace: The performance of gender by female World of Warcraft players'. *Convergence* 17, 323–42.

Estrich, S., 1987. *Real rape: How the legal system victimizes women who say no.* London: Harvard University Press.

Finn, J., and M. Lavitt, 1994. 'Computer based self-help groups for sexual abuse survivors'. *Social Work With Groups,* 17, 41–6.

'Gang Rape Photos on Facebook', 2010. *CBC News.* Retrieved 01.01.17 from http://www.cbc.ca/news/canada/british-columbia/story/2010/09/15/bc-pitt-meadows-rave-assault.html.

Giles, D., 2006. 'Constructing identities in cyberspace: The case of eating disorders'. *British Journal of Social Psychology,* 45, 463–77.

Hamilton, M., 2012. 'Does Tomb Raider's Lara Croft really have to be the survivor of a rape attempt?' *The Guardian.* Retrieved 01.01.17 from http://www.theguardian.com/commentisfree/2012/jun/13/tomb-raider-lara-croft-rape-attempt.

Haraway, D., 1991. *Simians, cyborgs and women: The reinvention of nature.* New York: Routledge.

Harris, A. (2005). Discourses of desire as governmentality: Young women, sexuality and the significance of safe spaces. *Feminism & Psychology* 15 (1): 39–43.

Herbst, C., 2005. 'Shock and awe: Virtual females and the sexing of war'. *Feminist Media Studies,* 5, 311–24.

Hernandez, P., 2012. 'Three words I said to the man I defeated in Gears of War that I'll never say again'. Retrieved 01.01.17 from http://kotaku.com/5914348/three-words-i-said-to-the-man-i-defeated-in-gears-of-war-that-ill-never-say-again.

HollaBack 2012. Retrieved 01.01.17 from www.ihollaback.org.

Hollway, W., 1995. 'Feminist discourses and women's heterosexual desire', in Wilkinson, S., and C. Kitzinger, eds. *Feminism and Discourse: Psychological Perspectives.* London: Sage Publications, pp. 86–105.

Hookway, N., 2008. '"Entering the blogosphere": Some strategies for using blogs in social research'. *Qualitative Research,* 8, 91–113.

Houser, D., P. Kurowski, and J. Worrall, DMA Design, Rockstar Vienna, 2001. *Grant Theft Auto III.* Rockstar Games, New York.

Hughes, D. 1999. *Pimps and predators on the Internet: Globalizing the sexual exploitation of women and children.* Kingston, Rhode Island: The Coalition Against Trafficking in Women.

Hughes, D., 2000. '"Welcome to the Rape Camp": Sexual exploitation and the Internet in Cambodia'. *Journal of Sexual Aggression,* 6, 29–51.

Illusion, 1999. *Biko.* Author, Yokohama.

Illusion, 2000. *Biko 2.* Author, Yokohama.

Illusion, 2004. *Biko 3.* Author, Yokohama.

Illusion, 2006. *RapeLay.* Author, Yokohama.

Jones, S., 1995. 'Introduction: From where to who knows?' in Jones, S., ed., *Cybersociety: Computer-Mediated Communication and Community.* London: Sage Publications, pp. 1–9.

Kelly, L., 1988. 'What's in a name? Defining child sexual abuse'. *Feminist Review,* 28, 65–73.

Kendall, L., 1999. 'Recontextualizing "cyberspace": Methodological considerations for online research', in Jones, S., ed. *Doing Internet Research: Critical Issues and Methods for Examining the Net*. London: Sage Publications, pp. 57–73.

Kimmel, M., and M. Mahler, 2003. 'Adolescent masculinity, homophobia, and violence: Random school shootings'. *American Behavioral Scientist*, 46, 1439–58.

King, S., 1996. 'Researching Internet communities: Proposed ethical guidelines for the reporting of results'. *Information Society*, 12(2), 119–27.

Kramer, E., 2011. 'The playful is political: The metapragmatics of Internet rape-joke arguments'. *Language & Society*, 40, 137–68.

Krawczyk, M., A. Stein, D. Jaffe, and K. Fay, SCE Santa Monica Studio, 2005. *God of War*. Tokyo: Sony Computer Entertainment.

Langelan, M., 1993. *Back off! How to confront and stop sexual harassment and harassers*. New York: Simon and Schuster.

Martinez, M., and T. Manolovitz, 2010. 'Pornography of gaming', in Riha, D., ed., *Videogame Cultures and the Future of Interactive Entertainment*. Oxford: Inter-Disciplinary Press, pp. 65–74.

Miah, A., 2000. 'Virtually nothing: Re-evaluating the significance of cyberspace'. *Leisure Studies*, 19, 211–25.

Morahan-Martin, J., 2000. 'Women and the Internet: Promise and perils'. *Cyberpsychology & Behaviour*, 3, 683–91.

Muise, A., 2011. 'Women's sex blogs: Challenging dominant discourses of heterosexual desire'. *Feminism & Psychology*, 21, 411–19.

Mystique, 1982. *Custer's Revenge*. Los Angeles.

Nicolson, P., 1993. 'Public values and private beliefs: Why women refer themselves for sex therapy', in: Ussher, J., and C. Baker, eds., *Psychological Perspectives on Sexual Problems*. London: Routledge, pp. 56–76.

Othman, M., and R. Latih, n.d. 'Women in computer science: No shortage here!' *Communications of the Association for Computing Machinery (ACM)*, 49(3), 111–14.

Overgaard, P., 1994. 'The scale of terrorist attacks as a signal of resources'. *Journal of Conflict Resolution*, 38, 452–78.

Parker, I., 2014. *Discourse Dynamics: Critical Analysis for Social and Individual Psychology*. London: Routledge.

Potter, J., and M. Wetherell, 1987. *Discourse and social psychology*. London: Sage Publications.

Potts, A., 2002. *The Science/fiction of Sex: Feminist Deconstruction and the Vocabularies of Heterosex*. New York: Psychology Press.

Ranganath, R., D. Jurafsky, and D. McFarland, 2009. 'It's not you, it's me: Detecting flirting and its misperception in speed-dates', in *Proceedings of the 2009 Conference on Empirical Methods in Natural Language Processing*. pp. 334–42.

Reid, E., 1995. 'Virtual worlds: Culture and imagination', in: Jones, S., ed., *Cybersociety: Computer-Mediated Communication and Community*. Thousand Oaks: Sage Publications, pp. 164–83.

Ritchie, A., and M. Barker, 2005. 'Feminist SM: A contradiction in terms or a way of challenging traditional gendered dynamics through sexual practice?' *Lesbian & Gay Psychology Review*, 6, 227–39.

Robinson, K., 2005. 'Reinforcing hegemonic masculinities through sexual harassment: Issues of identity, power and popularity in secondary schools'. *Gender and Education*, 17, 19–37.

Rockstar Games, 1997. *Grand Theft Auto*. New York.

Ross, M. (2005). Typing, doing, and being: Sexuality and the internet. *Journal of Sex Research* 42 (4): 342–352.

Salih, S., 2004. 'Introduction', in Butler, J., and S. Salih, eds., *The Judith Butler Reader*. Oxford: Blackwell Publishing, pp. 1–18.

Schwendinger, J., and H. Schwendinger, 1974. 'Rape myths: In legal, theoretical, and everyday practice'. *Crime and Social Justice*, 1, 18–26.

Sethna, C., 1992. 'Accepting "total and complete responsibility": New age neofeminist violence against women'. *Feminism & Psychology*, 2, 113–19.

Shanahan, T., 2009. *The provisional Irish Republican Army and the morality of terrorism*. Edinburgh: Edinburgh University Press.

Sharf, B., 1999. 'Beyond netiquette: The ethics of doing naturalistic discourse research on the Internet', in Jones, S., ed., *Doing Internet Research: Critical Issues and Methods for Examining the Net*. London: Sage Publications, pp. 243–56.

Sixsmith, J., and C. Murray, 2001. 'Ethical issues in the documentary data analysis of Internet posts and archives'. *Qualitative Health Research*, 11, 423–32.

Sprecher, S., P. Schwartz, J. Harvey, and E. Hatfield, 2008. 'TheBusinessofLove.com: Relationship initiation and Internet matchmaking services', in Sprecher, S., ed., *Handbook of Relationship Initiation*. Hove: Psychology Press, pp. 249–68.

Stanko, E., 1985. *Intimate intrusions: Women's experience of male violence*. London: Unwin Hyman.

Stanko, E., 1990. *Everyday violence: How women and men experience physical and sexual danger*. London: Pandora.

'Steubenville Ohio School Footballers Guilty of Rape', 2013. *BBC News*. Retrieved 01.01.17 from http://www.bbc.co.uk/news/world-us-canada-21823042.

Tosh, J. (n.d.). 'Rape is no joke, but the conviction rate is'. Retrieved 1 August 2012 from https://www.facebook.com/groups/283163171718067/ (closed group).

Wajcman, J., 2006. 'TechnoCapitalism meets Technofeminism: Women and technology in a wireless world'. *Labour & Industry*, 16, 7–20.

Weedon, C., 1996. *Feminist Practice and Poststructuralist Theory*. London: Wiley.

White-McAuley, J., 1999. 'Still "no surrender"? New Loyalism and the peace process in Ireland', in: Harrington, J., and E. Mitchell, eds., *Politics and Performance in Contemporary Northern Ireland*. Massachusetts: University of Massachusetts Press, pp. 41–56.

White, P., 2014. 'On the trail of Amanda Todd's alleged tormentor'. *The Globe and Mail*. Retrieved 01.01.17 from http://www.theglobeandmail.com/news/world/on-the-trail-of-amanda-todds-alleged-tormentor/article18935075/?page=all.

Whitty, M., 2003. 'Cyber-flirting: Playing at love on the Internet'. *Theory Psychology*, 13, 339–57.

Wilford, R., 1996. 'Women and politics in Northern Ireland'. *Parliamentary Affairs*, 49(1), 41–54.

Winnicott, D., 1997. *Playing and reality*. London: Tavistock.

Wiseman, E., 2013. 'The Slane girl Twitter scandal proves that women can't make mistakes'. *The Guardian*. Retrieved 01.01.17 from http://www.theguardian.com/lifeandstyle/2013/sep/01/slane-girl-twitter-scandal-women.

Wise, S., and L. Stanley, 1987. *Georgie Porgie: Sexual harassment in everyday life*. London: Pandora Press.

Wood, E. 2008. Consciousness-raising 2.0: Sex blogging and the creation of a feminist sex commons. *Feminism & Psychology* 18(4): 480–487.

# CHAPTER 9

# Heteronormativity as a Painful Script: How Women with Vulvar Pain (re)Negotiate Sexual Practice

*Renita Sörensdotter*

Sexual practices, or a lack of them, are part of everyday life that, in relation to cultural norms, constitute us as subjects. How we perform our sexuality is organised by what society, culture and the environment regard as good and bad sex, or not at all sexual. People with reduced sexual ability must actively respond to sexual discourses on what is considered 'normal' sexuality, since they are unable to perform certain expected sexual practices. Women with pain in the genital area, especially when the pain is localised to the vaginal opening, have difficulties with vaginal intercourse. This is particularly true for those living a heterosexual life, when they end up in a position of not being able to meet the ideal of vaginal intercourse. The 'script' for heterosexual sex assumes vaginal intercourse to be a given part of the sex act (cf. Hite 1976, 1981; Segal 1994). The sexual practice that is taken for granted is challenged. But the difficulty of participating in vaginal intercourse has different effects depending not only on the woman's age and sexual experiences, but also on how her partners and others regard sex.

R. Sörensdotter (✉)
University of Uppsala, Uppsala, Sweden
e-mail: renita.sorensdotter@gender.uu.se

© The Author(s) 2017
E. Rees (ed.), *Talking Bodies*, DOI 10.1007/978-3-319-63778-5_9

163

In this chapter I will show how norms for gender and (hetero)sexuality affect sexual practices, and how the sexual practices themselves challenge or reinforce sexual norms. The focus is on how the body's actions in relation to cultural norms contribute to shaping the subject and its space for (re)negotiation. I examine empirical material which comes from interviews with women who have had, or who continue to have, pain in the genital area, and who thus have difficulty in participating in vaginal intercourse. Norms for a gender-specific sexuality affect what is seen as sexually possible and impossible.

## VULVAR PAIN

As an anthropologist, I am more interested in cultural processes and meaning-making than in exact diagnoses; therefore I will not define my informants' diagnoses. Instead, focus is placed on the impact of their problems and how the informants relate them to discourses of gender, sexuality, and sexual practice. But to give an idea of the problems, I will briefly describe the diagnoses: vulvar vestibulitis/provoked vestibulodynia; vulvodynia; and partial vaginismus.

When suffering from vulvar vestibulitis/provoked vestibulodynia (the name of the diagnosis has shifted to the latter recently) the pain is localised at the vaginal entrance.[1] Some informants also have widespread pain across large sections of the vulvar area and would most likely be diagnosed with vulvodynia, which means a more generalised pain. At the same time, some of my informants have both generalised pain throughout the vulvar area, and distinct pain in the vaginal opening. Many also suffer from partial vaginismus as a result of vestibulitis, since the pelvic floor muscles become tense due to vulvar pain.[2]

Vulvar pain causes difficulties with sexual practice, especially with vaginal penetration, whether with a dildo, fingers or a penis (use of tampons, and gynaecological examinations are also problematic). The age at which the pain starts varies, but sufferers are usually in their teens at onset. Some informants have had pain from the first moment of penetration, for others the pain arrived after a few years of painless sex, leading to a different experience than if the pain has been there from the beginning. Those who have had pain after a few years of sexual activity report many other problems, especially repeated yeast infections[3]; overuse of medication for yeast infections; bacterial vaginosis; delicate mucous membranes; cracks; and sex including vaginal penetration despite continued itching, burning sensations and sharp pain.

## METHODOLOGY, MATERIAL AND ANALYSIS

I conducted semi-structured interviews with 21 women who have or have had vulvar pain. Informants were recruited through different internet forums; blogs about vestibulitis; and through personal contacts. Three of the women no longer suffer from pain; the others continue to experience pain. For all of the informants, problems started when they were teenagers. At the time of the interviews, the women's ages varied between 18 and 39 years old, and all of the women lived in Sweden. Fifteen of the interviewed women primarily practised heterosexual sex; one of them, despite not having had any experience of sex with women, defined herself as bisexual. Four had experiences of having sex with both women and men. One only had sex with women. One had no sexual experience with others at all.

The interviews were 60–150 min long and focused on the informants' own perceptions of themselves, the body, gender positions, sexual experience, relationships, and meetings with healthcare professionals. The stories are intense and voluminous and contain narratives from adolescence until adulthood. Interviews are, of course, also shaped in relation to other people's stories and cultural forms of storytelling (Stanley 1992; Good 1994). Life stories are constructed on the basis of selected parts of life where the events are interpreted and made into a culturally-shaped story structure. The interviewer's questions are shaping the story. I myself am comfortable talking about sexuality, but given that some people perceive it as too intimate, I left it open for informants to choose for themselves how much they wanted to be explicit. Most informants quite openly told me about their experiences of, and reflections on, the body, sexuality and relationships. Since this chapter focuses on sexual practice, and the body, it examines only a fraction of the huge amount of material that arose from the interviews.

In the interpretation of the material I have used discourse analysis to focus on how these women talked about, and related to, both hegemonic and alternative discourses of gender, sexuality and sexual practice (Burr 1995; Jørgensen and Phillips 2000). I assume that people are entangled in various discourses, with varying degrees of ability to influence, and break, the norms. In descriptions of sexual practices, I particularly searched for how informants talked of (hetero)sexuality, and how queer 'leakage' is produced by the stories. Making queer readings means analysing the material in relation both to normative heterosexuality and to the challenges of heteronormativity (Rosenberg 2002).

## EMBODIED SEXUALITY

The body becomes a central element in analysing sexual practice. Judith Butler argues that the materiality of the body is formed by the normative regulatory discourses in which it exists. No 'natural' unregulated body can be found; the body can only be interpreted and made sense of culturally. Norms for gender and sexuality determine how bodies are expected to act, in a way that shows identification with attributed sex (Butler 1990, 1993; see also Grosz 1994). In order to be an understandable and identifiable person, one is required to perform certain bodily actions, and, in a heteronormative culture, certain gender performances are expected. Although heterosexual sex is not always the same as heteronormative sex, heteronormativity structures the interpretations one can make about sexual practice (Butler 1990; Beasley 2010).

To imagine that discourses shape bodily materiality is, however, a narrow perspective, since the lived body is affected by situations that transform one's perception of self. Our body's material actions constitute, amplify and question gender identification. Elizabeth Grosz (1994) argues, with inspiration from the philosopher Spinoza, that the body is a process of continuous becoming. The body is active and productive. It both affects, and is affected by, other bodies (Grosz 1994; see also Deleuze 1992; Gatens 1996). Sexual practice affects bodies that meet, and bodies transform each other through the sexual practice that is performed. As we shall see, bodies are filled with meaning by the gender and the form of sexuality they enact. Bodies that come together sexually are also specific and shaped by discursive formations of gender, sexuality, class, race, ethnicity and body shape (Grosz 1994).

Sexuality is a concept that includes a multiplicity of actions, feelings, experiences, sensations and processes, in addition to policies, legislation and the media (Grosz 1994). Given that I take sexual acts as my focus I will confine my discussion to those practices categorised as 'sexual' in relation to sexual orientation or direction, that is, which bodies are desired sexually, and how sexual practice is constructed by, and constructs, the subject. In sexual practice, different conceptions and practices are brought together and shape the sexual situation, which may vary with time and partners. Perceptions about how sex 'should' be done may collide with the body's materiality and agency.

John H. Gagnon and William Simon argue that the sexual self is formed in relation to the gender-specific self. They place sexuality in everyday life, in an awareness of sex, but their use of the term 'sexual script' shows that there is a culturally constructed sexual dramaturgy, which interacts with interpersonal and intrapsychological sexual scripts.[4] Sexual scripts are interpreted, reinterpreted and put together in different ways, which may explain the varying ways in which individuals integrate and relate to sexual practices (Gagnon and Simon 1973; Simon 1966). This is in line with how Butler (1990) describes sexuality; the social governance of what is considered sex is produced culturally. Individually, however, the subject is constituted through a diversity of discourses. Normative images of how sexuality *should* be performed are created; while sexuality varies on an individual level. Discourses are diverse and paradoxical and there is space for movement and change. Vivien Burr (1995) mentions the concept of the 'skilled discourse-user' in order to show how, through knowledge of how discourses are organised, we can reflect on and compare various discourses and thus challenge a lifestyle portrayed as normative. The various sexual scripts a person encounters can thus be set up against each other, and challenged or upheld. For those women who experience vulvar pain, both their sexual practice and their relationship to their own bodies are changed (Sörensdotter 2012). When the body changes, the individual's experience of self is challenged, and a process of reclaiming and coming to terms with the body and identity starts (Seymour 1998).

## REAL SEX = VAGINAL INTERCOURSE

Which bodily interactions can be categorised as *actual* sex is not very clear. Several informants say that sex can be almost anything like cuddling, touching, oral sex and penetration, but for some informants, it is hard to imagine that sexual practices other than vaginal intercourse can be counted as 'real' sex. When I talk about non-penetrative sex with Christina, a 28-year-old female who has been pain-free for a few years, she says: 'I think it is mostly like foreplay. [...] It feels as if it is not completed. Like maybe taking a break and then one should do it for real'. She does not feel that she has been pressured to have vaginal intercourse: 'We should have non-penetrative sex, but when I was ill then I thought "no, but it's not for real". In some way, one is so orientated towards the performance, it [the penis] should go in, otherwise it is not for real. Although he may not actually have thought it was necessary'.

To make sex 'real' requires a very specific sexual act, 'it should go in' as Christina says—otherwise it's not really sex. Sexual acts such as oral sex, touching, and so on, are simply called other forms of sex by several informants. The sexual acts performed are graded in a hierarchy. Most informants having sex with men think that 'sex' is the same as vaginal intercourse, even if they point to other ways to enjoy sexuality, as Magdalena says: 'If I think sex, I think of penetrative sex'. In theory, sex can be all sorts of sexual pleasure, but in practice it means vaginal intercourse (Lundgren and Sörensdotter 2004). Vaginal intercourse is what is 'natural' and therefore desirable. The cultural script for heterosexual sex sets the agenda for what can be counted as real sex.

Since vaginal intercourse is presented as central to the heterosexual sex act, many of the informants tried to participate in it in spite of the pain. For some informants, vaginal intercourse brought so much pleasure that they did not want to give it up, and expected a certain amount of pain. Alexandra, who is 31 years old, says that sometimes, when the desire for vaginal intercourse sex is there, she calculates that it will hurt for a couple days afterwards, but that the pleasure is sometimes worth the pain: 'I can still have good penetrative sex and think it is nice though it hurts. [...] Yes, it will hurt and it will hurt afterwards, but it's worth it'. That the pain is mixed with pleasure makes it more difficult to handle for 36-year-old Kim: 'There is both pleasure and pain, for it is nice in there, but it hurts on the outside, or more at the entrance'. To opt out of vaginal penetration when it is pleasurable can feel difficult. It should be added that for some of the informants, it is neither possible nor desirable to have vaginal penetrative sex. Some also believe that they have great sex without vaginal penetration.

It is not always desire that drives women to participate in vaginal intercourse; some have a relationship where it is difficult to refrain from participating in it. Magdalena explains that she is trying to find ways to manage vaginal intercourse:

Magdalena:    I have sex anyway even though it hurts, I still have it and somehow I need it.

Renita:    Why?

Magdalena:    I do not know, for my peace of mind I think. The physical pain is less than the mental. But one can find positions that work better than others, because one has different spots that

are very sore and some positions works so that they do not
lie and press the spots all the time. It works, but it is not perfect and it has hurt every time, but it's bearable.

In Magdalena's case, beliefs about how sex 'should' be done force her
to continue. Most informants go along with sex (in the sense of vaginal
intercourse) even though they do not want to, sometimes because their
partner nags; sometimes for fear of losing their partner; and, above all,
because having sex in a specific manner is included in a couple's relationship (cf. Elmerstig 2009). Christina talks about how she got tired of difficult sexual practices that were filled with interruptions. After a half-year
break from sex she made a choice: 'Then I thought if I'm going to have
this my whole life, then I have to accustom myself to the pain. [...] I
told Micke that "It's over now, there is no pain". So we kept on having
sex for a year I think, although it was very painful'. To go through with
vaginal intercourse in spite of the severe pain increased Christina's pain
and led to constant lies to her partner. She wanted the sexual practice
in the relationship to flow smoothly, not because her partner had been
pressurising her (he was happy to have other forms of sexual practice),
but because of the belief that a sexual relationship must include vaginal
intercourse to be full and complete.

Lisa, who is 32 years old and no longer suffers from vulvar pain,
reports that in her teens she had a sympathetic boyfriend, but that she
herself was fixated on going through with vaginal intercourse:

> My boyfriend said, 'No, we do not need to have sexual intercourse' and
> 'We can have sex in a lot of other ways', but still I felt every time we had
> sex it was a stress. So then I bit into the pillow, and did not show, because
> I had the notion then, which I thankfully don't have now, about what sex
> should be; that it should always end with vaginal penetration.

With distance, several informants say that they do not understand how
they could have treated themselves so badly. As Kim says: 'What I get
angry at is that I myself have done it so many times though it has been
painful, and faked that it hasn't been painful, like that stuff, it is quite
bizarre that one exposes oneself to it'. Or, as Simone explains: 'I felt that
I was very active in this. [...] It was very important for me to be able to
do this and have it, and I don't think they [her sexual partners] understood the magnitude of what happened'. Several of those who no longer
participate in vaginal intercourse refer to age when they talk about why

they had vaginal intercourse in spite of the pain. They say they were younger then and did not understand that they should listen to their own bodies, and many think in retrospect that the pain was too high a price to pay.

It is possible to call the above mentioned sexual practice 'go-along-sex'. These women participate in vaginal intercourse because they want to feel like 'normal' heterosexual women having vaginal intercourse. Many perceive themselves not to be 'real' women if they are unable to participate in vaginal intercourse (Kaler 2006; Ayling and Ussher 2008; Sörensdotter 2012). They fulfil their prescribed gender norms by participating in vaginal intercourse despite the pain. In interactions with their partners, they take responsibility for performing their gender accurately. Vaginal intercourse is a way to prove one's heteronormative gender.

Another form of sex that is not based on the desire for having sex is 'nag sex'. Magdalena describes her previous boyfriend as reckless: 'He told me it was my problem, I should solve it. [...] He would rather have sex even if it hurt me, than try to cancel, because he thought it was so terrible for him. So then I went on to have sex even if it hurt'. Her current partner, by contrast, is very careful and stops immediately if he notices that Magdalena gets the slightest pain. They also try with various forms of sex and sex positions. However, the years spent with the former boyfriend still affect Magdalena: 'I have a lot of values remaining from that time. [...] I am unfortunately caught up in that idea that I do not want to be different. [...] Thus we can have oral sex, it is no problem, but then all of a sudden I think that I have to have penetrative sex'. Alexandra talks about a boyfriend who did not want to do the exercises a sexologist recommended for giving pleasure to one partner at a time. The boyfriend thought that sex had to be a merging; therefore he always wanted to have vaginal intercourse. Alexandra often went along with sex when she was younger to 'put a stop to the nagging' and because she was afraid of being left.

Having vaginal intercourse despite the pain is relatively common. Midwife Eva Elmerstig (2009) showed that out of 1,566 women aged 18–22 years, 47% went on to have vaginal intercourse even though they experienced pain. The study involved only women who have sex with men. The reasons these women gave for their participation in painful activities were that they were afraid of losing their boyfriends; they wanted to be a good girlfriend; and they wanted to satisfy their partner. Normative heterosexual relationships are based on the idea that the woman takes responsibility for the relationship, the feelings, and for the other's well-being. As a result, she also takes responsibility for the man's well-being and feels guilty if she cannot meet what she perceives to be his requirements (Holmberg 1993; Martinsson 1997). In the relationship, the body, and especially in this case the genitals, become an object that is being sacrificed in order to satisfy the partner, to keep the relationship stable and to gloss over problems with sexual intercourse.

## SEX IN A RELATIONSHIP

In long-term (heterosexual) relationships some of the women experienced guilt, and blamed themselves for the 'failed' sex act. Anna, who is 30 years old and has been married to her husband for ten years, has never been able to participate in vaginal intercourse. She is relatively satisfied with their sex life and thinks they are creative in their sexuality. But there are some concerns:

> Olle does not want it to be like this. And neither do I, of course, but it is. I feel sometimes like the villain, because I'm the one being wrong. […] If I had been the one to decide I'd be happy, but for Olle sometimes, it's a little difficult to accept, even after 10 years together [*sigh*]. But then, I am like this: 'But Olle we have so much variation and there is so much else to do, think how sad it is for those who only have the same sex the whole time'.

Anna has a good sex life, but her husband's needs pose a concern, although she describes him as nice and sympathetic.

As an effect of the genital pain, some of the women also sense a lack of desire. They are the ones constantly pulling away from their partners, saying 'no' and having to cancel sexual activities, as Alexandra explains: 'Never to be able to take the initiative yourself makes you turn off. Never to be the one who has lust first makes you become […] You end up at a disadvantage. You get a strange sexual power balance'. Alexandra explains further: 'That you never ever can be the one becoming horny first […] makes you a little disgusted by the other's sexuality. […] Male sexuality in this case becomes unpleasant'.

Sex, and the practices that it is possible to perform, have a certain status in the couples' relationships. Vaginal intercourse especially has such high status that it is difficult to renegotiate. It is not only in steady heterosexual relationships that vaginal intercourse is taken for granted;

the same goes for those who are single and looking for a male partner. Heterosexual informants without a partner experience a certain fear about telling prospective partners about their inability to participate in vaginal intercourse. Two of the women use the term 'false advertising', as 23-year-old Amelie explains: 'It's hard to even think about flirting and think about relationships and children; because no one wants a girl you cannot fuck'. It is not the pain that is difficult to explain, but the sexual inability in relationship to the heterosexual norm about how sex should be performed. Sandra, who is single, says that the norm today is to have sex on the first date and that it is consequently difficult for her to think about dating. She becomes the 'weird' one among her friends because she does not date men:

> Then I get this fear, to go home with someone the first time. [...] I think that guys can sometimes be a little clumsy, just put in their finger, you know this typical electrical whisk. Then I haven't any control. [...] Otherwise, I have to say: 'We're not going to have intercourse', because it feels like that is what guys expect that you should have.

The heterosexual script means that vaginal intercourse is expected to be included in sex, regardless of whether the woman is in a relationship with a man, or is single and looking for a man. Some feel that it is easiest to be single in order to avoid having to explain, and so as not to be expected to have vaginal intercourse, as Magdalena says: 'I felt that I was feeling better when I was single, because I did not have this pressure on me to have sex. [...] And I had really decided that I'd be single for now, because I cannot feel so psychologically bad again and have the pressure on to have sex all the time'. Magdalena told her boyfriend about the pain and the problems with vaginal intercourse after only a few weeks into the relationship. He took it well and has been very helpful in the treatment and is clear that he does not want to have vaginal intercourse in a way that hurts Magdalena. For Magdalena, however, it is difficult to let go of the idea that they must have sex with a certain frequency: 'Sometimes we have sex maybe a couple of days a week, and it's quite good because then I don't have to go around and think that now we must soon have sex again. I think about that very often: "It's been a long time"; "It's been many days"; "I feel sorry for him" and so on'. Apparently, single life was less complicated for Magdalena. Sandra also thinks it is difficult not being able to have vaginal intercourse: 'As soon as we began to make out, fondle, or anything, it was there: something I cannot do, I will not be able to endure the final stage. [...] I don't want to give him false hope'.

The women's statements say a lot about perceptions of men's sexuality. Men are portrayed as if they have to have vaginal intercourse, otherwise they will be unsatisfied and unhappy. An additional image of men's sexuality is that some of the women are stressing their gratitude at having a man who can do without vaginal intercourse, even when their male partner is satisfied and happy with their sex life. Shere Hite (1981) has shown that vaginal intercourse is important to most men having heterosexual sex, but a lot of men do not always want vaginal intercourse; they want more variety. Many also feel pressured by always being the one responsible for the sex act and for mutual orgasms. Several men also describe that they get more powerful orgasms through manual stimulation—above all by their own masturbation, while vaginal intercourse fills other functions, of closeness and being enclosed. Similar stories emerge in Hite's (1976) study of women; they get the most intense orgasms by masturbation and manual stimulation of the clitoris, while vaginal intercourse stands for closeness and intimacy.

Sexuality as practice is historically and culturally shaped, but it is also defined by interpersonal social interactions. Stories about sexual practice and what direction the desire takes can be found at the cultural level, as well as in people's own experiences. The informants talk about heterosexual sex as a prescribed script. First, foreplay; then the main act in the form of vaginal penetration by the penis; and a finale when the man has ejaculated. Even if there are stories about a variety of sexual practices, this script remains as the dominant frame of reference. Shere Hite's reports on women and men and their sexual lives very much confirm this, even though around 30 years have passed since the reports were published. Hite shows that problematic sexuality is, to a degree, based on a lack of knowledge and communication; many sexual interactions are based on beliefs about what women and men are expected to do in heteronormative practice (Hite 1976, 1981).

## THE LESBIAN DREAM

In relation to problematic (hetero)sexual practice, some heterosexual informants revealed that they wished they were lesbians, because it would allow them to have sex without a pressure to participate in vaginal intercourse. There would be no guilt, just pleasure. Everything would be easier. In this 'lesbian dream' we can find aspects of freedom and sexual negotiation. It is a dream where women are free to shape their own scripts for sexual practice. Lisa has given much thought to the status of penetration: 'I think now, if I had had sex with women, if it had been, but you cannot know, it's just what you might think, but it is precisely that [heterosexual sex] is so fixated with penetration'. Lesbian sexual practice is not expected to be fixated on penetration in the same way that heterosexual sex is. Several informants expressed a suspicion towards men and their sexuality, based on the experience they had of painful sex. Amelie, who feels a certain hostility towards men precisely because several have treated her badly, has a particular desire to have sex with women: 'I usually joke that I'm going to become a lesbian when I grow up. [*laughter*] I don't know, but I'm working on it'. Ellinor, who has also had difficult experiences with men, claims she no longer sees herself as heterosexual, although she has not yet had sex with any women.

The researcher Tasmin Wilton (2004) conducted focus group interviews with heterosexual women about their views on lesbian life and lesbian sexuality. Interestingly similar responses about the lesbian dream were revealed. The women in Wilson's study felt that a relationship with a woman would bring benefits such as intimacy, trust, better sexual satisfaction, equal responsibility and empathy. In addition, they would be freed from the bad parts of relationships with men such as poor hygiene, an obsession with computer games and sports, and overconsumption of alcohol. These women have—like my informants who dream of lesbian relationships as a kind of rescue—no, or only limited, experience of same-sex relationships. The lesbian dream does not show how women having sex with women are experiencing sexuality and everyday life, but rather reveals how heterosexual women *imagine* a more straightforward and more satisfying sexuality than they have experienced with men (Wilton 2004; see also Hite 1987).

The lesbian dream is most likely not a yearning for a lesbian identity, since this would mean to enter into a 'deviant' identity, having to 'come out'. Sexual identity and practice have in this case different meanings. Longing for the lesbian life is all about longing for another sexual practice in which sexuality is based on one's own desires; longing for a more intimate relationship. Sexual identification as a lesbian would involve a life transformation. The confusion of practice and identity shows the problems with the concept of sexual orientation as something true and delimited as an identity, since it prevents people from seeking a sexual pleasure which is most compatible with their own ability and willingness to partake in a particular sexual practice.

The four women who have experiences of having sex with both men and women describe sexual practice with women as more free and enjoyable, as Kim explains: 'I think it has been easier with women since we can choose what we want to do. There are so many different ways to do it. If I don't want her to get into me with a dildo just today, it is enough with a finger or nothing at all'. For Moa, the experience of having sex with women was a clear shift in her room for manoeuvre and influence in sexual negotiations:

> I could go into a different role sexually and become more, well, drop something [become less inhibited], I think, even though it is still a little problematic for me with sex. I became braver and could express more what I wanted. And to be the one who did more. The other way around I'm always the one that gets done to, I think, it is very much that way with men.

Moa takes the active role in sexual encounters with women, in contrast to her experience of sex with men where they have been more active, and so she has adopted a more passive role. Moa can still be attracted to men, but she opposes the form of sexuality that is expected of her: 'I get a bit panicked by the feeling that I would have sex with a man and that his dick would decide that it wants to enter me, and I don't want that'. For Moa, gender norms in relation to desired sexual acts stand in the way of an active negotiation of how sexual practice could be enacted with men. One explanation may be, as Alexandra says, that norms for sexuality are different for those who have sex with women: 'The sex one has with men is incredibly defined. The sex one has with women is not. Because there you decide on your own what to do'. Nowadays, Alexandra mainly has sex with women. She also practices BDSM in a dominant position and that means that she has even more control over her sexuality and sexual negotiation: 'You don't put up with BDSM [*laughter...*] It is much easier. [...] You have a different kind of sex. Vestibulitis is no handicap whatsoever. Especially since I'm dominant'.

Same-sex sexual practice is less pre-choreographed than heterosexual practice. There is more space to select practices that could be part of sexual interaction. In particular, it is possible to opt out of vaginal penetration without it becoming strange in relation to one's sexual partners. The Kinsey report on women's sexual behaviour showed that women prefer the sort of sexual practices that appear in lesbian sex. Women who have sex with women showed higher levels of orgasm. The report equated this with men's supposed inability to relate to women's sexual needs (Kinsey et al. 1953; see also Hite 1987).

## THE SPECIAL MAN

In a similar way to the talk of a freer lesbian sexuality, some women claim they have better sex with more cautious men. They describe this type of man as reluctant to take sexual initiatives, not pushing the sexual situation, but letting the woman do it; the same is true for men who are more interested in women's pleasure than their own, or who simply find their own enjoyment through women's pleasure. Kajsa, who is 30 years old, distinguishes clearly between men rushing into vaginal intercourse and men who let her take the initiative and decide whether to engage in vaginal intercourse or not. She was in a relationship with a man she describes as shy and cautious: 'There I found a sex life that was amazing. I got the time to listen to myself. I controlled the sex act. I decided if we were going to have penetrative sex. Then I had time to be turned on'. Kajsa and others suggest, however, that this kind of man is difficult to find, as Moa puts it: 'It might be quite different with a man too, but then it would be a quite special man, a very open man who also wanted to do it differently'.

Simone, who along with her first boyfriend was experimenting sexually, and who therefore had a good experience of sex with a man without fixation on vaginal intercourse, still believes it is easier to have sex with women. She sees few opportunities to meet men who can handle the kind of sexuality in which she is interested: 'Thus for me this coming out thing, it was very much just this, what a fucking relief to get rid of that heterosexual dramaturgy in sex. [...] So I would certainly be able to achieve that kind of sexuality, but which man would like that, is more my problem today'. Like some other informants, Simone means that these particular men are hard to find. Kim has not sought special men, but has tried to change the sexual practice in her existing relationships with men, but without much success:

> When you turn the roles, when I've done it and played [...] then they become so embarrassed, they are so unaccustomed to being the object.

[...] 'I want to watch you'; 'Shouldn't you stand there?' but then he becomes totally embarrassed by being looked at like that. [...] I have been doing that so much, so in all of the relationships, in the few relationships I've had with men, there has been so much fucking fuss about this kind of stuff. It has never been relaxed, but I have been so angry and provoked because I do things that I don't want and then I get mad at him because he is a man. [...] And then it's much easier with women.

The desire to be met with sexual creativity has not been successful for Kim. Instead, sex with men becomes awkward and disruptive. In the stories about 'special' men and attempts to transform sexual practice, it becomes clear that the majority of men are reluctant to change the heterosexual dramaturgy. However, as we have seen, there are informants who have a relatively good sexual life with their partners, although the heterosexual norm of vaginal intercourse as the only real sex persists.

## Renegotiations of Sexual Practice

Women living with vulvar pain must find strategies to deal with their experiences of the body and (im)possible sexual practices. Sometimes strategies lead to an enriched sex life; sometimes the inability to have vaginal intercourse feels like an ever-present lack. One strategy is for the woman to have control over the pace, pressure, intensity and position when having vaginal intercourse. Another strategy is that the woman takes all sexual initiative and stops when it does not feel good. She can choose to sit on top and control the pace during vaginal intercourse. Alexandra says that if people want to have penetrative sex in spite of the pain, 'then they should try to find out how to do it in the best way. [...] I don't think you should get caught up too much in making it impossible for one to have sex, but to think that there are other ways to do it'. She believes that it is important to find solutions, instead of getting distracted by physical limitations. To renegotiate sexual strategies and communicate about sexual preferences, however, is not simple, because sexual scripts are incorporated and made to seem natural. Sandra is not used to taking initiatives in how the sex act will be formed, but she practises thinking in new ways: 'Where I try to get better, I am the one that directs sex and I practise what I want: "I'd like to do this; you would want to do this"'.

Some, however, completely avoid vaginal intercourse and focus on other forms of sex or abstain completely from sexual activity. An important part of sexual renegotiation is time and age; it becomes easier to renegotiate sexuality with increased experience. Tove is 28 years old and has seen significant changes over time:

> When it started it was really hard. [...] There is a lot of different sex you can have, but it still feels like a loss somehow not being able to have penetrative sex. There have been quite a lot of tears and attempts and I've become really disappointed with myself because it's not possible. [...] But in recent years, this has not been the case: I've accepted it. Sure it is sad and I also know that it can be very nice to have penetrative sex, but then I think a lot is about that picture of what real sex is, the idea. But we have talked a lot about it, me and my boyfriend. Yes, it's been a journey that way, to learn about myself and my partner.

In a similar way to some other informants, Tove has learned to transform and manage her sexual practice through different experiences over a long period of time. In such a renegotiation of sexual practice, there is still sometimes a liability over the body's inability to participate in vaginal intercourse, as Anna says: 'There is some kind of internal pressure on me because I'm trying really to do everything for Olle, nothing like that creepy and disgusting in any way, but I always try, so that he is satisfied and happy, and then I'm satisfied and happy if he is happy and pleased'. Anna enjoys, as mentioned earlier, their sex life, but the thought that she cannot take part in vaginal intercourse still disturbs her. They try vaginal intercourse quite often even though Anna is satisfied with their sex life: 'Once we're together it's good. It's always good. It's just that it's not good in the real way, then: I have that in the back of my mind all the time. [...] But I'm always happy and Olle is too. He says he is, in any case. I don't know if he's lying to me, but I'm satisfied'.

Vulvar pain has meant that several of the women (and their partners) have been forced to challenge the norms of sexual practice. By the body's inability fully to participate in vaginal intercourse some women have been exploring more opportunities for sex. They have thereby as skilled discourse-users started positioning different sexual discourses against each other. A person with bodily pain has to relate to the body in a different way. If the pain is prolonged, constant, and distracting, it changes the conditions of one's way of life. The actions of the body need to be reorganised and the body reorganises itself (Seymour 1998; Sörensdotter 2012). Wendy Seymour (1998) describes the process as a recreation of the body as lived experience and a change in how the body is used.

## Sexual Norms and Sexual Practice

Vaginal intercourse between a man and a woman is seen as both normal and expected. To be understood as a heterosexual woman, vaginal intercourse with a man is a normative performative act of gender. When vaginal intercourse cannot be done, sexual practice is either absent or transformed. Some women are renegotiating their sexual practice over time, but the notion of 'real' sex as vaginal intercourse, is maintained as a reference point for those women living heterosexual lives, even when the body shows that other sexual practices are more beneficial. Women who have sex with women are situated in a queer context where sexual practice is less culturally choreographed and they therefore have greater opportunities to negotiate their sexual practice than women living heterosexually. There is, in other words, more room for sexual negotiation in a queer context that does not follow heteronormative sexual scripts.

Due to heterosexual normalised practice, that is, vaginal intercourse, culture has already formed the script for how sex should be carried out. The discourses of sexual acts are in a way pre-negotiated. Regardless of references to norms of sexuality, my informants, and other research on sexuality, reveal various sexual practices. Kinsey and his co-researchers showed in the 1940s the variety and diversity of people's sexual practices. They challenged the notion that people are either hetero- or homosexual simply by studying people's sexual acts (Kinsey et al. 1948, 1953; see also Jackson and Scott 2010). The Kinsey reports have been followed by research that indicates sexual variation across the world. Ford and Beach (1951), who have gathered anthropological research from many different places globally, shed light on how sexuality is shaped socially and culturally. They highlight that heterosexual vaginal intercourse is the most common form of sexual behaviour, but it is rarely the only practice that is done. They also mention the importance of stimulating the clitoris for women's orgasms (Ford and Beach, 1951, see also Masters and Johnson 1966). Shere Hite's (1976, 1981) well-known studies on sexuality also show that people have sex in varying ways.

Despite the sexual variation that appears to be common, the heteronormative script for how sex 'should' be done is a constant reference point. This is the case regardless of how sexual practice is experienced by the individual woman and her partner(s). Normative sexual practice can be transformed, but it requires a conscious renegotiation of the supposed consensus on how sexual encounters should be enacted. A renegotiation of sexual practice is, however, not made in a vacuum, but in the meeting with other bodies, wills and desires. Therefore, it can sometimes be difficult to change sexual patterns. This fact is visible in the resistance met by some of the women who have tried to renegotiate sexual practice. To change habits of the body and habitual thinking, characterised by cultural norms about right and wrong gender behaviour, is a serious challenge to take on. It requires that the skilled discourse-user navigate different forms of sexual script, and an individual approach is, of course, not enough. On a structural level, there needs to be a challenge to what sex means, and a consideration of how bodies of various shapes and abilities are limited by norms.

It is clear that some of the informants renegotiate the sexual script because of their vulvar pain. The pain drives them past heteronormative vaginal intercourse, since it hurts too much, and they find new ways to gain sexual pleasure. However, some become stuck in the feeling of not being 'real' women if they cannot participate in vaginal intercourse. By extending what is sexual, and particularly what is heterosexual sex, is it possible to find ways to gain pleasure based on the body's abilities, leaving behind the limiting effects of norms for gender and sexuality.

## Notes

(1) On diagnostic criteria for vulvar vestibulitis/provoked vestibulodynia see Friedrich (1987). It is also important to acknowledge that some medical researchers claim it is hard to differentiate between provoked vestibulodynia and vulvodynia, which makes diagnosis difficult (Edwards 2004; Binik 2010).

(2) Partial vaginismus can be seen as a defence connected to fear of pain, which leads to avoidance of vaginal penetration. Vaginal penetration can be performed to some degree, but it gives pain and soreness. Vaginal penetration is impossible at total vaginismus (Engman 2007).

(3) Recurrent vulvovaginal candida infection and oral contraceptives can be part of what causes provoked vestibulodynia (Ehrström 2007; Johannesson 2007).

(4) Sexual scripts can be divided into three levels: (1) cultural scripts created for instance in media, debates and politics; (2) interpersonal scripts that come from interactions in everyday life; (3) intrapsychological scripts that function on an individual level (Gagnon and Simon 1973; Simon 1966; Jackson and Scott 2010).

# REFERENCES

Ayling, Kathryn and Jane M. Ussher. 2008. '"If Sex Hurts, am I Still a Woman?" The Subjective Experience of Vulvodynia in Hetero-Sexual Women'. *Archives of Sexual Behaviour*, 37: 294–04.

Beasley, Chris. 2010. 'The elephant in the room. Heterosexuality in critical gender/sexuality studies'. *NORA*, 18(3): 204–209.

Binik, Yitzchack M. 2010. 'The DSM Diagnostic Criteria for Dyspareunia'. *Archives of Sexual Behavior*, 39: 292–303.

Burr, Vivien. 1995. *An Introduction to Social Constructionism*. London: Routledge.

Butler, Judith. 1990. *Gender trouble. Feminism and the subversion of identity*. London & New York: Routledge.

Butler, Judith. 1993. *Bodies That Matter. On the Discursive Limits of 'Sex'*. London & New York: Routledge.

Clellan S. Ford and Frank A. Beach. 1951. *Patterns of Sexual Behavior*. New York: Harper & Brothers.

Deleuze, Gilles. 1992. 'Ethology: Spinoza and us'. *Incorporations*. Ed. by Crary, Jonathan & Sanford Kwinter. London: MIT Press.

Edwards, Libby. 2004. 'Subsets of vulvodynia: overlapping characteristics'. *The Journal of Reproductive Medicine*. 11(49): 883–87.

Ehrström, Sophia. 2007. *Aspects on Chronic Stress and Glucose Metabolism in Women with Recurrent Vulvovaginal Candidasis and in Women with Localized Provoked Vulvodynia*. Stockholm: Karolinska Institutet.

Elmerstig, Eva. 2009. *Painful Ideals. Young Swedish women's ideal sexual situations and experiences of pain during vaginal intercourse*. Linköping: Linköping University, Gender and Medicine, Division of Women's and Children's Health.

Engman, Maria. 2007. *Partial vaginismus—definition, symptoms and treatment*. Linköping: Linköpings universitet, Faculty of Health Sciences.

Friedrich, E.G. 1987. 'Vulvar vestibulitis syndrome'. *Journal of Reproductive Medicine*, 32: 110–14.

Gagnon, John H. and William Simon. 1973. *Sexual Conduct. The Social Sources of Human Sexuality*. Chicago: Aldine Pub. Co.

Gatens, Moira. 1996. *Imaginary Bodies. Ethics, Power and Corporeality*. London: Routledge.

Good, Byron J. 1994. *Medicine, rationality, and experience*. Cambridge: Cambridge University Press.

Grosz, Elisabeth. 1994. *Volatile Bodies. Toward a Corporeal Feminism*. London: Routledge.

Hite, Shere. 1976. *The Hite report: a nationwide study on female sexuality*. New York: Macmillan.

Hite, Shere. 1981. *The Hite Report on Male Sexuality*. New York: Knopf.

Hite, Shere. 1987. *The Hite report: women and love: a cultural revolution in progress*. New York: Knopf.

Holmberg, Carin. 1993. *Det kallas kärlek. En socialpsykologisk studie om kvinnors underordning och mäns överordning bland unga jämställda par*. Göteborg: Anamma förlag.

Jackson, Stevi and Sue Scott. 2010. *Theorising Sexuality*. Maidenhead: Open University Press.

Johannesson, Ulrika. 2007. *Combined Oral Contraceptives—Impact on the Vulvar Vestibular Mucosa and Pain Mechanisms*. Stockholm: Karolinska Institutet.

Kaler, Amy, 2006. 'Unreal women. Sex, gender, identity and the lived experience of vulvar pain', *Feminist Review*. 82: 50–75.

Kinsey Alfred C., Wardell B. Pomeroy and Clyde E. Martin. 1948. *Sexual Behavior in the Human Male*. Philadelphia: Saunders.

Kinsey, Alfred C., Wardell B. Pomeroy, Clyde E. Martin and Paul H. Gebhard. 1953. *Sexual Behavior in the Human Female*. Philadelphia: Saunders.

Lundgren, Eva and Renita Sörensdotter. 2004. *Ungdomar och genusnormer på skolans arena*. Falun: Dalarnas forskningsråd.

Martinsson, Lena. 1997. *Gemensamma liv. Om kön, kärlek och längtan*. Stockholm: Carlsson Bokförlag.

Masters William H. and Virginia E. Johnson. 1966. *Human Sexual Response*. Boston: Little Brown.

Rosenberg, Tiina. 2002. *Queerfeministisk agenda*. Stockholm: Atlas.

Segal, Lynne. 1994. *Straight sex. The politics of pleasure*. London: Virago Press.

Seymour, Wendy. 1998. *Remaking the body. Rehabilitation and change*. Sydney: Allen & Unwin.

Simon, William. 1966. *Postmodern Sexualities*. London: Routledge.

Stanley, Liz. 1992. *The Auto/Biographical I. The Theory and Practice of Feminist Auto/Biography*. Manchester: Manchester University Press.

Sörensdotter, Renita, 2012. 'Pain and sex(uality) among women suffering from vulvar pain'. *Dimensions of pain*. Ed. by Lisa Folkmarson Käll. London: Routledge.

Wilton, Tamsin. 2004. *Sexual (Dis)Orientation. Gender, Sex and Self-Fashioning*. New York: Palgrave Macmillan.

Jørgensen, Marianne Winter and Louise Phillips. 2000. *Diskursanalys som teori och metod*. Lund: Studentlitteratur.

# CHAPTER 10

# Queer Wounds: Writing Autobiography Past the Limits of Language

*Quinn Eades*

### Writing/Righting the Wounded Body

Writing: first I am touched, caressed, wounded; then I try to discover the secret of this touch to extend it, celebrate it, and transform it into another caress.
Hélène Cixous, *Coming to Writing*, 1991, p. 45.

The first time I said the word 'wound' I was five. Summer in Sydney. Skelton Street. We lived in a four-storey terrace that teemed with children, adults, and cockroaches. In the mornings we stepped over people asleep on the floor on the way to the kitchen to make muesli. There was a three-storey bunk in our bedroom, pine struts knocked together, that wobbled when we climbed its frame to jump from the top to pillows on the floor. The grown-ups let us run. It was the seventies, and they were busy organising protests, or reading Adrienne Rich, or talking about feminism. Summer in Sydney, the endless afternoon. We played in the street, and thought we would never have to go home.

Q. Eades (✉)
La Trobe University, Melbourne, VIC, Australia
e-mail: q.eades@latrobe.edu.au

© The Author(s) 2017
E. Rees (ed.), *Talking Bodies*, DOI 10.1007/978-3-319-63778-5_10

The first time I said the word 'wound' it was a challenge, a lie, an attempt to get out of trouble. We were running in the street as the sun went down, the bitumen getting cold under our bare feet, and the grown-ups kept calling for us, and we ignored them. We ran. We ran but my mother came, eventually, to find us. When I saw her face I knew I was in trouble, and dropped to one knee:

'I'm wounded', I said, impressed by my own vocabulary.

'You're not. Get up. Walk. I've been calling you'.

'But I'm *wounded*'. She refused to look at the knee I cradled (it was, after all, an imaginary wound), took my hand and pulled me back to the house.

Jeanette Winterson writes that '[t]he wound is symbolic and cannot be reduced to any single interpretation. But wounding seems to be a clue or a key to being human. There is value here as well as agony' (2011, p. 221). The value of the wound in that moment, as the sun left and my mother stalked towards me in jeans and gym-boots, was its impressiveness. Not just a hurt, but a *wound*. A wound has the power to gather others around us. It suggests an ongoingness, a state of injury that is deep, that gashes through psyche as well as flesh. The value of the visible wound is this: it offers agony and relief. It draws to it empathy, sympathy, even love. It conveys a depth of suffering that has the power to become noble (Jesus was wounded, not injured).

Queer wounds are another matter entirely. Queer wounds, the ones received willingly at the hands of another, through trauma, from attack, these are the ones destined to be hidden, revised, obfuscated, and channelled into a forgetting that is most often labelled 'healing'. Queer wounds must be proved, shored up, and acted out; they must be constantly performed, because it is through the performance of the wound that we find a witness. The witness that is '*I*', that is the self, is never enough. And so queer wounds must be written, must be seen, and through being witnessed in writing, can become a source of power not only for the body that bears the wound, but also for those bodies who live proximal to the wound.

Kathryn Robson, in her 2004 book *Writing Wounds*, notes that '[t]he word 'trauma', derived from the Greek word for a bodily wound, [and] originally referred exclusively to bodily injury', but that '[i]n the nineteenth century, when the psychological effects of bodily traumas [...] were identified, 'trauma' came also to refer to the psychic wound engendered by bodily trauma' (2004, p. 29). In this important work, Robson moves to the site of the wound as the place where trauma narratives reside:

To remember and narrate trauma means, then, to attempt to write in and through wounds, through the holes within memory that represent the incursion of the past into the present. Yet how does one 'write (through) wounds'? (2004, pp. 27–8)

How does one write (through) wounds? With the fragment, with shards of poetry, with a figurative form of life-writing that is able to hold both the stories and silences of the traumatic experience; with a breaking down of the requirement to tell cohesive (healed) narratives. 'If the scar points to a story (of wounding and healing), a past that can be remembered yet left behind, the image of the wound figures the breakdown of narrative' (Robson 2004, p. 28). What you are about to read is writing (through) wounds—it is the performance Robson's image of the wound as a between place, or what Derrida would call a *hymen*, which is a veil; a piece of tissue so thin it can be seen through; 'a text within a text, a margin in a mark, the one indefinitely repeated within the other: an abyss' (Derrida 1981, p. 255).

Trauma theory has long accepted that any attempt to depict the traumatic event is at the limits of language—that it is impossible to write. This is the basis of Lacan's and Freud's theories of trauma and memory, whereby the impact of a traumatic event is delayed, then pushes its way repeatedly into the survivor's present, as well as leaving gaps or rents in memory where the subconscious has been unable to assimilate an encounter with the Real, and therefore 'represses' the memory of it (Lacan 1994; Freud 1986). The kind of 'memory that concerns Freud is not a conscious act that recalls the image or thought after it has passed away, but is unconscious, that is to say, a memory that has not been remembered' (Shepherdson 2008, p. 128).

I write these words as a trauma survivor, and I want to be clear from the start that of course there are individual and community traumas that take the form of memories that have not been remembered. I write these words with an intuitive and empathic understanding of a state of being whereby memory is not only dangerous, but terrifying. But I also write these words as a trauma survivor who simultaneously remembers and does not—who treasures the wounded places on and in his[1] body that carry memory for him—and who is suspicious of a popular vocabulary of trauma that requires survivors to heal, let go, and move on, most often through a therapeutic talking/writing/sharing practice that involves ordering traumatic events in time to create a cohesive, 'whole', narrative. Or in the words of Kathy Acker, 'I have no idea where to begin: repression's impossible because it's stupid and I'm a materialist' (1984, p. 172).

## NO LANGUAGE COULD CONVEY?

In 1811, writer Fanny Burney endured the surgical removal of her right breast with only a wine cordial (possibly laced with laudanum) for anaesthetic (Epstein 1986, p. 131). In a detailed letter, now housed in the New York Public Library, to her sister Hetty, Burney recounts the procedure moment by moment: the masked surgeons surrounding her, instruments descending, cutting, and most disturbingly, the feel of a scalpel scraping meat from bone:

> *When the wound was made, & the instrument was withdrawn, the pain seemed undiminished, for that air that suddenly rushed into those delicate parts felt like a mass of minute but sharp & forked poniards, that were tearing the edges of the wound [...]*

> *I then felt the Knife [rack]ling against the breast bone–scraping it!–This performed, while I yet remained in utterly speechless torture.* (Epstein 1986, p. 148; italics and brackets in original)

While Fanny remained utterly speechless with pain and horror throughout the operation, she was nevertheless able to describe it to her sister in great detail after the fact. This was not the case for her husband, Mr D'Arblay, who was present at the surgery, and wrote the following at the end of Fanny's letter, thus revealing his role as both witness and reader, or as having to 'see' twice:

> *No language could convey what I felt in the deadly course of these seven hours.* (Epstein 1986, p. 144; italics in original)

And in fact it is the witness, not the patient, who ends up experiencing (and then filling) gaps, due to Fanny's decision to keep most of the detail hidden. It is only upon reading the letter that he is able to come close to understanding what his wife has endured:

> *Besides, I must own, to you, that these details which were, till just now, quite unknown to me, have almost killed me.* (Epstein 1986, p. 144; italics in original)

There are some points of interest here. First, that the experience of unanaesthetised surgery removes Fanny's ability to speak, but not to write, and second, that for the (double) witness, what is taken is language itself. In her analysis of Burney's letter, 'Writing the Unspeakable: Fanny Burney's Mastectomy and the Fictive Body', Julia Epstein posits that

'Burney [...] reopens, relives, and recloses her wound by representing it in writing' (1986, p. 150), and goes on to say that '[t]o write her own medical history [...] was to re-undertake her own surgery; to control the probe, the knife, the wound, and the blood herself; to speak for the wound's gaping unspeakableness–the woman her own surgeon, both reopening and reclosing the incisions in her own body and in the body of her writing' (1986, p. 162). At the conclusion of her article, Epstein argues that Burney manages her state of trauma by writing herself out of subject and into object, and it is from this point that I suggest we move: it is possible to write the body not as object, but as subject-object, both. It is possible to write wounds, and to write trauma. It is perhaps less possible to write witnessing, as Mr D'Arblay's comment at the end of his wife's letter attests, but even so, it is not *impossible*.

If we accept that writing from the body is sometimes not cohesive, often not anchored in time, and riddled with gaps that are as productive as the spaces between them, then we accept that writing trauma is not always at the limits of language; that it is possible to write the wound.

## Boat/Leaf/Gash/Cunt (The Revised Wound)

This is not the first wound, but it is the one that reaches back to old cuts, and forecasts those to come later. It was made by a lover, scalpel in hand. I knelt at her feet, naked from the waist up, and shivered with darkness and cold. As she leant in towards me I anticipated pain, but when she made the cut all I felt was wind. The ice of air on flesh exposed. She sucked the blood as it seeped, then swiped the gash with antiseptic and covered it up. Five centimetres from top to bottom, it should have been stitched. It should have been stitched but we left it alone.

The cut was too long; it could not gather its edges together. The only thing this wound could do was to stay open, to slowly string cells across the gap. 'When it healed, I had the shape of a boat, of a leaf, of a gash, of a cunt' (Eades 2015, p. 6). The trauma is not where you think it is. This moment in time:

> floorboards, knees, cold, silverglint, moonlit, tongue in blood in cut, anti-
> septic, dressing, never shut,

was a treasure, a consent, a giving and receiving; was an 'axe for the frozen sea inside us' (Kafka 1977, n.p.). The trauma is not where you think it is.

When the wound had finally stitched itself together it had a way of drawing people to it, as if it spoke always of what had happened before. So when I took my boat/leaf/gash/cunt out into the world and the world couldn't help but stare, I found that I had to revise the moment (no one would hear of queer cut and seep as revelation or gift). I became convinced that this was a thing to be ashamed of, and made up stories for the curious: a nail sticking out of a garage door, an attack, a stumble while holding a sharp knife. I rarely wore singlets. I hid.

A queer wound is one that is not celebrated. A queer wound is hidden by the one who carries it, and by those lucky enough to lay eyes on it. A queer wound is an ill-begotten wound in the eyes of the world. Wounds that are not queer: war wounds, sports injuries and those acquired through accidents. Of course we will not forget stigmata, nor the hysteric and the psychosomatic, but these wounds belong in another place altogether; these wounds may be revered, studied, or pathologised, but they will not be celebrated either.

> These wounds that I list,
> from war,
> from sport,
> from a respectable fall,
> can't hold stigmata next to them.
>
> Opened palms that invoke
> blood on thighs,
> belly-ache,
> the smear of the not-conceived.
>
> Unstaunchable,
> stigmata will weep,
> will call,
> will seep.

Accidental wounds are sympathised with, and receive help in their healing. War wounds and sports injuries are both celebrated and commemorated. So the trauma? The trauma is here, in my first queer wound, on my right upper arm, the one that turned into a scar that invoked the void that was eventually revised. Revised not just by the stories that I told, but by a surgeon with his own scalpel, in an operating theatre where they kept me awake, their kidney-shaped bowls resting on my belly. They talked to each other like I wasn't there, and I shook so much the nurses had to move the bowls. I smelt burning flesh, felt the tug-tug of thread, and when it was over I walked myself out of a room that was so bright I had to squint. I was left with a thin red line, kept together by stitches that dissolved in the days that followed. I was left with a scar that couldn't invoke the first cut; it would only ever speak of the second. I was left with a scar that had lost its ability to draw the attention of others. My arm and the stories it told was revised, and in that revision the moments in time it held suffered an erasure born about by the respectability of 'healing'.

How much of healing, of 'letting go', is forgetting? What does forgetting do to the memory of pain? How do we commemorate queer wounds after an internally or externally motivated process of revision? If the therapeutic process of healing is based in the need to create (or to recreate) cohesive narratives of trauma, how do we make room for the illusive, the queer, the fragmented, the barely-remembered, the event that is experienced at the edges of the self?

We make room by telling the story of the wound, and of the traumatic event that the wound calls to. We make room by moving into language, movement, song, and poetry. We make room by allowing ourselves, and through writing, others, to see. Adrienne Rich, in her 1973 poem 'From the Prison House' wrote about the need for witnesses to see, and to remember:

> This eye
> is not for weeping
> its vision must be unblurred
> though tears are on my face
> its intent is clarity
> it must forget
> nothing.

And now I ask you this: can the eye not weep and simultaneously remember? Blurring is inevitable—from salt water, from time, from a light shining too brightly, from trying to see when twilight has begun its turn towards night—so is there a way to welcome the blur, the not-quite-seen? If the multiple narratives that the blurring of memory in relation to trauma produces can be read as a gap or a breach that should be valued, then the process of 'healing' trauma-based wounds can be reimagined. 'It is through the wound, the gap, the crack, or breach in being that power enters' (Campbell 2014, p. 212), and in order to keep this power, we must tell the story of the wound. How to do this? Through the poetic, the fragmentary, and the non-cohesive. Through the rejection of the linear narrative that requires us to always make sense of trauma. Trauma makes no sense. If we write this no-sense (which is also every-sense), we can move past the idea that trauma is at the 'limits of language' (Smith and Watson 2010, p. 283) and make our own corpus (Nancy 2008).

In her book *Trauma: Explorations in Memory*, Cathy Caruth discusses the need for individuals and communities to hear the truth in relation to traumatic events, and asks us to consider 'how we might perhaps find a way of learning to express this truth beyond the painful repetitions of traumatic suffering' (Caruth 1995, p. viii). But why this reluctance to repeat?

> To repeat is to produce and to alter, to make and to make anew. Repetition is a principle of irrepressible creativity and novelty; it would be impossible to repeat without making and without altering what is already made. Even to repeat 'exactly the same thing' is to repeat it in a new context which gives it a new sense. (Caputo, in Mazur 2005, p. 5)

In repetition it might be possible to find reframing, reunderstanding. Repetition is never truly repetition. One detail changes/it all/everything changes. Tell and retell. Repeat. Because every iteration will find some new way to speak.

## SUICIDE (THE GENERATIONAL WOUND)

Here, now, is the eye that weeps and simultaneously remembers. My grandfather, John Quinn: ghost-poet, returned from World War II untethered, up in the early mornings to beat his children to the day, to time, so he could write. Writing that failed to save, but left behind a slim blue book of poems: *Battle Stations*. And in these poems he caught on the page what was coming for him:

'Fugitive'
Lost in black nothing,
A tired fugitive hard pressed by time,
Here's sanctuary.

In a half-death let me lie,
Stripped free of pricking life,
Cloistered in warm oblivion,
Unending, unbeginning,

Safe in this citadel,
The dark tower of sleep.

Here no stars gleam,
Here no sun glares hotly at midday.
Only pale ghosts walk and, timidly,
Peep round the black bastions,
And panic back to timeless graves. [...] (John Quinn 1944)

So how do I carry this wound of his, a wound from a man I have never met? I carry his wounds on my wrists. His was a death made almost unspeakable by a single shot to the head, and my mother carries that death in her body, in the scream that she didn't let out when he died. I know him by his poetry and by photographs. My mother has his nose. And on her arms, the scars that speak of his going. Of course it is more complex than this—his suicide, the scars on her arms, the scars on my wrists—cannot be mapped so easily.

Cartographers know they're not really catching the coastline in ink. Early maps depended on a person with a sure eye, who hoped wind speed would remain constant. They perched at the prow of a boat, pen in hand, and followed the coastline as their vessel cut through the water. When they were unsure, they drew in dotted lines, or left places blank—occasionally they penned the curl of a question mark. These early maps are far more accurate than the ones we have now, laced as they are with the authority of satellite imaging and dots per inch, because they make room for the errant, the hard to pin down, the geographic event (Carter 2009, pp. 49–53).

Those moments, where the line breaks, are where poetry becomes possible. Time and place stretch, and make room for language, for expression, for the figurative. We should not pin down, or rewrite the gap, but instead leave it open on the page, to hold what it finds there. Carter asks us to consider that '...a new thinking (and drawing) practice does not abandon the line but goes inside it. The line is always the trace of earlier lines. However perfectly it copies what went before, the very act of retracing it represents a new departure'. (Carter 2009, p. 9) The lines on my mother's arms and on my wrists are the trace of earlier lines. They are made from razor blades wielded by our own hands. They are the calling back to a father gone too soon, a grandfather never met. They are an incomplete map, a connection, a wound made from a gunshot and a book of poems that couldn't save a life. They are writing.

'There, where you write, everything grows, your body unfurls, your skin recounts its hitherto silent legends' (Cixous 1991, p. 42).

The skin of my mother speaks, and says: I screamed at the side of my father's grave, I spoke aloud the cruelty of his leaving—I witness this. And the skin of my wrists, striated with scars, is a doubling, a witness of the witness, an echo, a way through. In his poem 'Ashes-Glory' Paul Celan wrote that 'no one bears witness for the witness' (1980, n.p.) but this is where I am: my skin recounts its silent legends and when the scars on my wrists echo the weals on my mother's arms we are joined. We are joined at a single corporeal moment that stretches back and forward through time. We are traced umbilically. We are the fragment that invokes the whole. The skin on her arms, on my wrists, makes room for poetry:

> Which is why fragments are necessary, here more than anywhere else. In fact, the fragmentation of writing, wherever it occurs [...] responds to the ongoing protest of bodies in—against writing. An intersection, an interruption: *this breaking into any language, where language touches on sense.* (Nancy 2008, p. 21; italics in original)

When bodies write (and particularly when wounded bodies write), they will use the language of the body to touch on sense. They will protest against the 'unspeakable', the 'limit', and the 'impossible' by speaking, by spitting fragments at anyone who will listen, by opening veins, by stumbling, by leaping, by incomplete mapping, by entering the gap or the gape.

Too often we are told that it is impossible to write trauma. That the mechanics of trauma mean gaps and erasures in memory, and therefore that what a trauma survivor can represent in language is limited, until those gaps are closed. There are two assumptions here. One is that language is only that which we speak or write. The other is that the gap is something that should be closed over, or healed. The gap here is what creates the fragment, which evokes Jean-Luc Nancy's protesting body inside the text. The fragment, and following on from this, the poetic, will always make their way into (and out of) trauma texts, if they are allowed to. In *The Space Between: Australian Women Writing Fictocriticism*, Amanda Nettelbeck writes that 'the stress in fictocritical texts on the fragment [...] might be read as signaling not so much a disappearance of value into a long, flat plain of relativity but rather a coming-to-grips with the contexts in which value is produced' (1998, p. 8). When we come to grips with the contexts in which trauma texts are produced, we may find that a collection of fragments has more to say about bodies, trauma and wounds than any cohesive narrative can.

The fragment I offer you here is the moment my mother held in a scream at the imagined graveside of her father (she did not go to his funeral because she was sure that if she did, she would start screaming and never stop), and then made that scream on her arms, the blood a tribute, a knowing, a relief. The fragment I offer you here is the picture of lines made from keloid, a writing from and of the body, about death, and a man that we carry with us, still.

## Dungeon (the Invisible Wound)

Here is the next queer wound: a wound that was made in the dark, with an unlocked door that I couldn't walk out of, at the top of a twisting set of stairs. Carpet grey in the curtained light. A man called John walking up them ahead of me, opening the door, letting me through, closing the door.

Closing the door.

It doesn't matter why I was there. It matters that I was there. It matters that I have been writing this wound now for twenty years, and whenever I sit down to do it again, this body remembers, and responds with fingers moving over keys while stomachtightens, tearspush, legstense, lungsstruggle, shouldershunch, breath ... Breath quickens when I know I will write this story again, and then tries to slow me into nothingness. If not enough oxygen can reach my extremities then maybe this body will cease its telling. Fingers move anyway. Breath carries enough light to keep going. The story is told. Again.

Again with the mirror wall, the four-poster bed with no mattress, a flat piece of polished wood where softness should be. Again with electric shocks through tongue and labia, rope burns on wrists, the small window that looked out over the corrugated rooftops of Sydney terraces on a warm August day. Again with do this, now this, on your knees, up, run with weights attached to nipples, beg, down, stay down, lick, suck, be blindfolded, be blinded with pain with endurance with no end no end no end no end.

There is an end. Five hours later there is an end. I walked into the room at the top of the stairs at 11 o'clock in the morning, and walked out the front door at 4 o'clock in the afternoon. Time carried on being unreliable, even after I left. Nights became infinite, and carried with them pictures and sensations from the five dungeoned hours, on repeat. I covered the rope burns on my wrists, and eventually the red-raw circlets left.

This is the invisible wound because it is the wound that I thought was impossible to speak. Counsellors didn't know what to do with me. If I'd been raped they would have sent me to the Rape Crisis Centre. One of them felt I'd been tortured, but the Centre for Refugees didn't know this kind of torture, and they didn't think I belonged there either. Another told me I should never have been in that room in the first place. It doesn't matter why I was there. It matters that I was there.

You may recognise the story I've just told. Not because you've read it before (you may have read it before), but because you've been taught how to read a testimonial. The telling will hold a sense of 'this, then this, then this'. It will be contained by time. You will read knowing the writer (the autobiographical *I*) survived. You will find yourself wondering if what I have testified is true:

> [b]ecause testimonial projects require subjects to confess, to bear witness, to make public and shareable a private and intolerable pain, [and] they enter into a legalistic frame in which their efforts can move quickly beyond their interpretation and control, become exposed as ambiguous, and therefore subject to judgments about their veracity and worth. (Gilmore 2001, p. 7)

The legal framework awaits every utterance of trauma, and it is a comfortable one in which to settle. This framework allows the reader of trauma stories to escape. The question that rings through the telling— '*how* could this happen?'—is replaced by the far less difficult—'*did* this happen?'. And now the reader is free. The autobiographical *I* becomes suspect, the confession is tainted, and bothersome or disturbing content is dismissed.

So again I must turn to the fragment, the poetic. When narratives of trauma are allowed to be fragmented, prismatic, unframed, spilling out, the application of a confessional and therefore a legal framework becomes problematic, if not near on impossible. Read this:

> It's between her legs, sliding always a little more painfully for her, for me. A spurt of white. Panic. Between life and death. Blue funk. (Brossard 1983, p. 15)

Brossard's fragment-writing will not be fitted, its truth is not automatically questioned, and this gives the reader (and writer) new relations to question: '[w]hat is philosophy if not a way of reflection, not so much on what is true and what is false, as on our relations to truth?' (Foucault, in Gilmore 2001, p. 144). So now the autobiographical *I* will tell the story of the invisible wound again, but in fragments, in the realms of the poetic, and will ask you to fly between gaps, to leave frames and confessions behind: to see relations to truth.

Slivershine the kettle in the kitchen
        is held by a woman in latex she
makes tea for her and the other
        girls (they are always girls here).

He wants to know about me
        why I am here what is a nice girl
so young
        what is a nice a nice a nice girl doing
here.

                <It does not matter why I am here ><It matters that I am here>

Up the stairs he takes
        he takes the day the year the decade from
me.

Up the stairs and into the room
        the door close/s it (does) not lock.

Stomachtightens, tearspush, legstense, lungsstruggle, shoudershunch, breath...

The way silver catches light.
Leather shines.
The bed is restraint. There are restraints. Movement is something to remember.

                Electric shock weight hung from lips a tongue burnt by fizz
                        a hiss.

                Later. Movement is something
                        to re/member.

Flesh carries the mark of rope for only so long.
        Red raw. Redraw. Re-draw.

Gun at my left flank, rope-burned wrists, shaking hands.

Closed door the lock that didn't click shut the bullet that wasn't shot.

                Outside the sun traced a path through the sky

a woman caught a bus
someone cast a line into the ocean and saw the shimmerglint
of the sinker sliver
g o i n g

d o w n.

## THERAPY (THE IMAGINED/IMAGINARY WOUND)

Now we come to therapy, the imagined and imaginary wound that comes from being asked to make the story of a wound cohesive, to tell the whole, with the beginning at the beginning and the end at the end. To probe into silences and gaps. To recuperate, recover, illuminate. To speak.

> The counsellor started by asking me about my desires. Slowly at first, and then more insistently. (Eades 2015, p. 117)

> I told the counsellor the story of the wound but it was a wound edged with shame, and with the utter belief that I was sick, and with the hope that she would fix me. (Eades 2015, p. 118)

I made that counsellor my witness, and she made me hers. We sat together in her room at the top of a different flight of stairs, where no gaps were allowed. Everything. I should tell her everything. And in that telling, I witnessed my self again in the dungeon. I cried like I would never stop. I broke inside the story I was required to speak aloud. I knew that this was meant to free me, to release me from the haunting I felt near leather-silver-electric-mirror-pierced-dungeon-weight, but saying it aloud in that room only seemed to lay it down more firmly under my skin. In *Trauma: explorations in memory* Cathy Caruth writes that '[t]o be traumatized is precisely to be possessed by an image or an event' (1995, pp. 4–5), and I was, possessed. But now what I think is that I was not ready to be unpossessed, that the haunting was also an animating, and that when I put every piece of that dungeon in order, I could not contain what was left.

It is possible that surviving trauma, that the therapeutic moment when trauma is expunged from the body (if there even is such a thing) is harder to endure than the traumatic event itself. That 'for those who undergo trauma, it is not only the moment of the event, but of the passing out of it that is traumatic; that *survival itself*, in other words, *can be a crisis*' (Caruth 1995, p. 9; italics in original). That five hours in the dungeon, and its subsequent haunting, had a peculiar way of holding me together, and the overall experience of attempting to 'heal' or to 'move past' that moment in time was worse, in some ways, than the event itself. Notice the language when we talk about healing? We move on, move past, let go of: the therapeutic goal is to assist the patient to keep the past in the past, and the present in the present, to re-establish temporal boundaries. In other words: the fragment that floats free, that is both then and now, must be reintegrated into the whole, so that the timeline of the self makes sense. Hauntings and 'holding on' are not permitted in the realm of the linear, the place of 'this, then this, then this'. If writing the wound is also, in essence, writing the body, and the therapeutic process is one that favours closing over or healing the wound, then it is clear that the body will need to fight to write.

Is it possible then that narrative therapy is in fact an attempt to quieten the body's desires to speak? What if the queer wound is a corporeal fragment that needs not to be healed, or let go of, but to be allowed to sit next to other corporeal fragments that together, make something that is greater than the whole? 'Perhaps *body* is the word without employment par excellence. Perhaps, in any language, it's the word *in excess*' (Nancy 2008, p. 21). So again we come to a fragmented or poetic writing of the body, which is a writing of wounds; fragments which will always be *in excess*—they multiply, they slip into unexpected places, they nestle between lines, the find their homes in silences previously thought to be unarticulatable.

How, then, do I write the imagined wound that is therapy? I write it through the body, because the body is:

Existence. Bodies are existence. The very act of ex-istence, *being.*
    Writing to bodies (what else do writers do?): something's being sent to being, or better yet, being's sending itself. (What else does thinking think?)
    It's from bodies that we have, for ourselves, bodies as strangers. Nothing to do with a dualism, a monism, or a phenomenology of the body. The body's neither substance, phenomenon, flesh, nor signification. Just being-excribed. (Nancy 2008, p. 19)

I write it in poetry. I allow the haunting. I do not prescribe timelines. I accept the stuttering of trauma in the present tense, as much as the keening sound it makes in the past tense. I give myself the body as stranger, and know that this body writing queer wounds is being-excribed, where excription is 'an effect of writing taken to its limit' (Hodge 2011, p. 3). If we accept Nancy's contention that '"Poetry" means, not a literary genre as such but the limit of "literature", of "writing"' (2008, pp. ix–x), then we must also accept that the limits of language are not to be found in the narrative gaps observed in the telling of traumatic events: it is by allowing these very gaps to exist within the poetic that we can begin to find our way.

## TOTAL LAPAROSCOPIC HYSTERECTOMY
## (THE TRANSFORMING WOUND)

Here is the last queer wound I will describe: some years ago a fibroid that had lived in my uterus since my twenties began to grow. My babies had both been born. There was a mention of pregnancy hormones kicking it into movement, into becoming vascular, into tripling its size in twelve months. A total laparoscopic hysterectomy was prescribed, while I stood in a backless gown covered in flowers, held the thick fabric closed, and imagined that part of me gone.

The surgeon told me they were taking my uterus, my fallopian tubes, and my cervix. They would leave me my polycystic ovaries, so I didn't catapult into menopause in my late thirties. When I asked what would happen to my vagina after my cervix was gone, I was told I would have a blunt end. I have written that surgery before, and I will write it again, but this is a place to write wounds, and the wound I write now comes from my blunt end.

After the surgery I bled:

The blood that seeps onto the pad between my legs gets darker, and slower, and finally, stops. And I think

I am closed.
I am not open.
I am was-open.
I am not edge/abyss/falling or flying/dreaming.
I am stitch.
I am sewn.
I am seam.

And I think

I am a seam. A seam is something we search along to find gold. I followed a seam of writing to be at this point on this page. A seam is a line on the surface that tells us to dig down. It is the marker of poetry, of the night: it is evidence of something lost that is soon to be found. (Eades 2015, p. 237)

After the surgery I bled, and a doctor I saw told me I had a seam, not a blunt end. I imagined blue stitching pulling together the place where my cervix had been, and saw not just a seam but a Derridean fold, first discussed when writing about Mallarmé in *Dissemination*, which is 'at once sex, foliage, mirror, book, and tomb' (Derrida 1981, p. 249). Derrida locates the fold in the lining of the *hymen*, 'in the angle or cleft, in the *entre* by which, dividing itself, it relate[s] back to itself (Derrida 1981, p. 229), and sees the *hymen* as having the ability to de-centre European philosophical concepts of time as a before-now-next continuum due to its 'confusion and continuity' (Derrida 1981, p. 210).

> To repeat: the hymen, the confusion between the present and the non-present [...] produces the effect of a medium [...] It is an operation that *both* sows confusion *between* opposites *and* stands *between* the opposites 'at once.' What counts here is the *between*, the in-between-ness of the hymen. The hymen 'takes place' in the 'inter-', in the spacing between desire and fulfilment, between perpetration and its recollection. (Derrida 1981, p. 212)

He goes on to define *hymenographies* as writings that describe membranes, films, veils, between-nesses, and traces the etymology of *hymen* back to 'a root *u* that can be found in the Latin *suo, suere* (to sew) and in *huphos* (tissue). *Hymen* might then mean little stitch' (Derrida 1981, p. 213).

So now I ask you to return to my cervix, removed. A blunt end become hymen, holding both fold and stitch. A place that was once moistly open, that moved to let blood out and semen in, that stretched and thinned and shook the core of me with pain to let two babies through, now a bed for theory, for a *hymenography*, a writing of the between, which is a writing of bodies, which is a writing of wounds. Can we (should we) consider the writing of queer wounds to be a kind of *hymenography*, achieved through the grafting of fragments and poetry, through a willingness to simultaneously write and not-write the gap or the void—to refuse the continuity of the line?

In her book, *Queer Phenomenology*, Sara Ahmed writes about compulsory heterosexuality and the contingent lesbian who is 'shaped by the pull of her desire, which puts her in contact with others and with objects that are off the vertical line' (2006, p. 94), and posits a theory of contact sexuality, where 'lesbian tendencies shape and are shaped by how bodies extend into worlds' (2006, p. 94). It seems that there is a comparison to be made here to the wounded queer body which, when it comes into proximity with other bodies, has the ability to pass on the wound.

In this instance, I am thinking of this body, that writes now (I find it almost impossible to say 'my' body, as if there's a subject that owns an object), as one that infects itself with wounds. There is a trajectory here. The hysterectomy is the fifth wound, but it is certainly not the last.

In a footnote on the word *hymen*, Derrida describes the botanical term '*dehiscence* [...] [t]he action through which the distinct parts of a closed organ open up, without tearing, along a seam. A regular predetermined splitting that, at a certain moment in the cycle, is undergone by the closed organs so that what they contain can come out' (Derrida 1981, p. 215). What if the wounded body, even after a wound has closed over, goes through a kind of *dehiscence*, whereby the spores of a wound take flight and position themselves elsewhere, either on the body that holds the originating wound, or on an other proximal, 'pulled' body?

I am thinking now about Fanny Burney, the woman who lived through an unanaesthetised mastectomy, and about my own hysterectomy, which left me feeling less woman and more man, which led me ever closer to a different pronoun, and to thinking forwards through time to my own double mastectomy, which produced another queer wound, with its own stitches and folds. I am thinking too of my mother, and our scarred and echoing arms. I am imagining a place where queer wounds matter, and are not edged by shame; where they are commemorated and celebrated for the between-spaces, the *hymenographies* they are able to produce; texts that matter: fragmented, poetic, gappy, and written with respect and love for the body that survives.

## NOTE

(1) Between the writing and publication of this chapter, I transitioned from female to male. Please note that while some of the wounds described in this writing are located in a female-bodied person, I use male pronouns.

## BIBLIOGRAPHY

Acker, Kathy, 1984. *Blood and Guts in High School Plus Two*. London: Pan Books Ltd.

Ahmed, Sara, 2006. *Queer Phenomenology: Orientations, Objects, Others*. Durham and London: Duke University Press.

Brossard, Nicole, 1983. *These Our Mothers Or: The Disintegrating Chapter*, trans. by Barbara Godard. Toronto: Coach House Quebec Translations.

Campbell, Marion May, 2014. 'Poetic Revolutionaries: Intertextuality & Subversion'. *Postmodern Studies* 50. Theo D'haen and Hans Bertens eds. Amsterdam and New York: Rodopi.

Carter, Paul, 2009. *Dark Writing: Geography, Performance, Design*. Honolulu, Hawaii: University of Hawai'i Press.

Caruth, Cathy, ed., 1995. *Trauma: Explorations in Memory*. Baltimore: The Johns Hopkins University Press.

Celan, Paul, 1980. *Poems*. Translated by Michael Hamburger. New York: Persea.

Cixous, Hélène, 1991. 'Coming to Writing'. In *'Coming to writing' and other essays by Hélène Cixous*, ed. by Deborah Jenson. Cambridge, Massachusetts: Harvard University Press.

Derrida, Jacques, 1981. *Dissemination*. Trans. by Barbara Johnson. London: The Athlone Press.

Eades, Quinn, 2015. *all the beginnings: a queer autobiography of the body*. Melbourne: Australian Scholarly Publishing.

Epstein, Julia L., 1986. 'Writing the Unspeakable: Fanny Burney's Mastectomy and the Fictive Body'. *Representations* 16, 131–166.

Freud, Sigmund, 1986. *Beyond the Pleasure Principle*. London: The Hogarth Press and the Institute of Psycho-Analysis.

Gilmore, Leigh, 2001. *The Limits of Autobiography: Trauma and Testimony*. Ithaca, New York: Cornell University Press.

Hodge, Joanna, 2011. 'Excription at the Edge of Sense: Reading Jean-Luc Nancy'. *Aesthetic Pathways* 2, 3–29.

Kafka, Franz, 1977. *Letters to Friends, Family and Editors*, no editor listed. New York: Schocken Books.

Lacan, Jacques, 1994. *The Four Fundamental Concepts of Psycho-Analysis*. London: Penguin.

Mazur, Krystyna, 2005. *Poetry and Repetition: Walt Whitman, Wallace Stevens, John Ashberry*. New York: Routledge.

Nancy, Jean-Luc, 2008. *Corpus*. Trans. by Richard A. Rand. New York: Fordham University Press.

Nettelbeck, Amanda, 1998. 'Notes Towards an Introduction'. In *The Space Between: Australian Women Writing Fictocriticism*, eds. Heather Kerr and Amanda Nettelbeck. Nedlands, Western Australia: University of Western Australia Press.

Quinn, John, 1944. *Battle Stations*. Sydney: Halstead Press.

Rich, Adrienne, 1973. *Diving into the Wreck: Poems from 1971-1972*. New York: W.W. Norton.

Robson, Kathryn, 2004. *Writing Wounds: The Inscription of Trauma in Post-1968 French Women's Life-Writing*. Amsterdam and New York: Rodopi.

Shepherdson, Charles, 2008. *Lacan and the Limits of Language*. New York: Fordham University Press.

Smith, Sidonie, and Julia Watson, 2010. *Reading Autobiography: A Guide for Interpreting Life Narratives*. ebook: Minneapolis, Minnesota: University of Minnesota Press.

Winterson, Jeanette, 2011. *Why Be Happy When You Can Be Normal?* London: Jonathan Cape.

# CHAPTER 11

# The Trouble with Body Image: The Need for a Better Corporeal Vocabulary

*Melisa Trujillo*

Our embodied experiences and the language we use to discuss them have been at the forefront of the social sciences for many years now, and will no doubt remain so for many more (e.g. Csordas 1994). Because our relationships in, of and with our bodies are so inherent to what it is to be human, it is hardly surprising that one of social science's great projects—not to mention that of most individuals going about their daily lives—is to find an adequate way of talking about embodiment. While acknowledging that language can never quite capture the complexity, surprising idiosyncrasies, and materiality of our lived experiences, it is nevertheless the primary way we have of sharing with others the confusing and uncertain realities of our embodied lives.

There are many different vocabularies used to talk about the body within the social sciences that we might employ in everyday life, for example, from feminism, queer theory, and poststructuralist approaches (ignoring for the purposes of this discussion the bodily vocabulary of the natural and medical sciences). These different vocabularies are deployed to different purposes, with varying political, ontological and

M. Trujillo (✉)
University of Toronto, Scarborough, Toronto, Canada
e-mail: melisasuetrujillo@gmail.com

© The Author(s) 2017
E. Rees (ed.), *Talking Bodies*, DOI 10.1007/978-3-319-63778-5_11

epistemological aims. And while they have proven highly productive within the academy, and have made some headway in popular culture and mainstream media, it is the psychological concept of 'body image' that has broken decidedly free of the ivory tower.[1] The concept of 'body image' is now widespread throughout mainstream media, is employed in pop psychology and in government policy, and is commonly used by individuals wishing to describe certain aspects of their embodied experiences.

The concept of 'body image', therefore, is now a term with its own logic within popular culture and the media, used often and indiscriminately by different actors within the neoliberal, sexist and racist economies of bodies that pervade Anglo-Western contexts, and which emphasise the acceptability of only some bodies and in some ways. However, the ways in which 'body image' is used popularly are often reductive and unhelpful in the project of (a) helping us to understand and talk about lived experience, especially when it comes to the intersectional aspects of our embodied lives, and (b) attempting to create interventions with which to help people understand and live their often complicated and difficult relationships with their bodies.

In this chapter I will provide an evaluation of the usefulness and relative merits of 'body image' for a feminist project that seeks to understand and alleviate troubled embodied experiences. I will examine the popular usage of 'body image' in two ways: first, I examine the ways in which the very popularity of 'body image' highlights some of its most useful attributes, that should be kept and built on in the quest for a better language of the body. These are its communicative advantage and psychological immediacy. Second, in critiquing the popular usage of 'body image' I delineate two main issues: 'body image's' problematic relationship to gender, and its false universality.

I will then use two examples of alternative vocabularies of the body to highlight key elements of a potential new language of the body. I will suggest that we need to come up with more creative, inclusive and descriptive ways of talking about the body, as we abut the limits of what 'body image' can bring to this endeavour. I will argue that, even without conducting more research, or raising more awareness of the issues currently discussed under the rubric of 'body image' (although doubtless we need more of both), we could change the parameters of our popular cultural discussions about bodies and embodied experience if we had access to a popular vocabulary that integrated the materially and socially embodied experience as a whole, and was accessible, conceptually rich and intersectional. Doubtless this is an idealistic exercise, but a necessary one, especially as we contemplate the next few decades of research into the complexities of embodiment.

## A Note on Language in this Chapter

A brief note on language: I have so far mentioned the long-term social scientific project of developing 'language(s)' adequately to describe embodied experience; the existence of different, potentially competing 'vocabularies' of the body that emerge from within and outside of those disciplinary efforts; and the 'concept' of 'body image'. Throughout this chapter I will refer to 'body image' as a concept, one that is part of a broader, popularly used vocabulary of the body (often in conjunction with discussions of beauty norms and ideals, body weight, sexual desirability, self-esteem and femininity) that emerges from psychology, but is broadly used outside of the academy.

However, thinking about 'body image' as paradigmatic also offers some insights about how it is deployed. According to *Merriam-Webster's Dictionary*, one of the definitions of 'paradigm' is 'an outstandingly clear or typical example or archetype' (2016). In this way 'body image' is indeed paradigmatic of a particular way of talking about embodied experience that is regularly employed by individuals, mainstream media, and even governmental agencies: one, as I will discuss, that is heavily focused on physical appearance and the emotional and psychological effects of individuals' appearance-related experiences. On the other hand, the second meaning of 'paradigm' that Merriam-Webster offers, 'a theory or a group of ideas about how something should be done, made, or thought about', succinctly describes the academic study of 'body image', which has in recent years sought to capture the complexity of embodied experience in ways that encompass the study of appearance, but also supersede it (2016). I will mostly use 'concept' to describe 'body image', but will occasionally call it a 'paradigm' in the sense of the first definition discussed above.

Finally, a quick note on how I use the terms 'vocabulary', 'language' and 'discourse' throughout this chapter. I use 'vocabulary' according to its definition in Merriam-Webster's Dictionary: 'the body of words used in a particular language' (2016). This is for two reasons: first, the vocabularies of the body that I describe have a primary term or slogan attached to them (e.g. 'body image' and 'black is beautiful'), along with secondary terms that I do not discuss in detail (e.g. 'beauty ideals' or 'black pride'). The primary terms and secondary phrases constitute that particular 'vocabulary' of the body. However, they cannot be described as fully-fledged 'languages'. Second, these vocabularies, while not being 'languages', are constitutive of certain discourses of the body, and it is as such that I treat them as having important social consequences in need of analysis and intervention.

I have avoided using 'language' as much as possible in favour of, where applicable, 'discourse', as I want to argue, along Foucauldian lines, that discourses are 'ways of constituting knowledge, together with the social practices, forms of subjectivity and power relations which inhere in such knowledges and relations between them' (Weedon 1987, p. 108). In this chapter, therefore, I am treating 'vocabulary' as building blocks for discourse—not necessarily deterministic, but constitutive of discourse in complicated and potentially fluid ways.

## Contextualising 'Body Image' for this Chapter

There are two potential contexts in which to examine the relative merits of 'body image'. The first of these is the research or academic context in which 'body image' has been an important concept within psychology for over half a century. Paul Schilder coined the concept of 'body image' in his book *The Image and Appearance of the Human Body* (1950), and by doing so moved the field from attempts to understand neuropathology, such as the 'phantom limb', to a more complex understanding of the need to examine psychological, social and cultural aspects of embodied experience (Pruzinsky and Cash 2002, p. 4). Schilder defined body image as 'the way in which the body appears to ourselves' (1950, p. 11). During the middle of the twentieth century scholars such as the prolific Seymour Fisher and Sidney Cleveland (Fisher and Cleveland 1968; Fisher 1970, 1986, 1989) and Franklin Shontz (1969) developed different aspects of the field, from psychodynamic theories to behavioural and cognitive approaches, and the late twentieth century saw the amalgamation of a significant corpus of literature on eating disorders and body image. A more recent definition of 'body image' comes from Thomas Cash, an eminent body image researcher who has said that, 'Body image refers to the multi-faceted psychological experience of embodiment, especially but not exclusively to one's physical appearance' (2004, p. 2; Banfield and McCabe 2002). Today, the field of 'body image' is thriving, and notably has its own international journal (*Body Image: An International Journal of Research*).

'Body image' research is a major contribution to the empirical research on embodiment, although there are certain methodological shortcomings to this body of work (e.g. Gleeson and Frith 2006). Indeed, Cash has said that the widespread focus of this research on eating disorders in young women has 'reinforced the limiting notion that body image is only relevant to girls and women, and only concerns body weight and shape. I firmly believe that the field must build upon yet transcend this narrow focus and capture the rich diversity of human experiences of embodiment' (2004, p. 2).

The primary way I will discuss 'body image', however, is as a vocabulary that is part of a popular, publically mediated discourse concerning what a person thinks and feels about their body, most often focused on what that body looks like and how well it fits into normative perceptions of beauty. Though the concept of 'body image' and, as Cash notes, its widespread focus on girls, women, bodyweight and shape, has emerged from psychological research, it has now spread widely beyond disciplinary confines. The translation, interpretation or filtering through of this research into the popular domain is the focus of this chapter. Discussions of women's bodies remain dominant, though there is a slowly increasing focus on men, people of colour and other bodies (e.g. Cohane and Pope 2001; Grogan 2008).

The sphere of popular culture and media is the discursive world in which people ordinarily live, and in which their psychic and material bodies are constructed. For most individuals, the wealth of research in the academy remains largely unavailable as an additional reference on 'body image', for two main reasons: first, obtaining physical access to academic work is difficult for those not affiliated to universities as the cost of access to academic papers and books is prohibitive for most people not able to access them institutionally. Second, most non-academics rely on the media to make research comprehensible and relatable. This is due to a number of factors, not least that the often dense language and oblique disciplinary boundaries and standards, as well as the backlog of knowledge one often needs to understand research, effectively exclude most people from interacting with it. It is often through media 'translations' that gaps and misunderstandings emerge in the interpretation of research. Apart from the issue of 'translating' academic research to the popular sphere, the language of 'body image' has also grown to academic research over the past few decades. I will discuss both issues in this chapter.

## The Relative Merits of the Concept of 'Body Image'

This section will examine the merits and disadvantages of the cultural dominance of 'body image', examining why it has become so popularly used, and where it hinders rather than helps a social project that seeks to understand and repair people's relationships with their bodies. Some powerful traits of the 'body image' paradigm include its psychological immediacy and communicative advantage, and any new vocabulary should also have these properties. However, it should also learn from the shortcomings of 'body image', namely its problematic relationship with gender and the misleading perception of 'body image' as universal explanation and panacea for diverse embodied experiences. In discussing these drawbacks, I will be drawing on examples from policy, industry and women's popular media. Although these examples are far from representative, they provide a snapshot of how 'body image' is used in popular mediated discourse from various perspectives.

## The Communicative Accessibility and Psychological Immediacy of Body Image

Why has 'body image' become so ubiquitous in popular discourse? I argue that it has achieved this popularity for many reasons, the most salient of which are its communicative accessibility and psychological immediacy. By 'communicative accessibility' I mean that 'body image' is instantly evocative of a broad range of things that fall under its purview (appearance, attractiveness, bodyweight and shape, etc.), while also being vague or broad enough to be used to describe any number of body-related things, whether or not they directly have to do with 'image'. 'Psychological immediacy' is both a function of communicative accessibility, and of the popularity of the term and the extent to which it is embedded in popular discourse. When one hears 'body image', it immediately conveys remembered anecdotes, news articles, statistics, and personal experiences to do with subjects discussed under the 'body image' rubric, thus reinforcing the association between those embodied experiences and discussions of 'body image'. This provides the term with psychological weight and pathos, as well as immediacy and readability.

The accessibility of 'body image' as a concept gives it a powerful communicative advantage over other vocabularies of the body. Because it is instantly recognisable and relatable to most people, as they grapple with questions of appearance, weight, attractiveness and conformity to beauty norms on a regular basis, 'body image' can be used in ways intended to both convey messages of varying complexity and enact social change. 'Body image' seems to provide a satisfying psychological shorthand explanation to reach for when faced with those aspects of embodied life that ail us in often profound and mystifying ways.

These two aspects of 'body image' enable it to be used by many different parties. Users, consumers, transmitters or beneficiaries of the 'body image' concept include policy-makers, the business world, media commentators and the general public.[2] The UK's All Party Parliamentary Group (APPG) on Body Image, for example, defines body image in its 2012 report, *Reflections on Body Image*, as 'how people feel about the way they look and the way their body functions' (p. 9). This report was the culmination of months of public consultation and a review of the academic literature, which sought to both establish the state of 'body image' in the UK at the time, and to make policy recommendations.

Similarly, within the beauty industry there are attempts to utilise the language of 'body image' to improve the image of certain companies—the Dove Campaign for Real Beauty is one notable example (2016b). This marketing campaign, spanning 2004–2011 and bookended by two 'large scale' studies, *The Real Truth About Beauty* (2004) and *The Real Truth About Beauty: Revisited* (2011) sought to 'widen' the 'definition of beauty' (ibid.) and Dove says that its research 'into self-esteem, *body image*, and body confidence uncovers the difficulty women and girls have in recognizing their real beauty' (2016a; emphasis mine). This is another example of the labile uptake of 'body image' vocabulary in popular discourse. In its language, this campaign reads women's primary 'body image' concerns as having to do with beauty and whether their bodies conform to dominant ideals of beauty (thinness, whiteness, etc.). In its remedy this campaign challenges the nature of beauty ideals by seeking to tell all women that they are beautiful in their own, individual and idiosyncratic ways, whether or not they conform to these ideals—all women are 'really' beautiful. This is a necessary and in some ways radical intervention. However, in doing so they are nevertheless reifying the idea that all women must be beautiful, and that being beautiful should remain one of the core pillars of identity-building and being-in-the-world for women. Moreover, while the models that Dove uses in 'Real Beauty' adverts are more heterogeneous in terms of body shape and ethnicity than those in other beauty companies' advertising, they remain nevertheless more or less normatively beautiful. This example highlights two key features of the communicative and psychological dissemination of 'body image' vocabulary: first, the associated vocabulary clusters around terms associated with beauty ideals, bodyweight and self-confidence/esteem. Second, it tends to reify the primacy of appearance when attending to people's embodied experiences.

It is clear, however, that, similarly to the APPG report, Dove's Campaign for Real Beauty is an attempt to understand and improve the lived experiences of people, in this case women, through a popular appeal to the language of 'body image'. In this case the communicative advantage and psychological immediacy of 'body image' is a real asset: women can immediately grasp the message of the campaign and relate it to their own lives by understanding it through the prism of 'body image'. These examples demonstrate what can be 'done' with 'body image', and are laudable both as awareness-raising and public intervention. Nevertheless they also point to problems with 'body image' that will be taken up in the next section.

## Body Image's Problematic Relationship with Gender

'Body image', on the face of it, should be a concept that applies to everyone, regardless of gender (indeed, in the academic literature this is more and more the case). However, gender is inexorably called on in the ways 'body image' is popularly used, whether explicitly or not. This creates two interrelated problems: first, gender is an important way that we organise our embodied lives, both personally and socially, and this needs to be explicitly acknowledged and examined through popular corporeal vocabularies (something that feminism has done exceptionally well, although because feminism is so culturally polarising this language does not benefit as much from mainstream popularity or usage). Second, without explicit acknowledgment of how 'body image' is embroiled in gendered representations of men and women, the often sexist ways in which it is used, for example in popular media, can be easily elided. This can also serve to allow highly problematic notions of gender to propagate without critique, serving to reinforce or even reify these ideas. However, when I argue that 'body image' should be 'explicitly gendered', I am not in any way saying that 'body image' should be used to reinforce the gender binary, or traditional ideas of masculinity or femininity, but that the ways in which embodied experiences and representations of bodies are shaped by gendered norms and structures should be explicitly examined.

The following example embodies some common tropes in the depiction of body image in the popular sphere, and is also a clear example of how body image research is sometimes 'translated' through the popular media. In this short online UK *Cosmopolitan* article entitled, 'Friday's big issue: body image', the subheading is 'Are guys more attracted to super-skinny or curvy women?' This short article reports on a 'new Australian study', which apparently found that men prefer 'curvy women over size zero models and athletic types' (2009). The emphasis in the article is on normative, heterosexual desirability and body size, as illustrated by the last two sentences in the text, the first of which tentatively asks, '*Should* it matter what size you are, as long as you're healthy and happy?' (emphasis mine). This is followed immediately by, 'Have your say on what guys really want'. If a reader then wanted a second look at this study and clicked on the hyperlinked 'according to a new study' in the body of the article, they would be redirected to a *Daily Mail* article entitled 'Gentlemen prefer Miss Average: The "perfect" centrefold body is ousted by homely shape of girl-next-door in new study', which discusses the study in a little more detail, citing it as a 2009 study from the University of New South Wales (I was unable to find the study in question). The *Daily Mail* article also discusses 'new German research' from the University of Regensburg, which seems to confirm the findings of the Australian study. The text is interspersed with photographs of celebrities of somewhat varying shapes and sizes to illustrate the points of the article. Nowhere in either article are either the Australian or German studies linked to directly, nor their titles or authors mentioned, making it impossible to check the veracity of the headlines.

The idea of 'body image', as I noted above, is rendered specifically through the lens of heterosexual desirability in this article. Indeed, the title of the piece, 'Friday's big issue: *body image*' (emphasis mine) seems almost a placeholder. As I argued earlier, the communicative accessibility of 'body image' is part of what makes it a powerful corporeal language, and this is what the article seems to appeal to: the language of 'body image' is a convenient shorthand for talking about an issue related to how women feel about their bodyweight. This article seems to also be calling up an interplay between the internal and external in its readers: the title of 'body image' appeals to readers to reflect on their internal self-body relationship, while the questions about 'what men think' of their bodies then calls on readers to think of the external world and their place in that particular constellation of (heterosexually desirable) bodies.[3]

In this example, representations of body image research and ideas are explicitly gendered, but also laced with heterosexist intonations and assumptions. It is assumed that women will (want to) immediately connect their own 'body images' with what men think of them and what bodies men find the most attractive. In doing so readers are encouraged to dissent and debate both the researchers' findings and the 'pressure' that they might have faced from men to 'lose or put on weight'. The individual reader is implicitly constructed as autonomously agentic, while simultaneously being urged to externalise her desires and self-perceptions to identify with those of men (Bartky 1990).

Such examples serve to reframe the 'body image dissatisfaction' many women experience, and which most feminist theorists would argue is a symptom of gender inequality and sexism writ large on the body (e.g. Bartky 1990; Wolf 1991; Firestone 1970; Bordo 1993; etc.), as either a matter of fact reality of women's existences or an essentialised flaw in their characters. It can also become a normalised and enduring exercise to be worked through and repeated by women over and over throughout their lives (for example through repeated cycles of dieting and exercise, or cosmetic procedures), rather than recognised as a pathological effect of gendered socialisation. This serves to hide the often gendered causes of body trouble; in other words, what is it about women's position and representation in this society that renders them so vulnerable to body dissatisfaction, so prone to act on their bodies in harmful ways, and so predisposed to spend an inordinate amount of time and money working on their appearance? The concept of 'body image' could be actively used to address these questions, but, as in the *Cosmopolitan* example above, often reinforces pathological gendered stereotypes and representations.

## False Universality: The Flawed Perception of 'Body Image' as Explanation and Solution for All Troublesome Embodied Experiences

I will use another example from the popular women's media to illustrate some of the features of false universality: a *Harper's Bazaar* article about Misty Copeland, who was made the first ever African-American principal dancer at the prestigious American Ballet Theatre (ABT) in June 2015 (Mooallem 2016). The article chronicles Copeland's feelings about this momentous promotion in conjunction with the opening of a Museum of Modern Art exhibition for which she was photographed 'channel[ling]' some of Edgar Degas's famous painted dancers. The article mentions a documentary, called *A Ballerina's Tale* (2015), in which Copeland starred: 'She was also the subject of a documentary, Nelson George's *A Ballerina's Tale,* which chronicled her triumph over depression and body image issues, as well as her comeback from a career-threatening leg injury in 2012'. This is almost a throwaway comment—the rest of the article focuses on combining details about Degas's life and paintings with Copeland's biography to create a myth-like story of a quasi-inevitable rise to stardom, drawing on Copeland's natural talent, dedication and modesty. Perhaps it is unfair to 'pick' on one sentence from a fairly lengthy article. And yet, this is a perfect encapsulation of the way that 'body image' is used as a catchall term, what I call 'false universality': the notion that body image is capable of explaining or encapsulating any number of self-body issues, no matter what they are. Copeland's 'body-image issues' are a key part of the narrative in the documentary, *A Ballerina's Tale,* and include a number of different elements. This narrative centres on Copeland joining ABT as a naïve 17 year old (as of 2017 she was 34 years old), a lone black woman in an industry dominated by white dancers, and being instructed by her teachers and the company's administrators that her 'athletic' (read: muscular) body type was a problem. Copeland had prominent muscles and large breasts and was urged to lose weight, which aggravated her sense of being out of place and eventually led her to experience disordered eating for a period of time.

The phrase 'body-image issues' in this article is used to convey a sense of shared understanding with readers about the struggle involved: perhaps Copeland had issues with her appearance, weight, or body shape. To a certain extent this is borne out: part of Copeland's 'body-image issues' *were* to do with weight and body shape. However, the reality is more complicated and deals with issues of institutional racism and highly restrictive beauty norms as a key part of professionalisation in the ballet industry, as well as social isolation and mental health issues. While 'body-image issues' is convenient shorthand, it does not adequately represent the nuance of the situation.

It will be useful to compare the interpretation of Copeland's story in the *Harper's Bazaar* article and *A Ballerina's Tale*. In the former, the focus is on Copeland's individual biography and accomplishments, as I mentioned earlier. In the documentary, however, directed by African-American writer and filmmaker Nelson George, Copeland's achievements are consistently placed within the broader cultural framework of Copeland as a rare black figure in a primarily white industry. Throughout the documentary, the viewer is introduced to various characters who shape the film's depiction of Copeland as one part of a broader collective of black women attempting to break new ground and effect social change. One of these is Copeland's mentor, Susan Fales-Hill, who introduces the teenaged Copeland to other successful black women as a way of showing her that there is a community available to her, even if one might not seem immediately accessible within the ballet world. The viewer also meets Victoria Rowell and Raven Wilkinson, who, as black women, had limited success as ballet dancers in previous decades. The documentary, therefore, appeals to a different notion of the self that is part of a collective, in this case one of African-American women pushing racialised cultural boundaries, and within which the bounded notion of the individualistic self in capitalism does not operate, perhaps alleviating some of the anxiety that comes with having to create oneself as an individual, rather than as one part of a larger whole (Gill and Scharff 2011, pp. 8–9).[4] In a sense, this appeal to the collective might be called a creation of kinship (or community) through tracing a genealogy of successful black women in white-dominated industries (Lawler 2012, pp. 47–49).

This connects with another aspect of 'false universality': that of the flawed perception of 'body image' being able to explain and find solutions for all self-body issues through 'improving' or 'changing' individuals' 'body image', for example. Body image, however, has a tendency to refer back to image and surface, again and again, without addressing the corporeal issues that have little to do with image and surface, but with identity, subjectivity, and gendered and other social norms. However, as the next example will illustrate, 'body image' is often framed as explaining a negative state of embodiment, or self-body relation. Although 'body image' does not in principle predetermine either a positive or negative self-body state, it often assumes a (most likely feminine) subject in distress. Even attempts to use the language of 'body image' in sophisticated and socially conscious ways often reify this implicit assumption, as the example of the APPG report that I introduced in a previous section illustrates. Consider this quotation from the preface: 'This inquiry has investigated the *causes* and *consequences* of body image *anxiety* in the UK

[...] As well as assessing the *problem*, we are proposing what can be done about it' (2012, p. 3; emphases mine).

In this report, therefore, 'body image' is very much constructed as a problem for which a solution is sought. In other parts of this passage, the phrases 'body image pressure' and 'body image dissatisfaction' are also used to describe the state of affairs that the APPG seeks to understand and remedy. This is perhaps unsurprising from a government-based initiative, but nevertheless shows that this association of 'body image' with the stricken embodied self is common and entrenched. Not only that, but while 'body image' is constructed as the problem, it is equally constructed as the solution—we must 'improve body image'. This circularity is troubling and, I argue, a hindrance to the project of discovering, articulating and, where necessary, resolving body-self issues.

## Towards a Potential New Vocabulary of the Body

What characteristics should a new or improved popular vocabulary of the body possess? Would an improved version of 'body image' that transcends its current limitations be adequate, or is an entirely new vocabulary necessary? It may be that the language of 'body image' may be expanded and added to, perhaps by new generations of interconnecting activist movements. Conceivably, the research emerging from psychology may succeed in 'capturing the rich diversity of human experiences of embodiment', and in developing a rich, accessible vocabulary with which to disseminate and popularise this new research (Cash 2004, p. 2). Perhaps, on the other hand, it might be necessary for a new corporeal vocabulary—whether from academia, activist movements or popular culture—to supersede 'body image' altogether. This could have the advantage of explicitly bringing into a popular vocabulary of the body a recognition and exploration of the multiple ways that class, race, gender and sexuality, among many other factors, shape embodied experience.

In either case, a new or improved corporeal vocabulary would ideally have several features that would allow it to become as popular as 'body image', but, crucially, would also allow us to imagine, identify and express more creative ways of thinking about our bodies. This vocabulary should be easily accessible to a general public and yet also have the potential to be conceptually sophisticated and academically rigorous. It should move beyond an unconstructive focus on image, surface and appearance. It should be explicitly inclusive of different aspects of embodiment (e.g. bodily functions and aptitudes, (dis)ability, sensations, mental health and appearance), without systematically privileging one over the others. It should also be intersectional, taking into account the multiple ways that embodiment is socially constructed, through sexuality, race and ethnicity, class, (dis)ability, and gender identity. This exhaustive list of ideal attributes runs the risk of any possible corporeal vocabulary collapsing under the weight of expectation. However, it is a good starting point from which to suggest more pragmatic suggestions.

## DRAWING FROM OTHER POPULAR VOCABULARIES OF THE BODY FOR INSPIRATION

In this section I will discuss two examples of other corporeal vocabularies, comparing them to 'body image' in order to identify features of these vocabularies that might enable us to get closer to a potential new vocabulary of the body.

The first example that I will discuss is 'black is beautiful', a slogan that emerged in the 1960s out of the Black Power movement in the United States (PBS: 'The African Americans' 2013). Although relatively forgotten today, its impact was notable at the time (Anderson and Cromwell 1977). It is worth examining here for two reasons: first, similarly to the 'body image' concept, 'black is beautiful' is catchy, easy to remember and highly evocative. It therefore has the communicative accessibility and psychological immediacy that 'body image' has, which, as we have seen, is a powerful advantage for a popular vocabulary of the body. Second, unlike 'body image', 'black is beautiful' emerged out of a social movement with specific social aims targeted at a particular group, and thus has some qualities that 'body image' does not.

'Black is beautiful' was a deliberate attempt to reconfigure blackness from abject to desirable, and address internalised racism, through, for example, appeals to the beauty of black skin (no matter how dark), natural hair (as opposed to chemically relaxed hair) and African facial features (Anderson and Cromwell 1977; 'For African-American College Students' 1995; PBS: 'The African Americans' 2013; Walker 2007). This was done through various means, including the long-running television show *Soul Train* (1971–2006), one of the first popular—and positive—depictions of African Americans on television, support from political and cultural actors such as the Black Panther Party, and advertising desirable products to black consumers (PBS: 'The African Americans' 2013; Walker 2007, p. 170). 'Black is beautiful' and the values it promoted, therefore, straddled the nexus of social, cultural, political, and economic interests. Where everything from educational attainment, economic status and social stigma had for decades depended to some degree on the exact shade of a black person's skin, 'black is beautiful' attempted to create a cultural environment that not only opposed and replaced oppressive racist stereotypes of blackness from the dominant white culture, but also sought to equalise the different 'shades' of blackness that existed ('For African-American College Students' 1995; Walker 2007). As Susannah Walker notes in her historical study on the beauty industry, *Style and Status: Selling Beauty to African American Women, 1920-1975* (2007), '[f]ew African Americans, inside or outside the beauty industry, challenged the ideal of shiny, long hair and light brown skin in the 1950s and early 1960s' (p. 170). In this context, a slogan like 'black is beautiful' would have carried considerable psychological immediacy and communicative accessibility for African Americans in the 1960s and 1970s.

One key difference is worth noting between 'body image' and 'black is beautiful' as vocabularies of the body. Because so much of the oppression that African Americans have experienced has been constructed and expressed onto their bodies, an anti-racist social movement about self-love that expresses that self-love through the body is a logical and effective strategy. This strategic approach to creating a popular language of the body is important to note because, unlike 'body image', which emerged from a popular translation of a systematic attempt to understand people's relationships with their bodies in an academic setting, 'black is beautiful' was a cultural intervention aimed at improving people's lives directly through changing consciousness. 'Black is beautiful' was part of a broader social movement—one could even say revolution—and drew from its values. Could there be an advantage to having a corporeal vocabulary that stems from a social movement? For example, a movement's system of values may be able to shape the vocabulary in question, and potentially guide a strategic plan for its deployment in society. In addition, being deployed as part of a social movement, the qualities of communicative accessibility and psychological immediacy discussed earlier could be intentionally created to have maximum cultural impact.

However, a concurrent disadvantage is that, as evidenced by the waning of 'black is beautiful' in recent decades, social movements tend to wax and wane over time. It may therefore be difficult to maintain the momentum of a particular corporeal vocabulary based on a slogan or campaign emerging from a social movement.

In addition, one key similarity between 'black is beautiful' and 'body image' is that they both inhabit the nexus between social, cultural, political and economic interests in their respective spheres. As such, their ability to draw together disparate actors in the pursuit of particular outcomes cannot be underestimated, nor can the potential benefits or damage resulting from this ambiguously powerful position. This ambiguity can be seen, for example, in the case of companies appropriating the rhetoric of 'black is beautiful' to sell—sometimes dubious—products: 'African American companies like Johnson Products and Supreme Beauty Products were first to [embrace the Afro], but white companies like Avon, Clairol, even hair relaxer producer Perma-Strate and skin bleaching cream maker Nadinola were soon promoting the "black is beautiful" idea' (Walker 2007, p. 171).

The second example I will discuss comes from Julia Serano's *Whipping Girl: A Transsexual Woman on Sexism and the Scapegoating of Femininity* (2007). In the chapter entitled 'The Future of Queer/Trans Activism', Serano highlights her concern about what she calls 'subversivism' within the trans/queer community. She defines this as, 'the practice of extolling certain gender and sexual expressions and identities simply because they are unconventional or nonconforming. In the parlance of subversivism, these atypical genders and sexualities are "good" because they "transgress" or "subvert" oppressive binary gender norms' (p. 346). She says of the queer/trans community, '[i]ts politics are generally anti-assimilationist, particularly with regard to gender and sexual expression' (p. 346). For Serano this is not a problem per se—the issue arises because, '[o]n the surface, subversivism gives the appearance of accommodating a seemingly infinite array of genders and sexualities, but this is not quite the case. Subversivism does have very specific boundaries; it has an "other"' (p. 347). In other words, in an effort to 'shatter the gender binary', Serano argues, many in the queer/trans community look down upon those with conventional gender expressions (p. 346). She identifies this 'often-unspoken category of bad, conservative genders' as being 'predominantly made up of feminine women and masculine men who are attracted to the "opposite" sex' (p. 347). In addition, she feels that this tendency also sidelines transsexual people, who are sometimes assumed to have transitioned in order to 'assimilate' into 'straight culture' (pp. 347–348). For Serano, in short, subversivism is an ill-judged reaction to gender theories of the last few decades that have highlighted the gender binary as the main—or only—source of sexism and gender-based oppression. Indeed, she argues that it sets up a new dichotomy, wherein some forms of gender and sexuality presentations are 'good' and others are 'bad' (p. 349).

The vocabulary in question regarding Serano's argument about 'body image' is that of 'shattering the gender binary' and the evaluation of people's gender and sexuality presentations as either progressive or regressive with regard to that binary. In a sense, 'subversivism' is about unintended consequences even with the best intentions; that by trying to undermine one binary as part of a socially progressive project it is possible to create new binaries that marginalise unexpected groups while reifying new hierarchies.

One similarity between the 'shattering the gender binary' vocabulary and 'body image' is that they both come from academia in some capacity—the context in which the former is used is activism, but it is an activism that is clearly theoretically grounded within gender theory. Indeed, it seems, from Serano's description, more closely grounded in academia than 'body image'. This highlights an important point: that perhaps the issues with 'body image' might not be resolved if the popular discourse were more closely grounded in the academic study of 'body image'—indeed, this might create different problems in its deployment.

A key difference between the use of 'shattering the gender binary' vocabulary and that of 'body image' is in the populations that have access to them: the 'gender binary' vocabulary that Serano discusses is deployed largely within the 'queer/trans' community, which she explains is 'a subgroup within the greater LGBTIQ community that is composed mostly of folks in their twenties and thirties who are more likely to refer to themselves as "dykes", "queer", and/or "trans" than "lesbian" or "gay". While diverse in a number of ways, this subpopulation tends to predominantly inhabit urban and academic settings, and is skewed toward those who are white and/or from middle class backgrounds' (2007, p. 345). In this way it is markedly different from those who can access the 'body image' concept: those who read popular magazines, watch television shows and listen to the radio will doubtless have encountered the term. Indeed, in the UK 'body image' is taught to children nationwide as part of the Personal, Social and Health Education curriculum (PSHE Association 2016). How does this difference in reach relate to the question of constructing an effective, popular language of the body? The queer/trans community as Serano describes it is one well placed to have a whole-person, intersectional, and theoretically-grounded approach to 'body-based' activism, given the long history of LGBT activism and its academic grounding. However, what Serano describes as 'subversivism' seems near-sighted and ultimately counterproductive, which poses the question: without assuming that the trend Serano has called 'subversivism' was deliberately created, what were the considerations and priorities that led to it taking the shape it has? This is ultimately a key question for the potential formation of any new vocabulary of the body.

## WHERE TO NEXT?

Based on the introduction to this section, in effect a 'wishlist' of attributes for an ideal corporeal vocabulary, and the two examples, which were more pragmatic illustrations of how vocabularies of the body fare in the 'real' world, several questions arise. The first two questions suggest avenues for creating entirely new vocabularies of the body, while the third brings us back to the question of what to do with 'body image' in the light of these findings.

First, the examples of 'black is beautiful' and 'shattering the gender binary' are focused on alleviating systemic injustice—racism, and gender and sexuality-based oppression, respectively, in a way that is not as apparent in 'body image'. Is having a specific social agenda, as opposed to the goal of providing an explanatory framework for embodied experience, more conducive to creating a useful and well-constructed vocabulary of the body? While the answer is not entirely clear, it seems that, at least in the case of 'black is beautiful', 'activist' vocabularies of the body can have a rapid effect on the populations they are targeting, but tend to rise and fall relatively quickly. Whether a short-lived, but impactful, vocabulary is better than a long-lived one with more ambiguous impacts is a question of perspective: is it better sharply to disrupt the system and then risk fading into history if the moment passes, or to create a long-lasting discussion within the current system that may, over time, effect change?

Second, 'body image' and 'shattering the gender binary' both emerged from academic research and theory, but are still problematic in a number of ways. Is it better for a vocabulary of the body to emerge from activism or academia? I would argue that these examples illustrate that a popularly accessible vocabulary of the body has to be constructed from the beginning through conversation between activism and academia, especially when attempting to create a social justice intervention that would be able to adapt successfully over time to changing social, political and economic conditions. Such a collaboration would also be necessary to create a corporeal vocabulary that would be popularly accessible as well as conceptually and strategically rigorous. In other words, I am arguing for a more strategic and conscious shaping of the vocabularies with which we create our bodily discourses.

Third, the vocabularies of 'body image', 'black is beautiful', and 'shattering the gender binary' are primarily focused on self-presentation and appearance as the basis for understanding various experiences of stigma, inequality and oppression; as well as the site at which these experiences may be healed or countered. Does this mean that any new popular language of the body would need to also focus on self-presentation and appearance? And what does this tell us about whether the best solution would be to reconceptualise the concept of 'body image', supplement it with other concepts, or discard it altogether in favour of an entirely new vocabulary? The strategic solution for the short to medium term seems clear: attempt to reconceptualise 'body image' to be a more sophisticated tool, or supplement it with a richer secondary cast of concepts that would include concepts relating to other bodily experiences than only those pertaining to appearance. In doing so, it might even be possible slowly to transition 'body image' over time to become an entirely different set of concepts and vocabulary, one more adept at addressing questions of 'whole-person' embodiment, and therefore influencing our discourses of the body.

However, the risk of attempting this strategic reformulation, if we consider 'body image' to be clearly embedded in discourses that reify physical appearance, is that of doing more harm than good in the time it takes for the 'body image' vocabulary to be slowly modified and improved. Which is of course not to argue that physical appearance is unimportant, but that it is often prioritised in 'body image' discourse at the expense of other facets of embodied experience. This has the effect of heightening the impact of negative appearance-related experiences rather than lessening them, as the primacy of being physically attractive to others is continually reinforced to individuals rather than diffused through attention to other facets of lived experience. A discourse of the body, on the other hand, that prioritised sensation, different bodily aptitudes, health—not as a function of appearance—and other facets of embodied experience would lessen the impact of appearance-based negative experiences considerably.

## CONCLUSION

The 'body image' paradigm inhabits a privileged position within contemporary Anglo-American societies in the multi-sited effort to address the huge variety of bodily experiences—often dissatisfied ones—that people experience. I argued that 'body image' has two traits that make it highly successful as a popular vocabulary of the body: communicative accessibility and psychological immediacy. Communicative accessibility refers to the instant intelligibility of 'body image' in a variety of different contexts, which makes it an easy catchall term for a variety of different bodily experiences. Psychological immediacy is a function of communicative accessibility, whereby the familiarity that most individuals have with the concept of 'body image' makes it a convenient and psychologically satisfying concept to reach for when faced with the need to explain a range of embodied experiences. These traits, I argued, are vital for any vocabulary of the body to have the sort of enduring success that 'body image' has had. I also highlighted certain problems in the way 'body image' is framed and communicated, namely its problematic relationship with gender, and false universality. Although 'body image' theoretically applies to everyone, in reality it is most often applied to girls and women, but in an unacknowledged way that creates two problems: first, this implicit focus leaves important ways that gender affects embodiment unexamined. Second, not explicitly addressing gender serves to hide and maintain the often sexist ways 'body image' issues are communicated, especially in the popular media. For groups whose bodies are already multiply marginalised through endemic gender-based violence, and objectifying and unrealistic beauty ideals, the dominance of the 'body image' concept may very well do more harm than good in terms of alleviating troubling embodied experiences.

I then discussed two examples of alternative corporeal vocabularies, 'black is beautiful' and 'shattering the gender binary' in order to highlight key similarities and differences to 'body image' and open a conversation towards a new or improved vocabulary. If there existed a conceptually rich, popularly accessible and intersectional language that integrated the whole embodied experience, I argue that it would change the parameters of the social project to understand and address troubled embodied experience. However, a more pragmatic project would be to modify and supplement 'body image' in order slowly to make it more sophisticated and productive in the long term.

I have argued that the language of 'body image' is limited and limiting in a number of ways, at least when occupying such a privileged position in popular discourse. The vocabulary we need to conceptualise is one that will address the 'what is the problem?' question as well as the 'what do we need to do about it?' question and offer solutions in a holistic, socially situated, intersectional and conceptually sophisticated way.

## NOTES

1. Although it could be argued that the language of feminism has also broken free of the academy, I argue that it would be more accurate to say that feminism emerged from popular activism and has been developed in that space as much as within the academy, and so represents a different relationship to popular discourse from that of 'body image', which is the focus of this essay.
2. I am not including in the 'popular' sphere educators or clinicians in the field, who, for the purposes of this chapter, I would categorise as belonging in academia. Such professionals dealing with the gamut of body-related pathologies, from eating disorders to body dysmorphia, almost universally use the concept of 'body image' in their work, a term which has enabled the therapeutic, public and professional fields that have grown up around it to have a common language and develop common goals.
3. I am grateful to Stu Marvel for her reading of the *Cosmopolitan* article.
4. I am grateful to Miriam Tola for her generous help with this analysis.

## REFERENCES

*A Ballerina's Tale*. 2015. [Film] Directed by George Nelson. New York: Urban Romances.

All Party Parliamentary Group on Body Image, 2012. *Reflections on body image*. London: All Party Parliamentary Group on Body Image and Central YMCA.

Anderson, C., and R.L. Cromwell, 1977. '"Black Is Beautiful" and the Color Preferences of Afro-American Youth'. *The Journal of Negro Education*, 46 (1), pp. 76–88.

Banfield, S.S., and McCabe, M.P., 2002. 'An evaluation of the construct of body image'. *Adolescence*, 37 (146), 373–393.

Bartky, S.L., 1990. *Femininity and Domination: Studies in the Phenomenology of Oppression.* New York and London: Routledge.

Bordo, S., 1993. *Unbearable Weight: Feminism, Western Culture, and the Body.* Berkeley, Los Angeles, and London: University of California Press.

Cash, T.F., 1990. 'The psychology of physical appearance: Aesthetics, attributes, and images', in T.F. Cash and T. Pruzinsky, eds. 1990. *Body images: Development, deviance, and change.* New York: Guilford Press. pp. 51–79.

Cash, T.F., 2004. 'Body image: Past, present, and future'. *Body Image,* 1 (1), 1–5.

Cohane, G.H. and Pope, H.G., 2001. 'Body image in boys: A review of the literature'. *International Journal of Eating Disorders,* 29, pp. 373–379.

Csordas, T.J., 1994. 'Introduction: The body as representation and being-in-the-world'. In: T.J. Csordas, ed. 1994. *Embodiment and Experience: The Existential Ground of Culture and Self.* Cambridge: Cambridge University Press. pp. 1–26.

Dove, 2016a. Our Research. [online] Available at: <http://www.dove.us/Our-Mission/Girls-Self-Esteem/Our-Research/default.aspx> [Accessed 01.01.17].

Dove, 2016b. The Dove Campaign for Real Beauty. [online]. Available at: <http://www.dove.us/Social-Mission/campaign-for-real-beauty.aspx> [Accessed 01.01.17].

Firestone, S., 1970. *The Dialectic of Sex: The Case for Feminist Revolution.* New York: Farar, Straus and Giroux.

Fisher, S., 1970. *Body experience in fantasy and behavior.* New York: Appleton-Century-Crofts.

Fisher, S., 1986. *Development and structure of the body image* (Vols. 1 & 2). Hillsdale, NJ: Erlbaum.

Fisher, S., 1989. *Sexual images of the self: The psychology of erotic sensations and illusions.* Hillsdale, NJ: Erlbaum.

Fisher, S., and Cleveland, S.E., 1968. *Body image and personality.* New York: Dover.

Gill, R. and Scharff, C., 2011. 'Introduction', in: R. Gill and C. Scharff, eds. 2011. *New Femininities: Postfeminism, Neoliberalism and Subjectivity.* New York: Palgrave Macmillan. pp. 1–17.

Gleeson, K., and Frith, H., 2006. '(De)constructing Body Image'. *Journal of Health Psychology,* 11 (1), pp. 79–90.

Grogan, S., 2008. *Body Image: Understanding body dissatisfaction in men, women, and children.* London and New York: Routledge.

Lawler, Steph, 2012. *Identity: Sociological Perspectives.* Cambridge: Polity Press.

Macrae, F., 2009. *'Gentlemen prefer Miss Average'.* Daily Mail, [online] 11 June 2009. Available at: <http://www.dailymail.co.uk/femail/article-1192142/Gentlemen-prefer-Miss-Average-The-perfect-centrefold-body-ousted-homely-shape-girl-door-new-study.html> [Accessed 01.01.17].

Merriam-Webster's Dictionary, 2016. *Merriam-Webster's Dictionary*. [online] Available from: <http://www.merriam-webster.com/dictionary/> [Accessed 01.01.17].

Mooallem, S., 2016. Misty Copeland and Degas: Art of dance. *Harper's Bazaar*, [online] 10 February 2016. Available at: <http://www.harpersbazaar.com/culture/art-books-music/a14055/misty-copeland-degas-0316/> [Accessed 01.01.17].

PBS: The African Americans. 2013. *Black is Beautiful: Afros, Soul Train and Self-Love*. [online] Available at: <http://www.pbs.org/wnet/african-americans-many-rivers-to-cross/video/black-is-beautiful/> [Accessed 01.01.17].

Pruzinsky, T., and Cash, T.F., 2002. 'Understanding Body Images: Historical and Contemporary Perspectives', in T.F. Cash and T. Pruzinsky, eds. 2002. *Body Image: A Handbook of Theory, Research, and Clinical Practice*. New York and London: The Guilford Press. pp. 3–12.

PSHE Association. 2016. *Key standards in teaching about body image*. [online] Available at: <https://www.pshe-association.org.uk/curriculum-and-resources/resources/key-standards-teaching-about-body-image> [Accessed 01.01.17].

Schilder, P., 1950. *The Image and Appearance of the Human Body*. New York: International Universities Press.

Serano, J., 2007. *Whipping Girl: A Transsexual Woman on Sexism and the Scapegoating of Femininity*. Berkeley, CA: Seal Press.

Shontz, F.C., 1969. *Perceptual and cognitive aspects of body experience*. New York: Macmillan.

Wolf, N., 1991. *The Beauty Myth*. London: Vintage Books.

Varnes, J.R., M.L. Stellefson, C.M. Janelle, S.M. Dorman, V. Dodd and M.D. Miller, 2013. 'A systematic review of studies comparing body image concerns among female college athletes and non-athletes, 1997–2012'. *Body image*, 10 (4), pp. 421–432.

———'For African-American College Students: More Black is now More Beautiful', 1995. The Journal of Blacks in Higher Education, (7), pp. 45–46.

Walker, S., 2007. *Style and Status: Selling Beauty to African American Women, 1920-1975*. Lexington, KY: University Press of Kentucky.

Weedon, Chris, 1987. *Feminist practice and poststructuralist theory*. Oxford: Blackwell.

# INDEX